Revitalizing Political Psychology

The Legacy of Harold D. Lasswell

Revitalizing Political Psychology

The Legacy of Harold D. Lasswell

William Ascher
Barbara Hirschfelder-Ascher
Claremont McKenna College

LEA LAWRENCE ERLBAUM ASSOCIATES, PUBLISHERS
2005   Mahwah, New Jersey   London

Lawrence Erlbaum Associates, Inc., Publishers
10 Industrial Avenue
Mahwah, New Jersey 07430

Cover design by Sean Trane Sciarrone

Library of Congress Cataloging-in-Publication Data

Ascher, William.
    Revitalizing political psychology : the legacy of Harold D. Lasswell /
William Ascher, Barbara Hirschfelder-Ascher.
        p.   cm.
    Includes bibliographical references and index.
    ISBN 0–8058–5206–9 (h. : alk. paper)
    1. Political psychology. 2. Lasswell, Harold Dwight, 1902–
I. Hirschfelder-Ascher, Barbara. II. Title.
JA74.5.A77 2004
320'.01'9—dc22   2004046928

In honor of Lisa Heumann Hirschfelder

Contents

Contents

Preface

This book grew out of two concerns. First, for the past quarter century political psychology has largely neglected the roles of affect, psychological needs, and the psychodynamic mechanisms that are crucial for understanding the full complexity of political behavior. Second, the connections between political psychology and the study of public policy seem increasingly tenuous. With notable exceptions, political psychology has focused predominantly on explaining individual or collective political behavior rather than trying to guide policy decisions that would be greatly aided by insights about how people react to symbols, how psychological needs shape their perspectives and predispositions, and how crises can undermine the defenses against destructive behaviors. These dimensions can be recaptured by explaining, defending, and extending the contributions of Harold D. Lasswell, who was unquestionably the dominant figure in developing political psychology in mid-20th-century America. Trained in the fields of pragmatist social science in America and psychoanalysis in Europe, Lasswell was the foremost figure in applying psychodynamic theories to politics. His framework and theories provide the best grounding for revitalizing political psychology. Yet, his framework also accommodates cognitive processes and social interactions ranging from communications (his model is still a prominent paradigm in journalism schools) to the policymaking process (his social process model is the heart of the policy sciences framework). This enables Lasswell's contributions, if properly understood, to resist the rejection of psychodynamic theories that has hampered contemporary political psychology.

In one respect, Lasswell's work is experiencing a renaissance, as witnessed by the republication of 10 of his books since 1990 as well as numerous articles, the posthumous publication of his 1,600-page magnum opus, *Jurisprudence for a Free Society* (1992), and the establishment of the Society for the Policy Sciences to further the applications of the Lasswellian framework. At least four organizations offer Harold D. Lasswell prizes: the American Political Science Association, the International Society for Political Psychology, the Policy Studies Organization, and the Society for the Policy Sciences. However, as Eulau and Zlomke (1999) pointed out, many who invoke Lasswell do so rather superficially. The use of Lasswell's framework and theories in political psychology, as well as in conventional public policy analysis, occurs far less often than one would expect in light of all the accolades. It is one thing to honor a pioneer as a historical figure, but quite another to recognize the continued relevance of the pioneer's contributions. This would be understandable if Lasswell's work had simply been eclipsed by advances in political psychology. However, this is not the case. Mainstream academic psychology has largely abandoned the crucial psychodynamic dimensions elegantly developed in Lasswell's work in favor of preoccupations with easily testable but rather narrow aspects of cognitive processing. Contemporary political analyses in the psychoanalytic tradition often neglect the socioeconomic and political factors that Lasswell so skillfully integrated with the psychodynamic considerations. As we demonstrate in this book, Lasswell's framework still provides an unexcelled guide for the analysis of current policy and political issues, while allowing for elaborations to expand and deepen his theories. Lasswell's incorporation of psychodynamic mechanisms within a broad social interaction framework avoids the reductionism and narrowness of early psychoanalytic theorizing. We hope that our review of Lasswell's configurative approach can help restore the status of psychodynamic functional theory to contemporary political psychology, which in recent years has largely rejected the utility of such theory. Lasswell's theories and our extensions demonstrate that these theories can be reintroduced within a framework that avoids the pitfalls of earlier Freudian efforts.

In this volume, we also show that Lasswell's pragmatist orientation offers an alternative conception of behavioral sciences to the dominant positivist paradigm in academic psychology. Thus, although this book focuses on Lasswell's contributions, we use his contributions and the debates over his epistemology as a window to examine broader issues in the behavioral sciences, such as the tensions between psychoanalytic approaches and contemporary academic psychology as well as those between pragmatism and scientific positivism.

In Chapter 1, we introduce the thesis that current political psychology has made progress in bringing more cognitive psychology into the study of political behavior, but has neglected the question of how a systematic evaluation of psychodynamic functional theory can add insight. We specify how Lasswell's work contains the seeds for a reinvigorated psychodynamic political psychology.

In Chapter 2, we explore Lasswell's seminal work on the displacement of emotion and beliefs from one object or target to another, and extend his theory to account for attributions of blame and shifts in value orientations and identifications. This chapter presents Lasswell's powerful framework for understanding the structure of belief systems, and addresses the role of the concept of the unconscious in accounting for displacements.

Chapter 3 reviews Lasswell's theories of the cognitive and emotional impact of political symbols and the dynamics of propaganda. It shows how Lasswell adapted the psychoanalytic distinction of id, ego, and superego to understand the multiple appeals of political and policy symbols.

Chapter 4 links personality and character analysis to democratic practice, showing how Lasswell's conception of democratic character is linked
with the values and expectations necessary to maintain the discipline
that democratic practice and fair dealing require. These concepts go far in
clarifying Lasswell's often misunderstood normative commitment. As the
source of the concepts of the "garrison state" and the "military industrial
complex," Lasswell's work on democratic character is crucial for understanding civil–military relations and the risks of militarization and the
contraction of civil liberties.

In Chapter 5, we assess the burgeoning field of leadership studies by
examining the key issues through the lenses of Lasswell's theories of elite
behavior and democratic leadership. Our analysis critiques the field of leadership studies, based on Lasswell's concerns over the risks to democratic
accountability posed by the current preoccupation with strengthening the
roles of charismatic and transformational leadership.

Chapter 6 focuses on political behavior in times of crisis, when the baseline character of leaders and the public often becomes distorted. Because
the political climate in crisis situations frequently reflects the erosion of
self-restraint and therefore the risks of destructive behavior, Lasswell presented approaches to preempt and discharge these destructive impulses.

Chapter 7 presents original applications—case studies and multicase
applications—of Lasswell's political psychology and our extensions of
his framework, in order to address contemporary political issues and to
emphasize the open-ended nature of Lasswell's framework. Five of the
applications diagnose intergroup conflicts around the world and the psychodynamic explanations that can help to guide strategies to reduce the
potentials for violence and the disruption of democratic practice. Other
applications look at U.S. domestic issues: how the debate on nuclear
energy is shaped by the symbolic linkages of the term *nuclear,* and how
the accountability of labor union leadership affects labor relations.

Finally, Chapter 8 clarifies the role of the political psychiatrist as one
who brings insight to the public and leaders about their own behavior—
especially, why they often approach public policy issues with distorted
expectations, priorities, and affects—rather than as a manipulator out
to control politics and policy through the arcane knowledge of political
psychology. This reinforces the appropriate interpretation of Lasswell's
contributions as a profoundly democratic theorist.

It is our hope that this book will help political psychologists to rediscover
the psychodynamic roots of political predisposition. Lasswell's framework
and the extensions that we present should assure them that they can rein-
troduce psychodynamic explanations without having to accept the reductionism that plagued the earlier psychoanalytic efforts to scale up to the
political and societal levels. Policy scientists, as well as political and policy
strategists, will benefit from greater familiarity with Lasswell's theories
of why particular political leaders or policies have compelling appeal,
how symbolic politics plays a role in these appeals, and how the political
and policy processes can maintain democratic and accountable practices.

Lasswell's warnings about the pitfalls of certain leadership styles should be heeded by experts and students in leadership studies and civil–military relations, and his foundational work on symbols and propaganda needs to be reinforced in the field of political communications. Certainly, students in courses on social psychology, political psychology, organization theory, and public policy studies would greatly benefit from exposure to the legacy and potential of Lasswell's general approach, as would students trying to master the scope and methods of political science.

ACKNOWLEDGMENTS

This project owes much to the continued commitment of the members of the Society for the Policy Sciences to understand and apply the extraordinarily rich framework that Lasswell and his many collaborators have developed since the late 1920s. The stimulating discussions under the auspices of this Society have focused on key aspects of Lasswell's political psychology as well as the policy sciences. We are indebted to many Society members, and in particular to Steven R. Brown, Ronald D. Brunner, Rodney Muth, Toddi Steelman, and Andrew Willard for invaluable guidance. Such guidance was also provided by our Claremont McKenna colleagues, John Farrell and Jay Martin, from both sides of the debate over psychoanalytic approaches. Several leaders in the field of political psychology, most notably Tom Bryder and Fred Greenstein, also provided penetrating reactions. We thank the readers for Erlbaum who provided additional insights on how to strengthen the book—Doris Graber, University of Illinois at Chicago, and Kenneth Hoover, Western Washington University. We also thank Emily Acevedo for her able research assistance.

We would additionally like to celebrate the virtue of having adult children—we prevailed upon Diana, Julie, and David incessantly to brainstorm on psychology and politics, always to excellent effect. Finally, we are grateful to Storm Ascher for demonstrating that psychological principles can be expressed in clear-cut and compelling ways. As an 8-year-old, her response to our explanation of the triple-appeal principle and the distinctions among id, ego, and superego was to note that it boils down to the devil on the one shoulder and the angel on the other.

Chapter 1

Introduction

THE UNFINISHED BUSINESS
OF POLITICAL PSYCHOLOGY

Political psychology is in need of revitalization to recapture its capacity to incorporate the emotional and psychodynamic roots of political behavior. To be sure, the field has made considerable strides over the past quarter century. First, as an interdisciplinary field that strives to understand the psychological bases of political behavior, it has strengthened its commitment to linking theory to issues of normative importance by focusing on such issues as citizenship responsibility, democratic commitment, interethnic tolerance, and willingness to engage in peaceful conflict resolution.[1] This commitment transcends the misguided "value-free" approach of some earlier research agendas.

Second, great theoretical progress has been made in accounting for how people process information and reconcile new information with preexisting perspectives (Alsolabehere & Iyengar, 1993; Ferejohn & Kuklinski, 1990; Lau & Sears, 1986; Ottati, 2002; Ottati & Wyer, 1993; Torney-Purta, 1989; Wyer & Ottati, 1993). Theories of "political cognition" have sharpened our understanding of how people cope with incomplete and inconsistent information about politics and policies. In the subfield of political socialization, which focuses on the development of political attitudes and predispositions among children and young adults, theories of cognitive and moral development have enriched our understanding of how political orientations change as individuals' cognitive and ethical capacities mature (Cook, 1985, 1989; Torney-Purta, 1989, 2000). "Political communication" has been analyzed far more systematically today than in previous eras. The theory of heuristics, developed by cognitive psychologists, helped to anticipate the simplifications that people use to understand complex politics and policies when confronted with uncertainty and limited analytic capacity (Kahneman, Slovic, & Tversky, 1982).

The study of political cognition has been undertaken through careful surveys, "laboratory" simulations, content analysis of political communications, and other empirical approaches. Except for the rare longitudinal study,[2] these tests, by their very nature, predominantly focus on current attitudes and only those antecedents that have currently measurable manifestations. As an essential element to understanding how life conditions affect political behavior, contemporary research strongly emphasizes identifying individuals' socioeconomic characteristics and linking them to beliefs and predispositions to action. Many of these studies meet the standard scientific conventions of explicit measurement, replicability, and statistical analysis.

Yet these accomplishments have come at a cost. A sound political psychology must be more than just a normative commitment and an understanding of political cognition. In order to link the full range of economic, sociological, and political conditions to political predispositions, a framework must be able to account for the impact of long-standing, deeply seated predispositions. In many circumstances, determining how individuals perceive the political situation is only part of the challenge; it is often far more difficult to determine why they have particularly strong affects in relation to the relevant actors and objects. Consider the often surprisingly positive reactions to clearly power-hungry, hyperaggressive leaders with questionable ethics and weak commitment to accountability. Consider also the acute animosity and associated stereotypes targeted toward ethnic groups with whom an individual has had little actual contact. To some degree these beliefs may be "learned," but often other forces must be at play to account for the intensity of these beliefs. These forces are distinct from the cognitive processing that is currently emphasized in theory and research, even if the cognitive processing is involved in shaping the resultant beliefs and predispositions. Richard Wyer and Victor Ottati noted:

> Although there have been many advances in our understanding of the cognitive aspects of political judgment, certain important considerations have been neglected. In particular, social judgments and decisions are often greatly influenced by affective reactions that are elicited by the people or objects being judged or by the information presented about them. The importance of taking these reactions into account is supported by evidence indicating that cognitive and affective process mechanisms are interrelated, with one often influencing the other. . . . However, the role of these affective mechanisms in political decision-making has rarely been investigated. . . . (1993, p. 296)

However, Wyer and Ottati's recommended research agenda is confined to survey-based correlations and "innovative experimental approaches," with no mention of approaches to distinguish the impact of affects originating from long-standing psychological needs, let alone to account for such affects (Wyer & Ottati, 1993). A decade later, George Marcus (2003) noted that the deficiency in accounting for the emotional or affective component of political belief systems persists. Even if theories of cognitive processing begin to account for the *results* of particular affects (assuming that the affects can be identified), they cannot fully account for the *origins* of affects. Therefore, they cannot identify which affects may have peculiar properties (e.g., rigidity or emotional exaggeration) due to connections with psychological needs quite apart from the immediate issue at hand.

This state of affairs came about because contemporary political psychology has largely eschewed efforts to model the internal dynamics that connect psychological needs to political predispositions.[3] *Psychodynamic functional theories*[4] focus on how internal psychological needs develop and shape attitudes, predispositions, and overt behavior. Some (although not all) of these needs are remote from the current and prior circumstances directly related to the political issue at hand. For example, an individual may hate a particular politician because of mental associations with hated teachers or relatives. Psychodynamic functional theory is indispensable for accounting for the drives and affects that both underlie these perspectives and explain why some predispositions are resistant to accommodation. How do these drives arise and get channeled in particular ways? How do personal histories generate the wide variations in political perspectives, apart from the typical considerations of economic and social standing or political experience? Psychodynamic functional theories presume that the impact of these earlier events or conditions is embodied in deeply seated psychological needs that become engaged in the current situation. Psychodynamic functional theory is necessary to understand why the same external stimuli, whether concrete events and conditions or political symbols, trigger different associations and, hence, different reactions from different individuals.

The functionality of psychodynamic theories does not necessarily mean that the attitudes or predispositions are beneficial or functional overall for either the individual or the polity. Psychodynamic functional theories are often employed to understand behavior that may relieve immediate psychological distress but is destructive to the individual and others in the larger sense. For example, blaming others may relieve a painful sense of guilt, but in the long run it may shape hostile attitudes that damage both the individual and the target of blame.[5]

Without psychodynamic functional theory, the models of sociopolitical linkages deteriorate into stimulus–response hypotheses that particular conditions produce particular responses in obvious, commonsense ways. If both stimulus and response are easily measurable, the weight of some relationships can be assessed through straightforward research designs. Yet, without psychodynamic functional theory we cannot fathom the idiosyncrasies of the political misfit, the abrupt shifts in political mood, the political manifestations of personal insecurities, the allure of political symbols that have no personal resonance to external observers, or the clinging to self-destructive beliefs and practices that have no apparent instrumentality. These require understanding the internal, preexisting psychological pressures impinging on specific individuals or segments of the population.

The Scope of Psychodynamic Functional Theory

Let us clarify the scope of psychodynamic functional theories that are in such short supply in contemporary political psychology. These theories encompass the processes that shape affects, meanings, associations, levels of attention, or predispositions in the service of drives or needs that are at some remove from the political situation at hand (Katz, 1960; Lane, 1959; Smith, Bruner, & White, 1956). Following is a partial list of possible mechanisms:[6]

- Affect flows from one object to another, not because of the straight-forward generalization from one like thing to another but rather because they are associated by overlapping symbol labels, serve some emotional function, or both. The function may be to fulfill a drive or to relieve anxiety. For example, a key component of Adolf Hitler's propaganda was to invoke the emotionally compelling symbol of "moral purity" and connect it to the Nazi agenda to preserve the supposed "purity of the racial stock."[7]

- Predispositions or beliefs may reduce internal conflicts. We are angry with A, but this uncomfortable anger is redirected to B; we had an urge to do X, which somehow threatens our self-image, and thus block out this urge or even develop a strong sentiment condemning X. Hence, the repertoire of possible psychodynamic functional processes encompasses, but is not confined to, the classical set of ego–defense mechanisms proposed by Anna Freud (1936/1966): compensation, displacement, emotional insulation, fantasy, identification, intellectualization, introjection, projection, rationalization, reaction formation, regression, repression, sublimation, and undoing.

- Holding particular attitudes may express values with which the individual wishes to be associated, to enhance either self-respect or standing among others (Katz, 1960). In some of these cases, the resulting attitude may be inconsistent with other political attitudes. For example, individuals who want to express their tough-mindedness may develop bellicose attitudes toward particular "antagonists" that cannot be explained on the basis of generalization, learning, or interests.

We use the term *dynamic* in a broader sense than its usage in Freudian theory. In psychoanalytic theory, *dynamic* (as opposed to *static*) relationships pertain to the "conflict of opposing mental forces" (Laplanche & Pontalis, 1973, p. 126). We can use the term *psychodynamic functional theory* to denote the broader conception of predispositions at the service of internal drives as well as of the management of internal difficulties such as anxiety, depression, low self-esteem, and so on.

Many psychodynamic functional theories invoke the *unconscious*. The unconscious can refer to the mental material outside of awareness or consciousness at a given moment. Alternatively, the unconscious as a system or set of dynamics can mean the processes (e.g., repression) that prevent material from coming into the individual's awareness at the conscious level. Therefore, the individual cannot act on this material with conscious deliberation, or report its existence to a researcher (Laplanche & Pontalis, 1973). Freud's evolving conceptions of the unconscious and those of various offshoots of psychoanalytic theory do not preclude that formerly unconscious material can come into consciousness—that is the essence of psychoanalytic treatment—but they presume that without special intervention, unconscious material exists in many or even all individuals.

WHY HAS PSYCHODYNAMIC FUNCTIONAL THEORY BEEN NEGLECTED?

We have asserted that psychodynamic functional theory is lacking in contemporary political psychology, but we have yet to explain why it is absent. Nor have we addressed the question of whether its absence is a necessary cost for achieving some other goal.

The Positivist Underpinnings of Contemporary Political Psychology

The neglect of psychodynamic functional theories by many political scientists and psychologists reflects the fact that exploring such theories does not fit within the still rather dominant paradigm of positivist research. The positivist dream is to discover true and certain general law theory,[8] approached through definitive empirical testing according to the conventional conception of the "scientific method." The goal is to discover *the* correct general theory through empirically based hypothesis testing that disconfirms alternative, false theories (hence it is often labeled *falsificationism*).[9] Parsimony is regarded as a great virtue; the continuing existence of contending theories and hypotheses is a sign of the incompleteness of the scientific project. Definitive hypothesis testing is so important that contemporary positivism has no tolerance for constructs that cannot be confirmed through direct observation. Equally importantly, the relationships that can be tested are limited in complexity and time frame. It would be a Herculean task to find definitive, confirmable, statistical evidence of a theory that links life history events to basic character qualities, these qualities to political predispositions, these predispositions to beliefs that emerge in particular political circumstances, and finally these beliefs to political actions under specific external political conditions.[10]

The commitment of mainstream political psychology to the positivist project is deep and pervasive. The most telling reflection of the restricted positivist mindset of much of contemporary political psychology is Richard Merelman's (1989) assessment of the state of political socialization.

He emphasized both critical tests and general law theories in no uncertain terms:

> Interest in political socialization among political scientists might reemerge more rapidly if proponents of these hotly debated paradigms recognize that research in political socialization offers them *crucial tests of their theories*. . . . It would be more satisfying to use political socialization research to help establish a single political theory, or at least to settle upon a single psychological theory of political socialization itself. *We all feel the lure of parsimony*. (p. 37; emphasis added)

Stanley Moore echoed this sentiment in the very title of his 1989 article, "The Need for a Unified Theory of Political Learning." Moreover, any perusal of *Political Psychology*, the flagship journal of the International Society for Political Psychology, would clearly reveal the predominance of research attempting to find and confirm *the* correct theory. The archetypical article begins with a description of a political issue and the related political behavior, cites two or more theories that have been invoked to explain the behavior, and then presents empirical findings to support one of the theories. Typically, this exercise links observable and current traits with observable and current beliefs and predispositions.

It should now be clear why psychodynamic functional theories are at a severe disadvantage in the eyes of researchers who hold to this positivist outlook. If theories must be definitively tested, those featuring nonobservable constructs representing internal psychodynamics do not qualify. Psychodynamic functional theories are complicated, and generally invoke mechanisms that cannot be proven through cut-and-dried empirical research. In particular, theories invoking the operation of unconscious processes and the impact of repressed material are inaccessible to the standard paradigm of the subject reporting to the researcher. When clever ways of eliciting possible effects of unconscious material are implemented, the skeptical reaction is that the materials emerge only because they are not truly unconscious, as demonstrated by their emergence.[11] Surveys, simulations, and other laboratory experiments cannot tap into the long-term development of basic psychological predispositions, nor can complex theories be easily tested by correlations of the variables accessible through these approaches. From a positivist perspective, psychodynamic functional theories are at a severe disadvantage.

The Disrepute of Psychoanalytic Theory

This problem is exacerbated by the disfavor of psychoanalytic theory and its offshoots in most contemporary circles of psychologists.[12] The well-known critique of psychoanalytic theory as untestable and unfalsifiable, especially because of the central role played by unconscious dynamics, is one prominent reason for its rejection (Erwin, 1996; Grünbaum, 1984) but so too is the doctrinaire stance of the most prominent variants of psychoanalytic theory. Insofar as each Freudian, Adlerian, Kleinian, Lacanian,

Jungian, or other psychoanalytic offshoot claims to be the true and certain theory, outsiders are likely to be skeptical of all of them. The pragmatist view that each approach should be valued for its insights, whether or not it is fully valid, is a dramatically different perspective.

The Pragmatist Alternative: Back to the Future

Sacrificing the insights of psychodynamic functional theory is unnecessary if we acknowledge the validity of the pragmatist approach to the development and application of theory. Today, we typically label the apparently new waves of philosophy of science with such terms as *postpositivist* or *postmodern*, inasmuch as their development followed the flourishing of the positivist applications of the past half-century. However, pragmatism already exhibited the insights shared with postpositivism that are crucial for justifying the status of psychodynamic functional theory: the recognition that ultimate certainty is unattainable and concepts are constructed and temporally bound, skepticism toward universalistic generalizations, and continued preoccupation with the ways in which seemingly straightforward language can mislead.

Let us compare contemporary positivism with the pragmatist approach that animated the remarkable developments in political psychology from the 1930s through the 1960s. This pragmatism also calls for empirical research, but the conception of developing, applying, and appraising empirically based theory differs greatly from that of contemporary political psychology. For the pragmatists, sets of propositions—or hypothesis schemas—are developed by learning inductively from experience. For William James, propositions were useful "leadings"; he maintained that knowledge consisted of working hypotheses rather than universal truths.

The core premise of pragmatist science is that theories are validated by their instrumentality in use (Farr, 1999; Rorty, 1982), not by the conventional scientific method. Theory is evaluated in terms of its contribution to effective practice. Therefore, we ought to subject hypotheses to empirical exploration in order to hone our capacity to know how they can be applied, but pragmatism is highly skeptical of the universalist claims of positivist science and rejects the possibility of a decontextualized, certain science. Instead, theory consists of a repertoire of insights, each of which will prove to have greater or lesser relevance for any given context. However, the relevance of each can only be determined as the specific context is explored, not in any a priori way that settles on certain propositions abstracted from specific contexts.

For the sake of the efficiency of this exploration, it is useful to determine which propositions have been prevalent in apparently similar cases, but propositions should not be discarded simply because they are disconfirmed by a test in a particular context. Instead, each proposition that is promising in terms of providing insight would prompt further probing in the particular case to determine how much credence the proposition deserves as a guide to addressing that case. Consider the proposition that rigid political attitudes may reflect a brittle adjustment to internal psychological tensions. This proposition may provide very useful insights into how to predict whether such attitudes are held by particular individuals and how to relate to them, yet this rigidity may instead reflect an unusually strong drive, or simply an uncompromising negotiating strategy. By the same token, an individual may cope with internal psychological tensions in ways that do not result in rigid political attitudes, but this does not diminish the utility of the availability of the proposition to explore in particular cases.

The pragmatist approach is particularly compatible with a postpositivist political psychology intended to guide policymakers and the public in pursuing the common interest in effective and democratic ways. Although positivist testing through controlled experiment, simulation, or survey can demonstrate the limitations of broad hypotheses, it cannot definitively confirm general laws guaranteed to hold in the specific applications at hand. Without one dominant assured law, the pragmatist comes equipped with multiple possibilities. Insofar as recognizing the importance of life histories, internal psychodynamics, and the plasticity of the political manifestations of psychological states is crucial for understanding political psychology, the positivist approach and its theoretical reductionism become insufficient.

Consider how some of the hard-learned lessons of political psychology from previous eras seem to have been lost. First, the insight that psychological drives can result in very different political predispositions, depending on contextual details, should discourage the efforts to try to cast correlations linking economic, political, and social conditions to political behavior as if they were meaningful generalizations. Yet this is the major research thrust of much of today's political psychology.

Second, another insight reached many years ago is the plasticity of both the meanings and content of attitudes and actions that carry the same label over time. Despite the impressive innovation that has gone into developing methods to understand meaning and tracing the changes in meaning over time,[13] many contemporary political psychology studies still treat political attitudes as if they were fixed. The self-defined conservative of today is not necessarily the conservative of 10 years ago; the willingness to engage in a political demonstration has different significance as the risks of participation change over time; any given depiction of racial attitudes will have different meaning as populations become more globalized and multi-ethnic.

A third lesson, learned with great difficulty, is that fundamental political predispositions, such as the willingness to uphold democratic practice, are manifested differently according to levels of deprivation and stress. The practice of ignoring this lesson is illustrated by the huge controversy that raged over the construct of the authoritarian personality. The initially promising approach of tying the personality type defined as "authoritarian" to undemocratic attitudes and behaviors has been widely rejected because survey and experimental simulation evidence has not shown the expected connections. However, the motivation behind the authoritarian personality research was to explore the reactions to the emergence of radically authoritarian political leadership—especially under the conditions of political and economic turmoil—clearly implying a level of stress and arousal that simply cannot be replicated by experiments or surveys. The fact that measures of developmental factors (e.g., childrearing practices), personality assessments, and political attitudes seem less highly correlated than the theory would predict may well be an artifact of weak methodology removed from the real world. Alternative methodologies, such as relying on psychiatric assessments of individuals confronted with real-world crises, have been decidedly scarce.

Fourth, the bulk of leadership studies now applaud the power of so-called transformational and charismatic leaders, without adequate recognition of the much earlier warnings about the negative potentials of these forms of leadership. In emphasizing the importance of change agents for organizations believed to be stagnant or unresponsive to emerging economic or societal needs, these approaches typically ignore the potential destructiveness of leaders who impose their needs for dominance and their twisted visions onto followers who lack the capacity to resist.

Fifth, the capacity to appreciate the complexity of the developmental aspects of political psychology has been weakened by the exclusion of long-term psychodynamics. Perhaps today's political scientists are simply less interested in origins of political predispositions than in the consequences of these predispositions, or regard the psychodynamic functional theories as unattractive because they are not definitively testable within the prevailing positivist paradigm. The longer-term, more holistic understandings of the development of critical political predispositions, based in the previous era on life histories and in-depth clinical studies, simply cannot be addressed by survey and experimental-simulation approaches. Therefore, the generational or age-cohort changes in political predispositions remain either unaddressed or are subject to ad hoc, commonsense explanations rather than the rich theorizing that flourished earlier.

REVITALIZING POLITICAL PSYCHOLOGY THROUGH THE WORKS OF HAROLD D. LASSWELL

If so much has been lost by the unwarranted neglect of the heritage of psychodynamic functional theory, where can we turn to recapture this holistic understanding of political psychology? Can we find thinkers who embraced the more realistic and useful pragmatist orientation, yet were also attuned to the insights that psychodynamic functional theory can contribute? Such a thinker would have to be a pragmatist who did not disdain the insights of psychoanalysis, but did not fall into the narrow, doctrinaire theoretical rigidities that have emerged from the infighting among proponents of the various offshoots of Freudian psychoanalytic theory. Pragmatism is not intrinsically hostile to psychoanalytic theory, but it is not particularly close, either. Daniel Robinson (1993) noted that "the pragmatic stance is neither consistent nor at odds with, for example, behaviorist, psychoanalytic, cognitive psychology. It is neutral across schools and systems, much as a yardstick is neutral as regards one length or another. The pragmatic test has to do with the extent to which one or another conception or method or perspective is serving our highest interests" (p. 641).

The obvious choice is Harold D. Lasswell, the political scientist who dominated the development of political psychology in mid-20th-century America. He was the brilliant innovator who pioneered the study of political behavior by bringing psychoanalytic theory into American political science. He systematized the study of symbols and propaganda through the development of rigorous content analysis techniques (Janowitz, 1968). His framework for assessing communications is still orthodoxy at journalism schools. As a lay psychoanalyst, Lasswell conducted psychoanalytic sessions and contributed to the body of psychodynamic functional theory through his articles in such journals as *Psychiatry* and his faculty status (1938–39) in the Washington School of Psychiatry. As an institution builder, he was instrumental in the founding of two prominent journals, *Public Opinion Quarterly* and *Policy Sciences*. He is revered as the founder of the policy sciences movement.

Heinz Eulau (like Lasswell, a past president of the American Political Science Association as well as a leader of the behavioral movement in political science) and Susan Zlomke judged that, "Harold Dwight Lasswell was, during his lifetime, an omnipresence as the most original and eminent of political scientists. . . . Lasswell's extensive and wide-ranging books, essays, and other publications remain extraordinarily rich sources of ideas, methods, and topics for the study of political behavior" (Eulau & Zlomke, 1999, p. 76).

Lasswell's status is enshrined in the Harold D. Lasswell prizes awarded annually by the American Political Science Association, the International Society of Political Psychology, the journal *Policy Sciences*, the Policy Studies Organization, and the Society for the Policy Sciences. He has been honored and assessed by Festschrifts, monographs, and compilations focusing solely on his work (Lasswell, 1997; McDougall, 1984; Rogow, 1969a), and innumerable analyses by political scientists either extolling or criticizing his views.

Yet aside from his unquestioned brilliance and prominence, what makes a revival of Lasswell's approach so compelling for today's political psychology? Lasswell's most prominent (and, to some, most notorious) contribution to political psychology was to bring psychodynamic functional theory to American political science. Yet, it is easy to overlook the more important contribution: transforming such theory in accordance with the principles of pragmatism. After all, Freud himself brought Freudianism to America, including his own applications to society and politics. Lasswell's true contribution was in adapting and disciplining the Freudian (and related) psychodynamic functional approaches by recasting reduction-ist, absolutist propositions into pragmatist hypotheses, securing a much stronger empirical base, and wedding psychodynamic functional insights with the broadest range of political, economic, and sociological explana-tions. Lasswell pursued the instrumental aspiration of pragmatism to broadly integrative approaches, taking into account the intricate interplay of psychological and nonpsychological factors.

Lasswell's metahypothesis, the "maximization postulate," presumes only that living creatures tend to act in ways perceived as making them better off—people strive to maximize valued outcomes. As a political sci-entist, Lasswell did not need to concern himself, as Freud had to, with the question of the ultimate origins of motivation in one drive, two drives, and so on. It was obvious to Lasswell that no matter whether drives originate from the single sexual instinct, the clash between life and death instincts, or the more complicated models of other offshoots of psychoanalysis, the sociopolitical result is that drives are channeled into a wide variety of pri-orities and preoccupations. Therefore, people will strive to maximize a wide range of outcomes (which Lasswell found convenient to categorize as power, wealth, well-being, skill, affection, respect, enlightenment, and rectitude), depending on *both* personal history and the social, political, and economic context. Lasswell was thus able to determine how different environments can channel drives into many different priorities, thereby providing the means to insert social and political institutions, culture, and pragmatic accommodations between the psyche and macrosocial trends. Because of the complexity of interactions, no universal, reductionist pat-terns are likely to exist. Therefore, Lasswell offered the bulk of his insights as hypotheses to be examined in particular contexts, and rarely asserted that any proposition would hold in all cases.

Lasswell saw the value of broadening the framework of political psy-chology to include the *possible* impact of unconscious material, and empha-sized the limitations of political analysis that presumes that individuals' behavior can be understood fully in terms of the motives and beliefs of which the individuals are aware. He did not reduce political behavior to unconscious drives and the irrational, but he left room for these phenom-ena in his schema.

Thus, in Lasswell's applications of this framework were paragons of interdisciplinary synthesis, integrating all aspects of individual psycho-dynamics and interpersonal exchange. This was epitomized by his bril-liant 1935 tour de force, *World Politics and Personal Insecurity* (Lasswell, 1935b/1965), a book of breathtaking scope and insight. Even Lasswell's most psychodynamically oriented analyses, such as his prescient 1933 article, "The Psychology of Hitlerism," invoked economic conditions (e.g., Germany's late industrialization, the hyperinflation and Great Depression of the interwar years, and the formation of unions and industrial car-tels), social movements (e.g., the German youth movements), and political institutions (e.g., the weakness of German parliamentarianism; Lasswell 1933/1948). Contrast this with Freud's speculations on politics and the social process (especially in *Group Psychology and the Analysis of the Ego*, 1921/1959; *Civilization and Its Discontents*, 1929/1961; *Totem and Taboo*, 1913/1950; and *Moses and Monotheism*, 1939) that were direct projections of individual psyche onto society, without taking into account the complexities of communications, hierarchy, organizational arrangements, and group interests.[14] Thus, Lasswell demonstrated far more care than Freud did in "scaling up" from individual psychodynamics to the societal level. In a characteristically tactful review of Freud's *Civilization and Its Discontents*, Lasswell (1931) wrote, "It is no doubt Freud's preoccupation with rectifying his theory of individual development that gives this essay a certain unexpected thinness, when it is critically considered from the sociological point of view. Freud seems to toy in passing with certain ideas, but sensing some of the methodological problems involved, draws hurriedly back" (p. 330).

Pragmatism also required empirical experience that went far beyond the introspection and intuitive clinical experience on which psychoanalytic theorizing was based. Freud relied almost exclusively on clinical sessions as his empirical base, whereas Lasswell sought out individuals in particular political roles for both standard and psychiatric interviews, developed content-analysis techniques for the systematic analysis of communications, and utilized careful histories rather than Freud's conjectures about the patricide of sons to wrest their sisters away from the father's sexual monopoly or Moses' transformation from pampered Egyptian prince to Jewish leader. Lasswell was, indeed, ferociously empirical. His 1948 compilation of some 16 essays was entitled *The Analysis of Political Behaviour: An Empirical Approach*, with a major section on "how to observe and record politics," which included a reprint of his 1941 proposal for a permanently ongoing "World Attention Survey," a remarkably ambitious project to chart and analyze the trends in prestigious newspapers' foci of attention through highly systematic content analysis. In the 1960s he co-authored the *World Handbook of Political and Social Indicators* (Russett, Alker, Deutsch, & Lasswell, 1964). Lasswell's view was that even if explanatory constructs need not be confined to observable constructs, true behavioralism (not to be confused with the profligate quantification and reductionist modeling that tried to appropriate this label in the 1970s and 1980s) required a vocabulary, framework, and modes of inquiry that could also focus on observable, empirical outcomes.

Lasswell's highly celebrated 1950 book *Power and Society: A Framework for Political Inquiry*, co-authored with the philosopher and semanticist Abraham Kaplan, provided the behavior-based vocabulary required to cast propositions in terms that are, in principle, testable. Bruce Lannes Smith (1969) described this book as "a formal and systematic statement (not unreminiscent of Aquinas' *Summa Theologica*) on the entire propositional structure of political science" (p. 51). Lasswell embraced one crucial tenet of logical positivism—that meaningful concepts must have empirical (but not necessarily observable) referents—but, as a pragmatist, Lasswell did not take the scientific-positivist step of presuming that these propositions need be invariantly true or that they were the only propositions providing insight for political analysis. Lasswell retained the capacity to use his behaviorally oriented framework to link drives and personality to predispositions to observable actions, even if some of the links are not directly observable.

WHO WAS HAROLD LASSWELL?

Lasswell's distinctive intellectual history elucidates how he succeeded in bringing psychodynamic functional theory into political psychology in accordance with the principles of pragmatism.[15] As a student (Ph.D. in political science in 1926) and young faculty member at the University of Chicago, Lasswell inherited scientific pragmatism from William James, John Dewey, George Herbert Mead, and his University of Chicago Political Science Department mentor, Charles E. Merriam.[16] This is clearly demonstrated in the aforementioned collaboration with Kaplan in writing *Power and Society*, a masterpiece of hypothesis schemas.[17] Bruce Lannes Smith noted that "[t]here is little doubt that Lasswell was predisposed to his later investigation of Freudian thought by his familiarity as an undergraduate and graduate student with John Dewey's pragmatism and with the 'social interactionist' psychology of the philosopher George Herbert Mead" (Smith, 1969, pp. 51–52). Even in his earliest writings, Lasswell held that "prediction [is] useful as a preliminary to control" (1923, p. 127); any reliable basis for prediction is therefore useful, and psychodynamic theories are valuable if they can provide any predictive power.

Lasswell was a Midwesterner (born in the small town of Donnellson, Illinois, in 1902), possessing both a firm belief in the ideals of American democracy and the skepticism reflected in Merriam's anti-corruption reformist crusades. On the one hand, political action could be healthy and constructive—Merriam himself was a Chicago City Council member and a mayoral contender, and other members of the Political Science Department shared the view "that to teach politics and to act politically were not conflicting aims, that their conjunctions might indeed be a new, modern necessity" (Karl, 1974, p. 30). On the other hand, politics could be corrosive and corrupt, and could give vent to the most hostile and destructive impulses. Lasswell's view that political psychology should serve to strengthen democracy was utterly consistent with the ethos of his background and training at Chicago.

The University of Chicago was not just the hotbed of the "new political science," it was also avant garde in sociology, psychology, philosophy, and anthropology. Lasswell, through connections at the University and the Social Science Research Council under Merriam's presidency, was in constant contact with the new behavioralists of the day, including John Dollard, Clyde Kluckhorn, Margaret Mead, and Edward Sapir. Many of these theorists were heavily influenced by Freud and by the functionalist perspective on the rise and persistence of beliefs and practices.[18] Lasswell was fully committed to this "functional" (as opposed to "conventional") analysis,[19] although more attuned to the microfunctionalism of Malinowski than the macrolevel, equilibrium-assuming structural-functionalism of Radcliff-Brown.[20] Kardiner and Preble (1961) best described Malinowski's functionalist approach as follows: "The functional view of culture lays down the principle that in every type of civilization, every custom, material object, idea and belief fulfills some vital function, has some task to accomplish, represents an indispensable part of a working whole" (p. 173). For Lasswell, then, the functional approach meant asking what function each belief or action serves, including functions that may be in the service of the psyche. To ignore that dimension would be to lose the holism of the analysis. In terms of the process of political cognition, the implication of the functional perspective is that political learning must be conceived not as a passive absorption of what is experienced or taught, but rather as a mechanism in the service of psychological and nonpsychological needs.

Rubbing shoulders with anthropologists, philosophers, psychologists, and sociologists also reinforced for Lasswell the interdisciplinary outlook championed by Merriam and other luminaries at Chicago who were committed to strengthening the social sciences as a whole. Later, in the 1950s, Lasswell discovered and brilliantly implemented another synergy among his intellectual and pragmatic commitments: that the best way to ensure the integration of the social sciences is to focus on real-world problems; any serious effort to address such problems clearly requires the insights of all social sciences. This problem orientation became the centerpiece of the policy sciences movement, of which Lasswell is the acknowledged founder and hero.

In the late 1920s and early 1930s, Lasswell, with the strong encouragement of Merriam, went to Europe to study both the dramatic sociopolitical changes and the new currents of psychodynamic functional approaches. In England, he studied at the London School of Economics, not such a surprising choice in light of the fact that as a 22-year-old recent college graduate he had co-authored a well-received labor economics textbook, *Labor Attitudes and Problems* (Atkins & Lasswell, 1924). Even in this labor economics textbook, the emphasis on attitudes and perceptions is apparent from the title per se.

Much more important, however, were Lasswell's travels to Berlin, Vienna, Paris, Budapest, and other cities to study psychoanalytic theory (and conduct supervised psychoanalyses) under Alfred Adler, Franz Alexander, Sandor Ferenczi, Karen Horney, and Theodor Reik, among others. Smith (1969) points out that Lasswell probably was "in some ways" predisposed to a positive reception of these approaches because of his earlier exposure to the works of Havelock Ellis, W. I. Thomas, Alfred North Whitehead, and George Herbert Mead, all of whom emphasized the importance of social and psychological connections and the importance of symbols. Yet, Smith acknowledged that these sociologists and philosophers could hardly be classified as Freudians. It was for Lasswell—with his deep social science training, commitment to progressivism and pragmatism, and first-hand exposure to psychoanalytic theories and techniques—to put it all together.

As an American outsider who could stand aloof from the intense infighting of the European psychoanalytic movements of the time, Lasswell could afford to savor rather than despair of the variety of the rapidly sprouting offshoots of Freudianism. Lasswell, despite his great admiration of Freud's contributions, chided Freud for becoming "less preoccupied in defending himself against his psychiatric colleagues than in perfecting defenses against his friends" (Lasswell, 1930/1960, p. 70), and he responded with intelligence and discrimination to the analysts who followed and then modified Freud. Lasswell was, indeed, part of the neo-Freudian movement to revise and sharpen Freud's original work. Lasswell was in an advantageous position to accept the basic thrust of psychodynamic functional theories without being wedded to one particular doctrinaire theory.

From this exposure and his remarkably fertile mind, Lasswell contributed a vast array of books and articles that developed and applied psychology to political analysis. The most relevant are *Propaganda Technique in the World War* (1927b/1971), *Psychopathology and Politics* (1930), *World Politics and Personal Insecurity* (1935b/1965), *Politics: Who Gets What, When, How* (1936b/1958), *Power and Personality* (1948b), and *Language of Politics: Studies in Quantitative Semantics* (1949). Among his articles and chapters, the most relevant are "The Triple-Appeal Principle: A Contribution of Psychoanalysis to Political and Social Science" (1932), "The Psychology of Hitlerism" (1933/1948), "The Study and Practice of Propaganda" (1935a), "The Garrison State" (1941), "Propaganda and Mass Insecurity" (1950), "Democratic Character" (1951), and "The Selective Effect of Personality on Political Participation" (1954).

In its most condensed form, we can summarize Lasswell's psychological model as follows:

> Political and policy goals (demands that are intricately linked with identifications and expectations) arise from values reflecting not only rewards from the external environment, but also from internal psychological dynamics. These include strivings originating from id, ego, superego, or some combination of these personality components (the "triple-appeal principle"); and the displacement of emotionally problematic private motives onto public objects. These factors determine not only the focus of demands, but also their intensity and rigidity. Distortions of political character, leading to irresponsible and undemocratic behavior, arise out of preoccupation with power (or, in some instances, with another value, e.g., wealth or affection) and emerge when deprivations of respect are overcome by the single-minded pursuit of power or the other value. The reaction of the populace to political and policy initiatives also reflects not only the direct content of the initiatives, but also their resonance with id, ego, and superego appeals, and with affects associated with other initiatives that share overlapping symbols (a key principle of propaganda). The appeals of leaders also reflect these influences, including charismatic and vicarious id appeals that may give rise to irresponsible leaders who are unaccountable to those whom they lead. The ability of the populace to maintain the self-discipline needed

to behave democratically and responsibly depends on the intensity of crisis and resulting anxiety, but can be countered with wise management of symbols, policies, and efforts to enlighten the citizenry about the psychodynamics behind their impulses.

This model and the broader analytical framework that underlies it demonstrate that political psychology can address the major problems of intergroup hostility, antidemocratic predispositions, abuse of power by nonaccountable leadership, inability to recognize true policy interests, and the sway of propaganda. It can trace the impact of earlier experience, on both the individual and group level, to account for otherwise inexplicable affects. It can revitalize how political psychology addresses emotion and predisposition in political behavior.

We analyze and extend Lasswell's contributions by focusing on four key aspects: the psychodynamic mechanisms drawn from psychoanalytic theory, the analysis of "democratic character" for both the public and the elite, the analysis of the role of symbols in political communication, and the classification of belief systems, which Lasswell termed "perspectives" and the "self-system." We take up each of these in turn.

Psychodynamic Mechanisms

Within his highly distinctive framework for linking drives to political perspectives (identifications, demands, and expectations), Lasswell incorporated psychodynamic mechanisms adapted from psychoanalytic theory. Two of the most notable mechanisms that he studied are explored in depth and extended in our analysis. The *displacement hypothesis* (the main subject of chap. 2) accounts for some of the most extreme and rigid political attitudes as they emerge from psychologically threatening intimate relationships, through "the displacement of private motives onto public objects." The *triple-appeal principle* (a core concept in our chap. 3, especially with regard to the analysis of political symbols and propaganda) capitalizes on the distinctions of the relations among id, ego, and superego processes to account for the attraction of certain individuals, political movements, and policies. This analysis goes far to explain the appeal of scoundrels and irresponsible policies as well as that of saints and sound policies. Lasswell cautioned that id, ego, and superego do not simply translate as impulse, reason, and conscience; our analysis clarifies the implications of the differences.

Democratic Character

Lasswell's character analyses captured the predispositions for behaving responsibly and democratically, in times of crisis as well as in "normal" times. In our chapters on the political character of the body politic (chap. 4) and on the character of political leaders (chap. 5), we present Lasswell's strategy of defining a cluster of mutually reinforcing traits of optimism, willingness to share, and freedom from narrow preoccupations with power or any other value. We contrast the current enthusiasm for transformational and charismatic leadership with Lasswell's concerns about the lack of accountability of leaders who attain power through appeals such as charisma or the indulgence of id impulses on the part of followers. We also demonstrate how Lasswell's analysis of character as comprised of both perspectives and the "intensity system" permitted him to grasp the effects of stress and anxiety on the capacity of individuals to maintain the self-discipline that democratic behavior requires. In chapter 6 on political climate, mood, and crisis, we review Lasswell's analysis of the potential impacts of acute provocations on the normal levels of observance of democratic norms.

Symbols

Lasswell understood the creation and communication of political symbols as the crucial connection between leaders and followers, between policy-makers and the public. He applied the psychoanalytic model of multiple associations to define the perception of a given object as a dense tangle of symbol associations, often subject to propagandistic manipulation. Lasswell also used this broader conception of subjective meanings to link political and policy appeals with the psychodynamics of relevant audiences. This insight opened up an entirely new line of inquiry concerning the associational strategies of propaganda. To explore these associations, Lasswell formalized content-analysis methodologies that are still practiced today. In addition to capturing the impact of symbol associations tapping into personal psychodynamics, his theoretical framework and methods for assessing political communication could also capture the more mundane—yet no less powerful—impacts of the sheer prevalence of specific political symbols in shaping the focus of attention. Lasswell's contribution to the theory of political communication and propaganda greatly improved the understanding of how the manipulation of symbols and their meanings shape the receptivity of political and policy appeals, through his remarkable insight that the apparent ambiguity of symbols with multiple meanings and connotations—considered a nuisance of definition by earlier communications analysts—is the key to the transfer of affect from one referent to another. His perspective on the meanings and associations of political and policy material transcends the content normally examined by political scientists and policy analysts.

Perspectives and the "Self-System"

Lasswell developed a refined and parsimonious framework for characterizing an individual's political orientation and predispositions to political action, outlined briefly in chapter 3. By distinguishing among identifications (how individuals symbolize themselves), demands, and expectations, Lasswell was able to connect political attitudes to the flow of political symbols as well as to the drives originating in psychodynamics. The concept of the self-system (utilized by George Herbert Mead [1934] and later adopted by many other social psychologists, perhaps most notably Albert Bandura [1986]) tied together these perspectives and the intensity of drives and predispositions. This combination is crucial to account for both the impetus to action and the impairment brought on by anxiety, which often threatens the ability to maintain the self-discipline needed for responsible, democratic political behavior. Indeed, as one of many indications of Lasswell's originality, his outline of the self-system anticipated the development of self-psychology by Heinz Kohut and others in the 1970s and 1980s (Kohut, 1971).

WHY HAS LASSWELL BEEN NEGLECTED?

Rekindling interest in a thinker who made his fundamental contributions more than a half-century ago is a daunting task, no matter how brilliant his contributions. In today's social and behavioral sciences, there is often a presumption that more recent work incorporates and eclipses what was done earlier. Yet, this is largely untrue for political psychology, which has lost many of Lasswell's insights. It is true that Lasswell remains honored, but, despite notable exceptions, the true impact of his ideas on political psychology and in political science in general has diminished. Based on an examination of citations of Lasswell's work, Eulau and Zlomke (1999) argued that many invocations of Lasswell's theory and framework are superficial, reflecting little understanding of his contributions. This also requires a short explanation, lest one think that contemporary political psychologists have simply and gracefully retired Lasswell as a theorist to be taken seriously, while still honoring his name in symbolic ways.

Part of the answer, to be sure, lies in the clash between positivist and pragmatist outlooks that we have already examined. Yet another factor is that the Lasswell remembered is often a caricature of the real Lasswell, mischaracterizing his efforts as simply the application of Freudian theory. Consider this rather recent summary by William McGuire (1993):

> Behind the 1930s introjection of Freudianism by many political scientists looms the father figure of Harold Lasswell . . . whose influence launched the use of Freudian notions of unconscious erotic (and thanatotic) motivations, of defense mechanisms that adaptively channel the expression of these drives, and of Freud's psychosexual notions of how oral, anal, and phallic frustrations of early childhood form the id, ego, and superego aspects of personality. (p. 15)

This seriously misrepresents Lasswell's approach. It incorrectly implies that Lasswell accepted a simplistic model of two drives. In fact, Lasswell was appropriately agnostic about the nature of primal motivations or drives, and rendered the issue moot by emphasizing the plasticity of expressions of drives. McGuire was also wrong in implying that Lasswell accepted the Freudian theory that conflicts of the earliest life stages define politically relevant personality characteristics. Lasswell focused far more on the struggles of the older child or the adolescent to maintain respect and self-respect than on the earliest stages. It is true that Lasswell made ample use of the id-ego-superego distinction, but the origin of these entities was essentially irrelevant to Lasswell's premise that the appeals to id, ego, and superego have different characteristics and consequences. The superficial equation of Lasswell's approach to psychoanalytic theory overlooks his remarkable accomplishments in transforming the Freudian impulse into sound social science.

Finally, the image of Lasswell may be one of broad-brush theorizing rather than careful empirical analysis. If the political psychologist is familiar only with *Psychopathology and Politics*, or *Politics: Who Gets What, When, How*, Lasswell may seem to represent an earlier era of impressionistic rather than systematic, empirical analysis. Familiarity with Lasswell's content analysis approaches to propaganda (e.g., *Propaganda Technique in the World War* [1927/1971]; *World Revolutionary Propaganda: A Chicago Study* [Lasswell & Blumenstock, 1939]; *Language of Politics: Studies in Quantitative Semantics* [Lasswell, Leites, & Associates, 1949]) would quickly disabuse anyone of this misperception. Ironically, Lasswell had thrown down the gauntlet to political psychologists to develop systematic measures to trace the observable manifestations of the dynamics that psychoanalysis offers for understanding political behavior.[21] With few exceptions,[22] this challenge has not been engaged.

EXTENDING LASSWELL'S LEGACY

If Lasswell's contributions had been static, without the possibility of being extended to broader areas and new phenomena, they would be of little use for deepening our understanding of political behavior. However, his legacy can be extended to a broader range of phenomena than Lasswell's applications encompassed, and can extend much more richly into the public policy arena. Lasswell's political psychology framework (as distinct from his specific theories and applications) was largely complete by the end of the 1940s. When he turned to developing the policy sciences, his efforts were not so much oriented to applying psychological theory to the policy process—although the policy sciences framework and his earlier work are certainly compatible—as they were to refining the analysis of the policy process and the interplay among values, institutions, and processes.

In this volume, we demonstrate that broadening and applying Lasswell's theories can generate fruitful insights into the policy process. In our chapter on the displacement mechanism (Lasswell's most prominent model for the genesis of political attitudes driven by internal psychodynamics), we develop a set of criteria for determining, in specific situations, whether invoking unconscious dynamics is a constructive way to account for attitudes toward public policy issues. Our efforts to extend Lasswell's framework and theories include a substantial broadening of the range of displacement mechanisms. Lasswell's "displacement of private motives onto public objects" may be extended to displacements from one public object to another, from one locus of responsibility or blame to another, from one value to another, and from one identification to another. We also show that displacements can rise out of conscious actions, without denying the possibility that unconscious dynamics may be responsible for some displacements. Furthermore, we outline the strategies most appropriate for clarifying the public interest when attitudes are subjected to these displacements. We argue that when the evidence of unconscious psychodynamics at play is weak, the most constructive strategies for clarifying and securing the public interest consist of revealing the discrepancies between objective conditions and the content or intensity of beliefs, directly addressing the issue onto which the affect has been displaced, or redirecting the displaced affect to less problematic foci. When unconscious psychodynamics are in evidence, more appropriate strategies include addressing the original problem that provoked the displacement, and applying essentially psychotherapeutic techniques to enhance citizens' self-insight into why problematic displacements had occurred.

We also show the compatibility of Lasswell's approaches to the more recent advances in cognitive psychology in order to understand reactions to political and policy initiatives. In several ways, especially through his theory of symbol associations and learning, Lasswell anticipated the work on decision making under uncertainty, such as the heuristics theory of Kahneman et al. (1982). The formation of attitudes toward political and policy initiatives can reflect both displacement and generalization. We additionally extend Lasswell's theoretical reach by employing the triple-appeal principle beyond its original scope, to understand the choices—and missteps—of the propagandists themselves. Our analysis of how propaganda is generated—and why it is sometimes ineffective—recognizes that leaders and propagandists are also subject to their own nonrational personality needs.

In exploring the implications of Lasswell's theory of democratic character, we develop an analysis of the strategies of intervention to address three types of individuals prone to undemocratic political predispositions: those who lack knowledge of democratic norms, those with character deformations that predispose to undemocratic behavior, and those who are pressed into undemocratic behavior by high levels of anxiety.

Finally, we assess the current theories of leadership through the lens of Lasswell's triple-appeal principle. In doing so, we reveal how the contrast between transactional and transformational leadership is overdrawn, as transformational leaders often shape followers' perspectives through the exchange of emotional rewards.

We offer this analysis in the hope that studying Lasswell can help us explore how a framework that can accommodate psychodynamic insights can be reconciled with contemporary psychology. Whether or not one accepts the existence or explanatory utility of unconscious psychodynamics, the Lasswellian framework can help bridge the gap between contemporary academic political psychology and the psychodynamic functionalist tradition. It can rekindle interest in the deep questions of emotion, psychological need, and life history and that have been neglected for decades.

Chapter 2

The Displacement Hypothesis

This chapter reviews and extends Lasswell's displacement hypothesis, his most direct and prominent application of psychoanalytic theory. Impulses and affects that are unacceptable on either an individual or a societal level are displaced or otherwise transformed in their focus or nature. In some instances, these displacements may occur without conscious awareness of the connection between the original and the resulting impulses or affects. This lack of awareness itself may complicate the resolution of political and policy issues, because lack of insight can hamper efforts to identify and resolve the issues of truly greatest concern.

Thus, Lasswell's framework for understanding displacement phenomena can incorporate the unconscious dynamics of Freudian theory. We believe that openness to the possibility of unconscious dynamics is necessary for a comprehensive behavioral framework, whether or not any particular instance of displacement entails unconscious mechanisms. Yet, Lasswell's fundamental notion of displacement is equally capable of facilitating the examination of alternative dynamics that do not invoke psychoanalytic premises concerning the unconscious. This is important for convincing political psychologists—skeptical about Freudian theory and the utility of the concept of the unconscious—that Lasswell's insights about displacement mechanisms are still compelling.

The displacement hypothesis invokes Freudian dynamics by positing that certain thoughts or emotions are so painful, threatening, or overwhelming that the individual will repress them, and redirect them onto more remote or otherwise less potent objects.[23] The impulses behind these thoughts or emotions range from hostility (aggressiveness, jealousy, etc.) to affection. Hostile impulses originally targeted at relatives or other close individuals pose obvious emotional risks, but less obviously problematic emotions may as well. For example, strong affection toward same-gender individuals often provokes anxiety in homophobic cultures, or an affection that is thwarted by an unresponsive parent may be displaced because of the emotional discomfort caused by the inability to express the affection or to receive reciprocation.[24]

In *Psychopathology and Politics* (1930/1960, p. 75), Lasswell presented his famous formula for one variety of displacement:

$$p \} d \} r = P$$

That is, private motives (p) are displaced (d) onto public objects, and then rationalized (r) in terms of the public interest, producing "political man" (P). This last step of rationalization occurs for some individuals more thoroughly than for others; in particular, those who come to be heavily involved in politics and public affairs.[25] This is because political figures typically must account for their political views more frequently and with greater polish and coherence than do ordinary citizens. However, Lasswell's hypothesis was that both political figures and ordinary citizens tend to lack insight into why their attitudes toward the derivative targets have come about; full, conscious insight would negate the reduction of anxiety accomplished by the repression of the original thoughts. Thus, a model of unconscious dynamics is an obvious (if controversial) way to explain how displacements may come about.

Using this formulation, Lasswell argued that some political attitudes are derived from impulses and affects originating in the smaller world of each individual's personal relationships. However, this was not a simple matter of generalization, such as "adulation for one's father leads to adulation of political authority figures." Rather, the displacement results in an inverse relationship between the orientation toward the original object and the secondary object: The intensity of affect toward the original object diminishes as the intensity toward the other increases.

A more general model can be formulated:

> Psychologically problematic affects, identifications, and demands are displaced onto other objects, and rationalized (partially or fully) according to the belief systems of the individual.

This formulation also specifies that displacement has impacts on both the original target of the threatening thoughts and emotions and on the secondary target of the displacement. Displacement leads to (a) attenuated and distorted affect, attention, and beliefs concerning the original object or issue; (b) exaggerated and distorted affect, attention, and beliefs about the objects or issues to which the displaced impulses come to be attached; and (c) possibly a further distortion of affect, attention, and beliefs toward yet other objects if the target of the original displacement no longer serves the function of discharging the original emotional threat.

This formulation allows for greater scope for displacement mechanisms; indeed, several important variants are found in Lasswell's own works. It also recognizes that rationalization may diverge from the public interest (e.g., observing the will of God, aiding one's family), but that some form of self-justification and reduction of dissonance is a likely by-product of the displacement.

Yet, for any of these variants, the question remains as to how—in terms of psychological processes—the displacement occurs, and in particular whether it involves the unconscious. This question is important not only in terms of whether to accept the displacement model in light of one's acceptance or rejection of the concept of the unconscious; it is also important because the resulting behavior, and the effectiveness of interventions, may depend on the nature of the psychological dynamics.

In this chapter, we review the scope of the hypothesis as Lasswell cast it and as it could be extended, as well as examine its status as an extension of Freudian theory. We look at the policy significance that displacements would have. We ask what is entailed in scaling up from individual psychodynamics to group psychodynamics, by reviewing group dynamics that can lead to displacements without unconscious psychodynamics necessarily playing a role. We also explain how the displacement hypothesis reflects the configurative breadth so valued by the policy sciences approach that Lasswell also pioneered (Torgerson, 1985). Although the displacement hypothesis is important in itself, its evolution is also a window on broader issues of political psychology and the policy sciences.

VARIETIES AND IMPLICATIONS OF DISPLACEMENT DYNAMICS

What is the scope of Lasswell's displacement hypothesis? We find in Lasswell's own work at least three modalities of displacement, and we develop two more that are consonant with his theory.

Private to Public Displacements

In its initial form, the displacement hypothesis posited that impulses toward *private objects* are displaced onto political objects. This mechanism is invoked to account for the remarkable levels of affect toward public figures. Just as Freud asked the fundamental question of how affects toward parents and other proximate objects emerge from the infant's internal, physical sensations, Lasswell tried to explain how intense affects come to be attached to public objects beyond what could be explained by rational deliberations. Lasswell also posited that the individual would interpret his or her impulse as part of a principled political-belief system. Both the intensity and the rationalization may insulate the displaced impulse from external factors such as new information, overtures at compromise, or changing objective conditions.

In considering the policy implications of the pervasive operation and influence of private to public displacements, it is useful to distinguish between two subvariants, according to whether the original object is self or other. When the initial affect is directed toward the self—for example, self-disgust or feelings of inadequacy—then one can easily imagine the connection between external conditions that may be addressable through policy. For instance, national or international economic depressions may create feelings of personal inadequacy that, insofar as they are psychologically intolerable, may be displaced onto government leaders, outgroups, or other public objects. Or, alternatively, changing social mores may loosen moral standards, inducing individuals to engage in behavior that they regard, on some level, as shameful. This model thus runs from societal-level trends and conditions to individual psychological states, then to beliefs and affects toward societal-level objects. We can contrast this with Durkheim's model, for example, in *Suicide* (1897), which begins with the same premise that external (e.g., economic and sociological) conditions would have an impact on the individual's mental state, but then assumes that the individual will internalize the effects and manifest them only in private behavior such as suicide. In contrast, when the original object is other than the self (e.g., a parent), it is much more difficult to see how policy actions can have an impact aside from long-term efforts to alter deep cultural patterns associated with pathologies in dysfunctional family dynamics.

The mode of displacing private motives onto public objects (the prominence of which is perhaps unfortunate in overshadowing many other politically relevant forms of displacement) was emphasized in Lasswell's *Psychopathology and Politics* in part because of his effort to develop the personality profile of "political man": an individual who is driven by preoccupation with public affairs. Anyone can displace private motives onto public objects (e.g., rioting against the prime minister who comes to represent a resented authority figure), but the "political man" has undertaken the rationalizations that make the individual comfortable in public life because his or her beliefs and actions are held to be consistent with the general interest.

Second, Lasswell invoked displacement as a mechanism to account for attitudes toward public objects that originate in attitudes toward *other public objects*. Consider his (1936b/1958) interpretation of anti-Semitism: "Plainly the Jew was available as the symbol which more than any other could be utilized as a target of irrelevant emotional drives. The hatred of the country for the city, of the aristocracy for the plutocracy, of the middle class for the manual toilers and the aristocracy for the plutocracy could be displaced upon the Jew" (p. 45).

Third, *blame and responsibility* may be displaced to avoid the distress of being held accountable for unacceptable behavior. The concept of projection of one's undesirable qualities onto others is obviously at play. Self-justifying interpretations of political history abound, whether in the form of scapegoating, which places blame on others, or shifting anger or disgust from self to abstractions such as communism or capitalism (Freud, 1940/1969). Lasswell's interpretation of anti-Semitism was also congruent with this form of displacement. In "The Psychology of Hitlerism," published in 1933, Lasswell argued: "Since the Germans hate most in themselves, as a collective unit, cultural diversity and intellectual virtuosity (qualities which they simultaneously admire), it is scarcely surprising to discover that they have turned upon the Jew as the most typical exponent of their own limitations" (cited in Rogow, 1969b, p. 136).[26]

Fourth, several dynamics may involve displacements from one *value cat-egory* (power, enlightenment, wealth, well-being, skill, affection, respect, rectitude) to another. Freud recognized the possibility of such shifts, con-veying these dynamics in terms of shifts in instincts.[27] One possibility is that holding particular values may be unacceptable to the individual. Perhaps they are unattainable, and therefore pose the risk of depression, self-disgust, or other emotional distress because of failure. The frustrated artist may become the hard-driving, successful entrepreneur, or the dis-appointed aspiration for wealth could be displaced onto aspirations for power or respect. Perhaps the original impulses are unacceptable in light of the individual's need to be upstanding and worthy of self-respect and the respect of others. The phenomenon of "sublimation"—the transforma-tion of an unacceptable impulse into a more acceptable one—is relevant here. Thus, some people turn their backs on their own acquisitiveness, or find their own cravings for power to be inappropriate, and redirect their self-demands to other values.

It is worth noting that Lasswell's matrix of value categories permits us to explore whether a given preoccupation with one value may have arisen from the sublimation of an impulse related to another value, without pre-suming that the original impulse is of a sexual nature. Lasswell's value framework allows for this possibility, inasmuch as the affection and well-being values can encompass both the emotional and physical-drive aspects of sexuality, yet one does not have to presume that sublimations arise solely from the displacement of sexual impulses. In contrast, Laplanche and Pontalis (1973) pointed out that sublimation:

> is postulated by Freud to account for human activities which have no apparent connection with sexuality but which are assumed to be motivated by the force of the sexual instinct. The main types of activity described by Freud as sublimated are the artistic creation and intellectual inquiry. The instinct is said to be sublimated in so far as it is diverted towards a new, nonsexual aim and in so far as its objects are socially valued ones. (p. 431)

Another possibility is that instead of experiencing the emotional distress or practical difficulties of acknowledging a particular value deprivation, the individual will displace his or her dissatisfaction onto other values. Lasswell's argument in this regard is that the psychological pain of being preoccupied with deprivations concerning one value would provoke a shift to preoccupations with other values. Consider the case of high levels of distress that a "rugged individualist" may feel in admitting to himself or herself the pain of disapproval by others. In such cases, the associated anger may be displaced onto other emotionally charged preoccupations, such as wealth and power. Such displacements may make it extremely hard to resolve policy conflicts because of the difficulty of identifying the true source of dissatisfaction. For example, a low-income group that seems to be uncooperative and "ungrateful" for a city government's initiative to provide its members with public housing may be reacting less to the economics of the initiative per se than to the disrespectful way they have been treated by the city government.

Fifth, threatening *identifications* may be displaced onto alternative identifications. The avoidance of self-hatred is often cited as a cause of rejecting otherwise obvious ascriptive identifications. Such self-hatred could arise from either the distress of being a member of a reference group that has oppressed others, or being a member of a group that is oppressed, marginalized, or disrespected. Thus, displacement of identifications can be a defense against both guilt and humiliation. For example, many observers of colonial India pointed to "self-hating" Indians who disdained traditional Indians and emulated the British ("identification with the aggressor").[28] Hero worship may also reflect the displacement of unsatisfactory personal identifications onto those of admired individuals, ranging from athletes to politicians or even fictional characters (Martin, 1988), although hero worship may have other causes as well, such as the need for security.

POLICY CHALLENGES OF DISPLACEMENT

It is important to point out that Lasswell's view of psychodynamics did not envision individuals as being impervious to external influences. Rather than presuming that these mechanisms operate strictly through individuals' personal psychodyamics, Lasswell proposed that these displacements could originate in many types of stress that challenge personal insecurity, status, and so on, and can be manipulated through propaganda, especially by targeting particular symbols that would become the objects for displacement. The global context of the 1930s described by Lasswell in *World Politics and Personal Insecurity* (1935b/1965) was rife with economic deprivation and physical threat. The first task of the "political psychiatrist" and the "politics of prevention," he argued, was to redirect civic energy away from actions of war and revolution onto safer human activities (p. 20). The political psychiatrist, he urged, also should help the citizens to put political leaders into proper perspective, so that these leaders could at the same time be held accountable but also enjoy support when they earned it. This requires—where justified by objective conditions—moderate and moderating attitudes toward political leaders.[29]

As policy scientists, we care about displacements when they result in attitude content and qualities that hinder efforts to resolve political and policy issues constructively. The five major obstacles to resolution can be classified as rigidity, impairment, distraction, intensity, and lack of accountability.

Rigidity renders political and policy positions unresponsive to learning and less amenable to compromise. Psychoanalytic theory attributes the origins of rigidity to the brittleness arising out of repression and displacement; therefore, the question of whether displacement involves constrictive mechanisms identified by Freud is relevant to the prediction of rigidity. Rigidity may also reflect the difficulty of achieving emotional discharge if only the secondary target is addressed and not the original source of psychological distress. This presumes the "artificiality" of the emotions associated with the target of the displacement.

Impairment of working ability may be the result of the "neurotic incapacity to concentrate or arrive at conclusions" (Lasswell, 1948b/1976, p. 95) that could arise from the whole range of repressions and other psychodynamic mechanisms, such as obsessive thought disorders, ambivalence, and persistence of no-longer-relevant behaviors (perseveration).

Distraction from the problems that would have to be addressed if tensions and dissatisfaction are to be reduced is the obvious outcome of displacement from one value category to another or from one public object to another. Consider the current anti-immigrant movements in Western Europe. Insofar as other issues—such as family disintegration, political inefficacy, or economic disappointment—are the true sources of resentment and hostility, the painful conflicts between anti- and pro-immigrant factions may exhaust the finite supply of goodwill and leaders' political capital.

The *intensity* of attitudes and affect, beyond what would be justified by "logical reflection" (the term Lasswell introduced in *Psychopathology and Politics* (1930/1960, pp. 29–30), may have a similar effect as rigidity, in making it more difficult for the individual to change his or her position when opportunities for compromise arise. In addition, more intense attitudes are more likely to provoke more extreme behavior.

Accountability is threatened by displacements of blame and responsibility, and by hero worship involving intense displacements of identification. Both self-responsibility and the accountability of leaders are compromised by scapegoating and hero worship.

What can be done about displacements that lead to problematic political behavior or policy impasses? Five broad approaches are available:

1. *Informing the individuals and groups about the discrepancies between objective conditions and the content or intensity of their beliefs.* This rational/cognitive approach presumes that conventional information (in contrast to some sort of psychotherapeutic intervention) would provide sufficient enlightenment of the individuals involved to realize that their displaced beliefs or affects are inappropriate. Lasswell advocated techniques such as the "social planetarium," a systematic display of the broadest range of potentially relevant trends and conditions designed to focus attention onto issues so that individuals can be aware of how their objectives might be affected by their stances and policy choices. He also envisioned mass communication as being useful in illuminating the public on how and why widespread attitudes may be out of kilter in terms of the public's own interests (Lasswell, 1948b).

2. *Applying essentially psychotherapeutic techniques designed to provide to involved individuals enough self-insight so that they can overcome the issues*

that led to problematic displacements. This approach presumes that self-insight requires dismantling the psychological defenses that not only cause the displacement but also block recognition of the dynamics of defense. If the obstacles to self-insight are believed to be in psychodynamics involving the unconscious, then "deeper" approaches would be preferred over the rational/cognitive approach. For example, one-on-one therapy of various kinds is proposed to provide insights into true motivations, whereas group therapy ("one-to-few patterns with either brief or prolonged expert supervision"; *Power and Personality*, 1948b/1976, p. 199) is proposed to bring insight to small groups. On the mass level, Lasswell suggested everything from mass hypnosis to insight provided by mass media fictional characters such as Donald Duck, whose "cartoon image stands for the one who loses self-control; and he enables a person to laugh at his own foibles, as well as to be reminded of them. . . . Mass therapy of destructive prejudices may be facilitated by this method" (*Power and Personality* 1948b/1976, pp. 200–201). Lasswell also pointed to the British government's tactic of permitting the free forum to allow individuals to speak their minds, vent their frustrations, and thereby "prevent crowds from reaching the level of intensity, unity and ruthlessness that releases their destructive potential" (1968, p. 677).

More recently, psychodramas, such as the so-called truth and reconciliation programs in South Africa, have been conducted as deliberately cathartic events. It is important to keep in mind that in Lasswell's schema this notion of the political psychiatrist determining the deep roots of displacement does not imply a philosopher king model in which the expert does "what is right for the patient" regardless of whether the patient accepts the diagnosis. In *Psychopathology and Politics* (1930/1960), the role of the political psychiatrist was not to dictate policies based on his or her conclusions about the motives of the body politic, but rather to help the public understand its own motives.

3. *Addressing the issues related to the original problem that provoked the displacement.* This obviously entails identifying the origins of the displacement, with great enough certainty and credibility to justify the effort. It also requires the willingness and resources to address what is identified as the source of the original problem. Some original issues may simply not be amenable to a given policymaker's efforts (e.g., if the displacement originates in anger toward a parent, there is little that a policymaker could do about it). It is more likely that displacements from one value category to another could be addressed through efforts to target the initial problem.

4. *Addressing the issue onto which the affect has been displaced.* Whether or not the secondary issue is at the "root of dissatisfaction," it is at the focus of attention and the individuals regard it as meriting attention.

5. *Redirecting the displaced affect to another, less problematic focus.* This may entail bringing greater focus of attention to different issues, objectives, and symbols, or trying to create new identifications. Lasswell had this in mind when he wrote, in *World Politics and Personal Insecurity* (1935b/1965), that "[t]he special province of political psychiatrists who

seek to develop and to practice the politics of prevention is devising inge-
nious expedients capable of discharging accumulated anxieties as harm-
lessly as possible" (p. 20).

ARE THE CONCEPTS OF "REPRESSION" AND THE "UNCONSCIOUS" NECESSARY?

Lasswell was open to the broad range of psychoanalytic theories and
approaches, and even chided Freud for paying more attention to attacking other figures in psychoanalysis than the enemies of psychoanalysis
(1930/1960). Yet, he was explicit and unapologetic about his reliance
on Freud and the concept of the unconscious. As late as 1948, Lasswell
devoted an entire chapter in *Power and Personality* to "Political Reality and
the Unconscious." Today, one of the enduring bases for rejecting Freudian
theory has been the rejection of the concept of repression to the unconscious. The anti-Freudian movement has raised questions of whether
repression into unconsciousness occurs, whether it can ever be verified
empirically, and whether the unconscious is a useful concept. Some philosophical analyses and reviews of the experimental evidence question the
distinction between the preconscious (as material not currently at the
focus of attention, but can be made so by the individual), and unconscious (as material that eludes awareness because of repression; see Erdelyi, 1992; Erwin, 1996; Farrell, 1996; Hart, 1982). Their argument is that
if "unconscious" material can be made conscious through the assistance of
a psychoanalyst, how is this different from the preconscious, which also
takes mental labor to recall?[30] On the one hand, the existence of unconscious material that is irretrievable under any form of mental labor cannot
be demonstrated; on the other hand, materials that come into consciousness through heroic efforts (e.g., extensive psychoanalysis that overcomes
defense mechanisms) might have been manufactured by the effort rather
than representing preexisting unconscious material.

Other models and metaphors have been proposed to account for the
seemingly irrational behaviors addressed by psychoanalytic theory. For
example, Abelson's (1981) script theory explains irrational behavior by
invoking previously learned scripts that are triggered by particular conditions; Skinner's stimulus–response learning (or habit learning) has long
been another alternative (Ferster & Skinner, 1957). Therefore, many have
rejected the existence of the unconscious and its utility as either scientific
concept or loose metaphor.

Is the validity of the concept of the unconscious necessary for the validity and utility of Lasswell's displacement hypotheses? Our conclusion is
that the displacement hypothesis is useful even if one does not invoke
the unconscious, but is even more so because of the option of invoking
the unconscious as a hypothesis. Preconscious and conscious mechanisms
can culminate in suppression of affects or beliefs, and then displacement,
without a "dynamic unconscious." In addition, these displacements are

enabled by group dynamics as well as by individual psychodynamics. These alternative mechanisms can account for levels of affect that have different content and intensity than what would be called for by "logical reflection." Let us explore whether conscious mechanisms can have the same effect of transferring affect and attitudes from one object to another, resulting in less intense affect toward the original object and more intense attitudes toward the secondary object that do not fit the objective situation.

Conscious Suppression and Redirection

Obviously, to a greater or lesser degree, people can consciously avoid focusing their attention on distressing information and thoughts, and instead redirect their attention to objects that hold greater psychological or practical reward. Any pattern that Freud, Lasswell, or other psychoanalytically oriented observers have offered as an example of displacement involving the unconscious could conceivably be construed as the result of conscious choice to ignore the initial impulse and redirect attention onto the secondary object, or even as temperamental disposition. This is so even if these observers inferred the operation of the unconscious because of the qualities of the resulting attitudes (e.g., their rigidity or intensity) or the characteristics of those holding the attitudes (e.g., their impaired, "neurotic" behavior).

"Spillover"

High levels of negative affect may influence a broad range of objects, as generalized anger, resentment, and so on. For example, a common explanation for the rise of Nazism and hostility toward Jews, Gypsies, and others during the interwar years is that the economic hardship and international humiliation of Germans created enormous anger and resentment that could be directed toward any target consistent with German beliefs that such targets were condemnable. One could imagine that, in focusing their hostility toward reachable outgroups, some Germans were distracted from objects of more direct responsibility for Germany's travails, such as the French and British demands for reparations. Thus, the pattern of anger displaced from the French and British to the Jews and Gypsies can be modeled without recourse to unconscious dynamics.

A contemporary example of this pattern is found in Ukrainian language policy. The government of independent Ukraine, largely powerless to punish or demand redress for past and present damage done by Russia, has been exacting a form of revenge against ethnic Russians who are Ukrainian citizens in the Crimea by imposing stringent language policies restricting the teaching and use of Russian. This policy apparently has strong support from ethnic Ukrainians. The rationalization is a combination of principle ("We must do everything we can to restore Ukrainian, which has been impoverished by Russification") and overt revenge ("*They* did it to us; we will now do it to them"). The displacement entails the disavowed—but not necessarily unconscious—shift in who "they" are.

Erroneous Generalization

Inappropriate generalization may shape attitudes of inappropriate valence and intensity. Conflicts with one outgroup may be generalized to hostility toward other outgroups, whether or not it is justified by objective conditions. Some European settlers in the New World displaced their fear and hatred toward especially aggressive Native American tribes onto the full range of tribes. Yet, generalization is inevitable because we are always in a situation of incomplete information and limited capacity to get detailed information about as-yet-unfamiliar cases. Whether or not the generalization is a justifiable shortcut depends on how costly it would have been to obtain better information, and how much the attitudes were fueled by emotion rather than reflection. Nevertheless, generalizing along the lines of "They're all that way" can lead to misleading conclusions and inappropriate policies.

Mutual Reinforcement

The muting or intensification of political attitudes can also result from the group dynamics of mutual reinforcement, through which each individual is inhibited or goaded by the others, and the acceptability or unacceptability of extreme behavior is heightened by the fact that others engage in the same behavior.[31] The classic example is the rioter who irrationally destroys property important to his or her own community.

Information Biases

Many mechanisms can account for what amounts to suppression of information that reduces the focus of attention on one object, and encourages information and greater attention regarding other objects. With respect to distressing information, one might expect that individuals would be sensitive to the risk of disapproval if they communicated about an objectionable matter, and that more positive attitudes would gain greater social acceptability. They may believe that others need no reminder of the matter. They may be motivated to find and be swayed by other information that denies or minimizes the validity or salience of the objectionable matter. They may develop alternative narratives or myths that neutralize the salience of the objectionable matter.

For example, consider postevent and contemporary Turkish attitudes toward the 1919 Armenian genocide (see also the treatment of this case in chap. 7). We would expect that few Turks would choose to communicate with other Turks about Turkish culpability in the genocide. Most Turks who are aware of the accusations would presume that other Turks are also aware. In terms of alternative attitudes, information, and myths, it is more acceptable for Turks to expound the view that many deaths occurred during the chaos of World War I and its aftermath, and that Armenians, perhaps in league with the imperialist Russians, were merely casualties among many others. The complementary, alternative myth, then, would be that Armenians today have exaggerated the genocide in order to justify their political aspirations for a reunited Armenia.

The displacement associated with this repression may come about because Turks react to hostile accusations by becoming angry themselves; such anger, in turn, may spill over to antagonism toward their accusers. Turkish leaders, perhaps sensing that Turks might feel consciously threatened or humiliated by Armenian accusations, may try to take advantage of Turkish anger to level accusations against Armenians. These events may culminate in attitudes toward Armenians that are not constructive for Turkish interests. In short, although unconscious feelings of guilt could be invoked to explain nonrational Turkish reactions, other mechanisms are available.

Lasswell recognized these possibilities in a 1967 essay on "Political Systems, Styles and Personalities," in which he noted that a collective

> demand is *repressed* when further support is not tolerated publicly or privately. *Collective repression* is not necessarily as deep as individual repression, which, strictly defined, relegates the repressed impulse to the out-of-consciousness, where it is prevented from reappearing at the full focus of waking attention by the anxieties generated by the defense mechanisms of the superego. (1967, p. 340; italics in original)

IS IT IMPORTANT TO INVOKE THE UNCONSCIOUS?

The fact that patterns tantamount to displacement can be explained without invoking the unconscious does not negate the importance of the distinction between conscious and unconscious displacements. Two crucial questions persist: Are attitudes resulting from possible unconscious displacements qualitatively different from attitudes that do not involve the unconscious? Are certain kinds of interventions likely to be more effective if the attitudes result from unconscious displacement? An affirmative answer to either question would make the issue of the unconscious highly relevant to both prediction and choice of action.

Regarding the qualities of attitudes arising out of unconscious displacement, psychoanalytical (and presumably many other psychological) theories would predict that such attitudes would be characterized by rigidity and high intensity. They would also predict that the individual is more likely to show signs of impairment in relating to the issues associated with such displacements.

Regarding the choice of interventions, the existence of unconscious displacement would call for the psychotherapeutic approaches as opposed to the rational/cognitive approaches. Some would insist that in order to uproot deeply entrenched myths that deny recognition of objectionable matters, it is necessary to resort to manipulated "psychodramas" that serve the parallel function of psychoanalysis. For example, if complacency about racial injustice is reinforced by denial that discrimination exists, or by myths that existing relationships and circumstances are acceptable, then a dramatization of racial injustice (e.g., films of lynchings) may be the form of psychodrama that could overcome the repression.

Moreover, if it were known that a displacement involved the unconscious, we would call for intensified efforts to overcome the intensity and rigidity that the attitudes would likely exhibit. This hypothesis is rooted in the idea that unconscious displacement defends more strongly against the original impulse than does a conscious displacement or one that simply involves disavowal of the initial distressing material.

Furthermore, should the unconscious play a part, we would be more skeptical about the efficacy of simply addressing it through the secondary issues. With unconscious displacement, the beliefs and affects with respect to secondary issues serve a psychodynamic need that does not go away with the mere resolution of the issue.

Finally, if we review the rationales for choosing alternative metaphors— such as scripts, self-deception, or habits of mind—we would note that the skepticism toward the unconscious is directed toward its utility as an explanation and guide to the treatment of individual psychopathologies.[32] Yet, for political psychology, these alternatives do not help us explore whether political actors are behaving with or without awareness of the motivations of their actions. Again, one may challenge in any given case whether this is true, but a framework for exploring the possibility that political actors are blocked from insight of these motivations without special interventions must have room for the unconscious.

THE EPISTEMOLOGY OF THE DISPLACEMENT HYPOTHESES: REDUCTIONISM VERSUS CONFIGURATION

Lasswell's clear admiration for Freud and psychoanalysis, and his own involvement in trying to strengthen the scientific basis for psychoanalytic theory and practice (Rogow, 1969b), raise important questions about Lasswell's political psychology. Did Lasswell commit the same errors of absolutism and reductionism that have led to a widespread rejection of psychodynamic functional theory by academic psychologists in the current era? Were the early critics of *Psychopathology and Politics* correct in asserting that Lasswell reduced politics to simplistic psychopathology?

These are particularly important questions, because Lasswell's most lasting contributions to political science and the policy sciences rest on an antireductionist embrace of the configurative approach.[33] This approach reflected nothing less than the broad movement to reintegrate the social sciences following their fragmentation in the 20th century. The configurative approach calls for a focus on how multiple factors fit among one another, rather than which factor or factors are the most important. To accomplish this, it also calls for a broad initial mapping of potentially relevant factors, which implies a refusal to exclude a priori any categories of affects, beliefs, or actions from the analytic framework (although Lasswell's framework does exclude metaphysical and other nonbehavioral concepts, such as "natural law"). The configurative approach also focuses on process, which can often be represented as temporal, causal linkages.

Although *Psychopathology and Politics* was received by some as notoriously reductionist and antirationalist, this criticism was a misreading. In that book (1930/1960), Lasswell wrote, "Besides the conscious subjective experience there is a rich unconscious life which [the psychoanalyst] is especially proficient in exposing. Thus our movements are not alone the outcome of simple conscious processes; they are said to be 'over-determined' by a variety of factors" (p. 253). By *over-determined*, Lasswell meant that the same outcome has multiple, mutually reinforcing causes. This principle, also termed *multi-functionalism* or *multiple determination* and most extensively elaborated by Robert Waelder (1936, 1963), was adopted by Freud in his later writings (1917/1935). Lasswell, having kept abreast of the advances in psychoanalytic theory, must have recognized the broadening of the causal models that Freud and others in the psychoanalytic movement were embracing.

The key point here is that Lasswell, along with the maturing psychoanalytic theory, recognized that the unconscious as well as the conscious have to be analyzed. Over-determination signifies that subjectivity reflects multiple impacts of conscious and unconscious factors that converge to form a complex attitude. There are two hurdles to the establishment and persistence of a belief: its consonance with unconscious needs and its credibility vis-à-vis the external world as it is consciously perceived and interpreted. These perceptions and interpretations may be heavily influenced by the unconscious needs, through selective attention, dismissal of dissonant information, substitution of symbols, and so on, but the external world is there nonetheless. In short, Lasswell was not posing the unconscious dynamics of the displacement hypothesis as an alternative framework to the analysis of rational interests and conscious cognition, but rather as an enriching addition to the framework of analysis.

By contrast, in his early writings Freud posited displacement as the ultimate origin of attitudes. To put the difference in its starkest form, for Lasswell it was imaginable that, in a perfectly (psychologically) healthy body politic, no displacement would take place, and all political attitudes and interactions would be in the rational pursuit of selfish or unselfish interest; whereas for early Freud it was unimaginable that attitudes could form without the displacements from infancy.

This difference may reflect not only the differences between early and later psychoanalytic theory, but also the subtle but important distinction between the questions that Freud and Lasswell addressed. Freud faced the most fundamental, virtually physiological question of how infants, initially experiencing only physical sensations, can develop *any* orientations and affects toward external objects. Freud offered an explanation of how sensation could become emotion, and how affect could leap from the internal to the external. Freud's neurophysiological model gradually evolved into a more psychological, abstract model (Strachey, 1965). The purely physical models of discharge of excessive excitation could not account for the nature and quality of emotions that formed vis-à-vis external objects; therefore, the basic transmutation from physical sensation to specific, externally targeted affects required explanation. One can argue that Freud was not so much a reductionist in rejecting other explanations of the origins of attitudes, as he was a pioneer in proposing a mechanism in a vacuum of theories about origins. Consistent with this interpretation is the fact that Freud was open to the multiplicity of causes of later attitude formation. For example, Freud acknowledged that some attitudes result from simple response generalization (Erwin, 1996). Once an affect or belief was attached to an external object, it could be altered by either psychodynamic mechanisms or the more open, conscious dynamics of learning, generalization, and "logical reflection."

Lasswell, in addressing the development of *political* attitudes that are obviously formed later in life, resorted to psychoanalytic theory not to identify the single, primal source of such attitudes, but rather to explain why (a) the *content* of certain political attitudes runs contrary to the attitudes we expect individuals to hold to pursue their conscious objectives, (b) the *intensity* of political attitudes is either too low or too high to be explained by the more mundane factors of pursuit of conscious objectives, and (c) different types of "political character" arise in people who devote themselves to politics and public affairs. Like Freud, Lasswell recognized learning, generalization, and "logical reflection" as potential origins of attitudes, as illustrated in his earlier books on the labor movement and economics and his later works on international legal sanctions.

With respect to content, Lasswell identified attitudes that would be quite different if it were not for psychodynamics, but did not imply that all attitudes require these mechanisms. The same holds with respect to intensity. At the beginning of his famous chapter on "Politics of Prevention" in *Psychopathology and Politics* (1930/1960), Lasswell stated that "[p]olitical movements derive their vitality from the displacement of private affects upon public objects" (p. 173). The key term is *vitality*. Insofar as politics and political leaders are truly relevant to interests, they will be subjected to attitudes of a particular intensity; it is when the intensity is significantly greater or lesser that psychodynamics warrant exploration. Several examples of greater intensity have already been offered. As an example of surprisingly low intensity, Lasswell noted that even when conditions in a country are poor, the people often do not express antagonism toward the highest, fatherlike rulers who are ultimately responsible. He cited the aphorism that "it is a principle of the British Constitution that the King can do no wrong and his ministers no right" Lasswell (1930/1960, p. 181).

Lasswell differed from Freud in one other respect that is crucial for understanding Lasswell's antireductionist epistemology. Although Freud may not have been reductionist in developing his displacement mechanism, he certainly was reductionist in his efforts to reduce the number of primal drives or instincts that account for psychodynamics. He expressed that it was a great accomplishment to reduce the number of instincts that need to be invoked (Freud, 1920/1950). Perhaps this was also part of Freud's project to find the primal roots of complex behavior in the earliest expressions of emotion and drive, and to draw psychology closer to the biological concepts of evolution through the "life instinct."

Lasswell considered Freud's commitment to narrowly sexual drives as "obstinate," and applauded *Beyond the Pleasure Principle* not because it reduced the number of instincts, but rather because it added to what Lasswell saw as Freud's previously unitary model of instinct (Lasswell, 1930/1960). Lasswell saw multiple political types (agitators, administrators, and theorists), hybrids of these types, and myriad types of deprivations that could lead to different stances.[34] Without having to worry about how this proliferation originated in the undifferentiated neuropsychology of the infant, Lasswell could afford to acknowledge the multiplicity of motives in any aggregation of individuals, although he may have been prepared to explain the genesis of the political attitudes of any given individual on the basis of a predominant drive (e.g., the drive for deference). This presaged Lasswell's development of the social process model, with its eight values and the insistence that none can be ignored as potentially important for understanding human behavior. What Lasswell admired about Freud was not his simplifications, but rather the fact that Freud tried "systematically to treat every manifestation of the individual as part of a related whole" (Lasswell, 1930/1960, p. 23).

In this vein, it should be noted that Lasswell claimed no originality for applying the displacement hypothesis to political beliefs and actions. For example, in *Psychopathology and Politics* (p. 180) he cited the interpretation of the prominent Viennese psychoanalyst, Paul Federn, that the 1927 Vienna riots involved self-defeating anger by the Viennese public in lashing out against a sympathetic regime, explained by displacement of anger toward authoritarian father figures. Lasswell saw his contribution as the interweaving of psychological factors and the rational calculation driven by perceptions of objective conditions. This was the basis of the "configurative analysis" that Lasswell introduced in *World Politics and Personal Insecurity* (1935b/1965) as *the* method for his analysis of values.

CONCLUSIONS

The displacement hypothesis is much more than a historic curiosity. Its applications and extensions, many found in Lasswell's own writings, cover a broad range of political and policy phenomena, and provide continuing insights for both diagnosing seemingly irrational behaviors and developing analytic approaches to address these behaviors.

Lasswell's displacement hypothesis addressed two questions: How do political attitudes in general arise? How do we explain anomalous political attitudes and anomalous intensity of political attitudes? Using his configurative, comprehensive approach, Lasswell acknowledged obvious motivations and rational choices, but also embraced the influences of less directly understood impacts in order to formulate an integrated model.

Thus, the focus on displacement reinforces rather than undermines the commitment to *comprehensive* analysis. If we credit the European lineage of Carus, von Hartman, and Freud for discovering and exploring the unconscious[35]—arguing that rational, consciously instrumental motives and considerations are only part of the relevant set of factors—we can credit Lasswell for bringing in politically and policy-relevant motives and considerations that are either unconscious or unexamined. A fundamental policy sciences critique against other analytical frameworks is that they truncate the set of motives available to explain and predict behavior. For example, strong variants of rational choice theory assume that simple, conscious, stable, obvious motivations characterize each class of actors: business executives are presumed to be exclusively interested in maximizing the firm's profits or stock value; politicians are exclusively interested in maximizing their security in remaining in office, and so on. For policy scientists, motivations may be highly complex, conscious or unconscious, changing, and nonobvious. The "discovery of the unconscious," reflected in the displacement hypothesis that unconscious motives are fundamental for understanding political attitudes, provides for greater complexity than does the rational choice framework.

Chapter 3

Symbols, Personality, and Appeals: Lasswell's Contribution to the Political Psychology of Propaganda

Harold Lasswell made three profound and enduring contributions to the understanding of how the manipulation of symbols and their meanings shape the receptivity of political and policy appeals. He first developed a perspective on the meanings and associations of political and policy material that goes far beyond the content normally examined by political scientists and policy analysts. In stark contrast to the conventional view of a political figure or policy proposal as the sum of objective attributes, Lasswell offered a much broader vision of the complex, multifold, subjective meanings of political and policy objects. He applied the psychoanalytic insight of multiple associations to develop the view that an individual's perception of a given object is defined by a thick tangle of symbol associations, often subject to propagandistic manipulation.[36]

Second, Lasswell used this broader conception of subjective meanings to link political and policy appeals with the psychodynamics of relevant audiences. This was epitomized by the direct application of psychoanalytic personality theory in his 1932 article, "The Triple-Appeal Principle," which explored the ways that reactions to sociopolitical phenomena are shaped by the demands coming from the id, ego, and superego. Finally, Lasswell provided an encompassing heuristic framework for exploring the full range of reactions to symbols, whether crafted on the basis of psychoanalytic insights or from more straightforward, naïve models based on focusing attention on obviously positive or negative symbols.

This chapter is divided into five sections that explore and extend Lasswell's contributions. First, we examine Lasswell's broad, original conception of "symbols" and associations. This conception enabled Lasswell to treat the ambiguity of symbols as one basis for accumulation of emotional energy. Second, we study his earliest "triple-appeal" differentiation for determining the personality structures that symbols and propaganda can address: the *id*, *ego*, and *superego*, as these terms emerged from the psychoanalytic framework. Regardless of whether these distinctions are held as valid representations of the personality, we can show how this differentiation can be used to understand the propaganda of both nondemocratic and democratic governments. The third section explores Lasswell's further differentiation of appeals according to which component of *perspectives*—identifications, demands, and expectations—is the target of the appeal. This analysis deepens the practical understanding of how political and policy proposals can tap into both individualized and mass yearnings. The fourth section clarifies Lasswell's definition of, and orientation to, propaganda, in order to link it with his perspectives on democracy and the crucial importance of free communication.

Our fifth and final section tries to assess Lasswell's contributions to the study of propaganda and symbol manipulation in light of more recent paradigms in psychology. Much of what Lasswell contributed to the study of the psychological bases of political and policy appeals was in broadening and enriching the framework of analysis. The logically exhaustive categories of perspectives (identifications, demands, and expectations) and values were wedded to the psychoanalytical categories of id, ego, and superego to provide a rich map for asking theoretical questions. Yet, Lasswell also offered theoretical insights into the dynamics of reactions to symbol manipulations and political and policy appeals that we can both extend and evaluate. We raise the question of how much of his theoretical analysis has been rendered obsolete by later developments in psychology.

SYMBOLS, MEANINGS, AND ASSOCIATIONS

For Lasswell, the primary link between objective reality and subjectivity was the symbol. In the semantically careful *Power and Society* (1950), Lasswell and his co-author, the philosopher Abraham Kaplan, left "symbol" undefined, but then went on to say that "[a] symbol is whatever has meaning or significance in any sense" (p. 10). Elsewhere, propaganda is the "management of collective attitudes by the manipulation of significant symbols" (Lasswell, 1927a, p. 627); it "refers solely to the control of opinion by significant symbols (Lasswell, 1927b/1971, p. 9). Lasswell's key insight was that symbols evoke multiple and varying associations. Symbol manipulation is feasible only because of this potential variability. In contrast to the Jungian project of discovering *common, universal* meanings of symbols, Lasswell's perspective was that the potentially idiosyncratic and variable nature of symbol meanings opens up the exploration of how symbols can be manipulated by efforts to change meanings and associations. The study of propaganda becomes a study of these manipulation efforts.

Symbols, Lasswell acknowledged, are by their nature of "ambiguous reference." But instead of trying to remove the ambiguities, as required by the scientific use of concepts (and as Lasswell and Kaplan accomplished in their 1950 work *Power and Society*), Lasswell's study of symbols was the examination of these ambiguities and their potential for shaping emotional responses to symbols. Although the symbol itself is a stable, objective entity (a word, a phrase, a flag design, even a physical action), its meanings and associations are not the same for different people or at different times, and they are not fixed for a given individual or group. On the one hand, a symbol can be attached to a new object, lending that object some of the symbol's significance; on the other hand, the new attachment may change the overall meaning of the symbol. For example, the use of the cross as the symbol of the Crusaders, as opposed to the insignia of their feudal lords, lent meanings of piety, unity, and self-sacrifice to the Crusades, in contrast to the alternative interpretation of conquest for power and riches. In taking on this new connection to Christians, undoubtedly the cross took on new meanings for Muslims. In all likelihood, the cross and related symbols took on far greater connotations of menace than they had previously held, when all were, to some degree, associated with a religion that Muslims had respected as a precursor to Islam.

As a symbol comes to be associated with a new object, the attitudes toward that object may change the meaning of the symbol. Note the potential for mutual influence that the previous example presented: The Crusades, as the new object, take on connotations from the preestablished symbol, whereas the cross, as the preestablished symbol, takes on some of the meanings of the new object. Contrast this with William Jennings Bryan's (1896) "Cross of Gold" rhetoric to dramatize the plight of debtors under tight-money policy. Invoking the symbol of the cross was a brilliant way to bring the martyrdom connotations of the cross to the money supply issue, but it is doubtful that the fundamental meaning of the cross was much influenced by Bryan's appropriation of the symbol.

The simple premise is that people tend to regard objects in the terms in which they are symbolized. To take a contemporary example, Palestinians are trying to extend the label of "racism" to the Israeli treatment of Arabs. Racism has an incredibly complicated set of meanings and associations, from colonialism, anti-Semitism, and apartheid to stereotyping and socioeconomic discrimination. Insofar as Israel's treatment of Palestinians comes to be regarded as racism—whether appropriately or not according to lexical definitions—the condemnatory attitudes associated with the idea of racism will inevitably color the attitudes toward Israel.

Intellectual Heritage

In this respect, Lasswell was building on the age-old concept of associationism, not as a theory of the origins of consciousness but rather as a way of defining the subjective meaning of symbols. Plato and Aristotle had emphasized the central role of concept associations in thinking; the

19th-century Continental and British associationists argued that links among concepts are the essence of thought; psychoanalysts stressed the importance of associations for uncovering repressed material through the technique of free association. Lasswell viewed the individual's perception of any object or label as encompassing all available meanings and associations. Yet, unlike the classical associationists, Lasswell took the associations more deeply into personality and psychodynamics. Whereas the classical associationists marveled at the "train" of associations, emphasizing the fact of association rather the overall emotional consequences, Lasswell viewed the multiplicity or ambiguity of associations as the source of heightened affect.

He did this for two reasons. First, he recognized that associations involve more than the simple triggering of trains of memory. The classical associationists cited frequency of past association, vividness, recency, congruity in emotional tone, and similarity as factors that predisposed one association to be triggered over another. These mechanisms were essentially physiological. William James, the great American psychologist-philosopher, saw associations as the result of simultaneous excitation of "nerve tracts" (James, 1890/1950). Yet, this model did not ask why any two objects had earlier been associated—why the nerve tracts somehow connected with each object had been excited at the same time. Second, nothing in this model allowed for personality and desires that would make one particular object come to be associated with another. Using psychoanalytic theory, Lasswell expanded on the "vividness" dimension by proposing that the idiosyncratic needs of the personality cause particular associations to be triggered and to endow the appeal with especially high affect. The closest the classical associationist theory came to this insight was in including "vividness" as a factor, but it did not aspire to understanding the psychodynamics that would make one association more vivid than another, nor did it assess how the association, once established, could contribute affect to the triggering symbol.

Lasswell was concerned not only with the likelihood that the presented symbol would evoke a particular association, but also with the strength of the symbol as a trigger of emotional reactions, and, conversely, with the availability of a given object to be evoked because of its emotional charge. The distinctiveness of Lasswell's framework is its guidance for exploring *personality characteristics* and *internally generated demands* that would either trigger a particular association or heighten the emotional reaction resulting from the association. It should be noted that the associationists recognized the idiosyncrasies of associations (James reported many highly elaborate personal "trains" of associations), but they did not venture into psychological (let alone psychoanalytic) explanations for these associations.[37]

Lasswell offered a framework for mapping the idiosyncratic needs of the individual's personalities, beginning with the Freudian distinctions of id, ego, and superego. He also adapted the insight on condensation symbols that Freud developed in his *Interpretation of Dreams*, to recognize that it is the cumulative affect triggered by a particular symbol or appeal that evokes multiple associations. "Condensation" in dreams gives rise to multiple meanings (Freud, 1900/1965). Freud noted that "[t]his ambiguity of the symbols links up with the characteristic of dreams for admitting of 'over-interpretation'—for representing in a single piece of content thoughts and wishes which are often widely convergent in their nature" (1900/1965, pp. 388–389). Lasswell's University of Chicago colleague, the remarkable linguist Edward Sapir, wrote that condensation symbolism, "a highly condensed form of substitutive behavior for direct expression . . . strikes deeper and deeper roots in the unconscious and diffuses its emotional quality to types of behavior or situations apparently far removed from the original meaning of the symbol" (1934, pp. 493–494). For the propagandist, using the symbol with multiple meanings can attach the emotion of one association to the association intended for manipulation. For example, if "liberalization" can gain positive affect from prior associations, it can bring that affect to the new initiative also labeled as "liberalization."

Lasswell viewed these affect-laden associations as the outgrowth of psychodynamic development from childhood on. In *World Politics and Personal Insecurity* (1935b/1965), he wrote:

> The environment of the infant and child is teeming with words of ambiguous reference, which take on positive or negative significance long before there is enough contact with reality either to define their frames of reference, or to distinguish those whose frames of reference are wholly indeterminate. As an "adult" the individual continues to respond to these articulations in many childish and juvenile ways, often imputing some special and even awesome significance to them. Such words are 'law and order,' 'patriotism,' 'a gentleman and a soldier,' 'truth,' 'justice,' 'honor,' 'good,' 'bad,' 'loyalty,' 'duty,' 'Germans,' 'French,' 'Negroes,' 'national hero,' 'good citizens,' 'national interest,' 'king,' 'constitution'; but these words do not stand alone in primitive concentrations or irrelevant affect. The whole of our vocabulary, plus our non-verbal symbols, is caught in the mesh of early structuralizations of this kind, so that the inner meaning of our symbols is never revealed except through the technique of free fantasy. (p. 30)

Lasswell's conception of linkage through condensation symbols is consistent with more recent theorizing about the "heuristics" that people use when confronted with new situations involving uncertainty in interpretation and expectation. Tversky and Kahneman (1974) emphasized the "representativeness heuristic" as one of the main mechanisms for making inferences about a new phenomenon for which there is only limited information; the individual places that phenomenon into a given class (e.g., classifying certain environmentalists as "radicals") and then presumes that the characteristics of the most representative instance of that class (e.g., antiwar radicals) will be shared by the new phenomenon. The overlap of symbols by labeling is obviously a framing factor that can increase the likelihood that a particular class will come to mind. In tracking affect as well as the more restricted cognitive processing of the Tversky and

Kahneman model, Lasswell's model similarly recognizes that a particular class is more likely to be chosen because of the strength of the affect that had previously been attached to it.

THE TRIPLE-APPEAL PRINCIPLE

The second psychodynamic insight that Lasswell brought to bear was the analysis of demands welling up from the different processes in the personality. Lasswell's first contribution in this regard was the "triple-appeal principle." In *World Politics and Personal Insecurity* (1935b/1965), Lasswell wrote, "Symbols are often organized within the personality so that they are principally related to the ego, superego or id, although it is clear . . . that these connections cannot be exclusive" (p. 49). The basic premise of the triple-appeal principle is that "the meaning of any social object to any particular person is to be interpreted in terms of its appeal to one or more of these main divisions" (Lasswell, 1932, p. 525).

Perhaps Lasswell's most intriguing application of the triple-appeal principle was presented in a fascinating 1950 article on "Propaganda and Mass Insecurity," in which he assessed the needs for different forms of propaganda facing polities of different types. For totalitarian regimes, Lasswell argued that the id impulses of aggression and fear that one would expect to be created would induce the regime to create appeals that would ensure that aggressive impulses would "be turned downward and outward" (Lasswell, 1950, p. 19). Scapegoating of nonconformers and highly emotional rallies would both squelch dissent while at the same time provide for catharsis to reduce the insecurities that are either created by or accompany the totalitarian state. The need for love is directed to the top of the hierarchy, where it is "so blended with fear that it leads to unlimited abnegation to the leader, the party, and the dogma" (Lasswell, 1950, p. 19).

Directing aggression "downward and outward" is more straightforward for some ideologies than for others. Communist symbolism can easily target the "oppressive" and "decadent" classes as well as foreign enemies. Yet, corporatist ideologies, including Fascism and Nazism, emphasize that all occupational groups or class segments are, in principle, legitimate. Therefore, other bases for stigmatizing the targets of aggression must be found. Minority ethnicities portrayed as undermining cohesion and societal integrity thus offer an alternative target.

To address ego demands arising in the totalitarian state, effective propaganda is likely to be designed to blunt the normal processes of reality-testing and contestation of disfavored policies, by emphasizing the dangers of dissent and nonconformity while ensuring security for obedience. The external world is portrayed as so complicated, and perhaps so rife with conspiracies, that ordinary individuals cannot fathom reality or policy choices: "The ego functions of most of the members of the community must be deliberately starved, atrophied, and trivialized" (Lasswell, 1950, p. 19). The institutions of inquiry, information, and interpretation, such as independent newspapers, are stigmatized as disloyal. Routinization through the repetition of symbolic acts that emphasize leaders' control and safety in unquestioning discipleship will feed into the ego demand for security.

For superego demands, the challenge for totalitarian propagandists seeking power is to discredit the existing sources of authority and propriety. Lasswell theorized that superego guilt can be projected onto the existing authorities and mores. Speaking of the appeal of Marxism prior to a Communist takeover, he noted that the

> symbolization of the environment as immoral facilitates the projection of individual guilt feelings from the self to the symbol of the environment. The individual origin of the guilt feelings is not necessarily related to any rational link to the particular aspect of the environment which is criticizes. Any obscure stresses between incompatible unconscious structures may generate guilt feelings, from which the individual may relieve himself by changing his symbolic definition of the environment. The process in question may be indicated, subject to the limitations previously made on such forms of statement, thus: "I am guilty of immoral impulses: I therefore deserve punishment; but the environment is immoral: the environment should therefore be punished." (Lasswell, 1935b/1965, p. 100)

Once the totalitarian regime is established, the superego challenge is to reconcile the remaining superego demands with the appeals to id impulses. In channeling aggression "downward and outward," the totalitarian regime risks violating moral strictures (observed in most societies) against unwarranted attacks against outsiders. The effective propaganda strategy, therefore, is to emphasize obedience as the predominant moral imperative, leaving other "moral" decisions in the hands of leaders who, by the combination of their prior sacrifice and their mastery of the complex ideology, are asserted to be the only ones in a position to judge definitively between right and wrong.

Another strategy addressing superego demands is to take advantage of potential associations between symbols of the regime's defining ideology and preexisting superego needs. As early as 1933, Lasswell identified Germans' perception of their own declining morality as a significant superego preoccupation (1933/1948). Nazi propaganda capitalized on the ambiguous associations of "purity" as pertaining to both moral integrity and ostensible racial purity. The semantic overlap in the use of the term can be viewed as an ambiguity, and a modest goal of propaganda would be to invoke racial purity in order to engage the concerns over moral purity, thus heightening support for Nazi separatism. The yet more ambitious objective was to unify the two concepts on a cognitive and theoretical level, so that rather than seeing the meaning as ambiguous, they would be understood as two aspects of the same broad and coherent phenomenon. Thus, Nazi propaganda tried to explain the decline in morality as being due, in part, to the degeneracy of racial mixing. It was not simply a matter of moral purity coming to mind when racial purity was invoked, or vice versa. Nor was it simply that the emotions linked to fears of moral decline were transferred to the concern over racial mixing. More than this, a new ideological basis for the association was established.

Another symbolic response to superego demands is to promise a highly moralistic long-term vision of the future that would warrant suspending moral strictures in the shorter term. Lasswell wrote that totalitarian propagandists "provide a grandiose and all-comprehending Valhalla of images of world-shaking destiny and glory" (1950, p. 21). Such chiliastic symbolizations appeal not only to superego needs, but also to id impulses. Lasswell noted that the sweeping nature of the vision of the Marxist future appeals to the impulse of cravings for omnipotence; the classless society appeals to "deeper yearnings for the reinstatement of that happy time in infancy when one was the center of the world" (1935b/1965, p. 134).

Finally, the propaganda of the totalitarian regime has to address the initial anxiety that arises when the ego and superego demands clash. Such an initial clash occurs when individuals accustomed to taking civic responsibility seriously cease to be politically active because of the dangers involved, pitting moralism against self-preservation. This creates anxiety that symbol manipulation can address by symbolizing civic duty as participation in mass events that submerge individuality while at the same time leave no opportunity for participation in the sense of articulating demands: "All the pageantry of marching thousands, of flapping banners, of uniforms and weapons is no act of debate. It is an act of incitement, and it is aimed eventually at the abolition of even the need of incitement by instilling a rat-like fidelity to the stimulating cue word and a deep emotional catharsis through the ceremonial liturgies of great occasions" (Lasswell, 1950, p. 20). The appeal of leaders portrayed as omniscient therefore also serves the purpose of reassuring the individual that his or her responsibility is not being shirked by passivity to the potentially objectionable aspects of the regime's policies and actions.

For democratic regimes, the situation is obviously more complicated because more actors are capable of employing the media of mass communication. We can speak of the propaganda strategies of the government (and even different actors within government), of political parties, of interest and advocacy groups, and of the news media. We can also address the question of what propaganda strategies, employed by the various actors, are best suited to the maintenance of democracy.

Political party leaders and propagandists build on the id impulses of party supporters by emphasizing the excitement of competition and victory, the affection that comes with party solidarity, and aggression toward competitors. For the legitimacy of the democratic regime, politics and policy disputes must be portrayed as engrossing conflicts that can indulge these competitive impulses, but without the risk of system instability that would arouse high levels of anxiety. For ego demands, democratic symbolism must stress both the efficacy of efforts to affect policy and also the capacity to understand political and policy issues. The anxieties that a democratic government must address in "normal times" arise out of the ego-based concern of particular groups that others' interests are better represented—that "insiders" can take advantage of money, superior expertise, and informal connections to gain special advantage despite the trappings of democracy and openness. The symbols have to reinforce the idea that individuals, or their representative groups, can chose rationally and pursue their interests. Political parties, as well as interest and advocacy groups, must invoke symbols of unity of interests ("What's good for General Motors is good for America").

In times of particular stress or threat, the challenge instead is to manage the anxiety and the risk that democratic institutions will be seen as inadequate for handling the crisis. As early as 1930, in *Psychopathology and Politics*, Lasswell recognized that political conflicts are rarely fully resolved; after all, they entail "who gets what, when, how."[38] Thus, the management of conflict in democratic societies is not so much the elimination of conflict as it is the management of conflict levels through symbolic acts as well as efforts at compromise. In "Conflict and Leadership" (1966) Lasswell wrote:

> Instead of exacerbating contradictory positions [leaders] may define the situation symbolically. . . .
> The task of leaders is to invent or accept formulations that change the perspective of contending parties. Instead of accepting as final the symbols in which demands are initially stated, leaders settle on statements that put these interests in a new framework that gives prominence to common interests. (p. 214)

Is there an analytic advantage to retaining the tripartite structural distinction as Freud articulated it? Lasswell (1932) pointed out that the id-ego-superego distinction does correspond roughly to less theoretical distinctions, such as impulse, reason, and conscience. However, he cautioned that "much distortion is involved in this usage" (Lasswell, 1935b/1965, p. 48). There are two reasons to believe that the less pretentious concepts of impulse, reason, and conscience cannot simply substitute for id, ego, and superego.

First, in psychoanalytic theory the id, ego, and superego do not have a one-to-one correspondence to impulse, reason, and conscience. It is not just the superego that is theorized as carrying conscience; in *The Ego and the Id* (1923/1960), Freud wrote that the ego "strives to be moral" (p. 79).[39] Similarly, the same demands for security and control can stem from ego or id; yet, according to psychoanalytic theory, the origins of the demand will determine its nature. The infantile yearning for security through isolation would be more characteristic of id impulses than of the ego-based search for security based on rational engagement. The primitive id demand for omnipotence can be contrasted with the ego demands for an appropriate modicum of control. The harsh quality of conscience arising from the superego differs from the ego desire to be upright.

Second, according to psychoanalytic theory, id, ego, and superego are dynamically related in ways that are not conveyed by the atheoretical constructs of impulse, reason and conscience. Lasswell (1935b/1965) pointed out that "[t]he three main personality structures are not to be thought of as rigidly separated from one another; the superego and the ego are not categorically cut off from the impulses of the id, but are properly to be conceived as complications in original impulse which have arisen in the whole process of elaborating these drives in relation to one another and to surroundings" (p. 48).

This restatement of the Freudian interrelations (the ego develops to advance id impulses in the face of obstacles from external reality; the superego emerges as ego-based inhibitions come to be internalized) is the basis for various hypotheses that presume greater interrelationships among these personality components than one might presume for the more theoretically neutral concepts of impulse, reason, and conscience.

A crucial hypothesis is that on the conscious, rational level the individual is not fully cognizant of the impact of symbols that appeal to id or superego impulses. The tendency to rationalize impulses contributes to this lack of awareness, in providing the individual with a seemingly instrumental reason for actions or attitudes driven by id or superego impulses. Thus, behavior is not simply a matter of the unified, conscious, rational individual deciding how to trade off the gratification of urges, the rational self-interest, and conscience. According to psychoanalytic theory, the id makes itself known through profound emotional pathways (e.g., complicated "love-hate" mixtures; aggressiveness colored by indignation, etc.) as well as by consciously perceived desires; the superego is expressed through anxiety and depression as well as by consciously perceived recognition of moral appropriateness. Therefore, the accommodation of conflicting id, ego, and superego impulses may be far more complicated than—would not be confined to—the conscious balancing of impulse, reason, and conscience.

This tripartite hypothesis also has important implications for the role of the "political psychiatrist." Insofar as the impact of propaganda has effects that are not comprehended consciously, the political psychiatrist can contribute by enlightening the public that some appeals are deceptive in terms of whether the public's interests are truly served. This unmasking role is parallel to the psychiatrist's task of helping the patient understand how unconscious forces drive attitudes, emotions, and actions. If all appeals— whether to impulse, reason, or conscience—were fully understood, this function would be unnecessary.

Two additional hypotheses concern the inverse intensities of id, ego, and superego needs at any point in time. On the one hand, Lasswell argued that satisfying the psychological needs associated with any one of the components of personality would heighten the demands arising from other personality components:

> During periods of slow social change, an equilibrium is maintained among these forms of expressions through which human impulses pass. During periods of rapid social change, the direction and intensity of the readjust-

ment may be predicted according to the following principle: Prolonged ego and superego indulgences (expediencies, mores) precipitate redefinitions in directions gratifying to the id (counter-mores); prolonged ego and id indulgences initiate redefinitions gratifying to the superego. In general the meaning of this formula is that periods of disregard of the prevalent body of authoritarian patterns generate insecurities which are favorable to the reimposition of new controls, or to the revalidation of the older controls; periods of intensified discipline generate insecurities which favor the spread of deviational symbols and practices. (1935b/1965, p. 50)

Thus, prosperity engenders asceticism, permissive times provoke Puritanism and other forms of fundamentalism, and Puritanical mores provoke hedonism or Bohemianism. The implicit premise of finite "psychic energy" enabled Lasswell to formulate such remarkably high-level macrosociological theorizing about political-cultural change.

However, in some instances it is not the satisfaction of id, ego, or superego appeals that prompts the rise of the others, but rather the suppression of one for the sake of maintaining the others. In particular, the acknowledgement of self-interested instrumental motives (i.e., ego motives) may undermine the superego demands that rationalize or justify aggression. In many circumstances self-sacrifice is crucial for the individual to avoid the negative self-perception that his or her actions are essentially selfish. The fundamental implication for understanding the triple-appeal principle is that an appeal to all three components will not always be the most effective. The suicide bomber may be attracted by the idea of self-sacrifice; the hospital volunteer may find the offer of even low remuneration to be repugnant. For Americans who supported the use of violence to secure the independence of Northern Ireland from Britain or Armenia from Turkey,[40] personal gain was strongly rejected, even though an outside observer might wonder whether the interactions among pro-independence advocates actually do provide personal benefits, at least on the social level. In terms of strategies of persuasion, ego appeals and superego appeals may present the greatest dissonance. In times of peace, the most effective recruitment for the military may be the challenge to "be all that you can be," but in times of war it may be "Give me liberty or give me death."

The Predominance of the Management of Anxiety

Lasswell's modeling of these dynamics in the context of "rapid social change" begins with indulgences and then culminates with insecurities. Although appeals to id, ego, and superego conceivably could be directed to the satisfactions of positive yearnings (in contrast with the clear function of displacement to cope with the psychic threat of painful emotions), the challenge in periods of change is viewed as the relief of anxieties. The basic premise of Lasswell's analysis of the triple appeal is that personal *anxiety* is the primary "raw material" that presents the major challenge—or opportunity. The very titles of Lasswell's key works on political psychology highlight the pivotal role of insecurity; the implication is that the central problem facing political leaders is how to handle anxiety arising from insecurity. Hence, Lasswell concentrated far more on the management of anxieties than on the actualization of positive aspirations. Of course, the interwar years in Germany, the Depression years in the United States, World War II, the Cold War, and the periods of rapid social change during which Lasswell wrote gave ample justification for focusing on insecurity and anxiety.

Of course, Lasswell understood that other targets for symbol management, in addition to insecurity and anxiety, could be equally important. These include libidinous impulses, the drive for feelings of superiority, moral indignation, and so on. In the "Triple-Appeal Principle" (1932), Lasswell wrote that "politics involves appeals to hatreds, omnipotence, lusts, and submissive urges; economics includes appeals to powerful acquisitive, retentive, and potentially expulsive drives; and science offers much opportunity for isolated imaginings, aloofness from any ordinary demands of society, and underlying sadistic designs against the reality which it pretends to serve" (pp. 533–534). Yet, it is nonetheless obvious that Lasswell's basic outlook in the 1930s and 1940s was a dark view of the forces that drive the appeals. Perhaps this could be attributed to stylistic hyperbole, yet the absence of positively cast aspirations on Lasswell's list may also reflect the preoccupation of the psychoanalytic orientation with ominous drives and the management of anxiety. The prominence of anxiety and problematic drives reflects the dual psychoanalytic premises that psychodynamics largely concern the struggle to cope with emotionally or socially challenging impulses, and that anxiety is more mobilizing than other psychological manifestations.

PERSPECTIVES

Lasswell's overarching model of human action begins with the logically exhaustive categories of impulse, subjectivity, and expression. We have reviewed the origins of impulse. Now we turn to how these impulses are mapped onto the cognitive schemas that undergird attitude structures. We have seen that the mapping of impulses prompts the exploration of id, ego, and superego as origins of drives; some are straightforward, whereas others involve such complex psychodynamics as displacements and projections. However, the mapping of subjectivity requires a further differentiation, which Lasswell addressed by defining three categories:

- *Identifications:* Self-definition of the individual as a member of particular categories or groups of individuals.
- *Demands:* Expressions of desired outcomes, based on values (Lasswell & Kaplan, 1950). Demands range broadly in terms of their intensity, from mild preferences to assertions of inviolable rights.
- *Expectations:* Beliefs about past, present, or future states of affairs, apart from demands or identifications.

The impulses welling up from the id, ego, or superego may be manifested as demands, but they are also conditioned by the nature of the individual's identifications and expectations. Lasswell and Kaplan (1950) noted that "[c]ertain identifications, demands and expectations tend to be clustered, as in the case of the person who is strongly identified with humanity as a whole; he is likely to support a world order, and to cherish some optimism about at least the long-range prospects of mankind" (p. 25). Yet, it is important to note that it is not simply a matter of the consistency among identifications, demands, and expectations. On the one hand, they are in dynamic relationship with one another (Lasswell, 1935b/1965); on the other hand, inconsistencies among identifications, demands and expectations frequently exist: "A perspective need not be a logically unified whole, and indeed seldom is. It may include 'stray' identifications, demands and expectations, so to speak, as well as integrated interests, faith and loyalties. It may even include in varying degrees, conflicting commitments of the ego and the self" (Lasswell & Kaplan, 1950, p. 25). Thus, relationships among identifications, demands, and expectations can reveal the psychodynamics that reflect conflicting impulses. Although pressures toward cognitive consistency may tend to reduce these inconsistencies, when they are found they provide a window onto the personality of the individual.

Because perspectives are expressed as statements (whether thought, spoken, written, or otherwise communicated internally or eternally), they come to be represented by symbols. A crucial corollary is that they are influenced by the symbols originating and adopted from other sources. Some symbols resonate with a given individual because they are consistent with either existing perspectives or with the adaptability to a particular perspective. Existing symbols of identification, demand, and expectation may be modified in meaning by the ways that propagandists express them. For example, an individual who identifies himself or herself as a Muslim may be influenced by Muslim fundamentalists to strengthen that identification, adopt the restoration of Palestine as a demand symbol consistent with that identification, and accept the ultimate success of the *intifada* as an expectation symbol.

Identifications

Lasswell gave great prominence to the symbols of identification. They shape a wide range of psychopolitical behavior, from the modeling of personality to the formation of political groups (1935b/1965). Their intensity determines how far people are willing to go to further the interests of the groups with which they identify. This is in keeping with the centrality of the psychoanalytic processes that culminate in identification. Laplanche and Pontalis (1967/1974) argued that "[i]n Freud's work the concept of identification comes little by little to have the central importance which makes it, not simply one psychical mechanism among others, but the operation itself whereby the human subject is constituted" (p. 206).

In keeping with their commitment to behavioral definitions, Lasswell and Kaplan defined identifications as ways that "a symbol user symbolizes his ego as a member of some aggregate or groups of egos (X identifies with the Ys if X symbolizes X as a Y)."[41] Thus, for example, the identification as a Muslim fundamentalist occurs if an individual regards himself or herself as such. The indicators can be overt symbol processes—speech, written statements, visualization, auditory "calls," or numerous other direct symbol manipulations—or by internal or externalized acts such as joining a Muslim fundamentalist organization. Identifications are cognitions—some are emotionally laden, some are not. Yet, when Lasswell wrote about the psychological processes of identification, he focused on the narrower subset of identifications that are accompanied by emotional attachments, generally but not exclusively positive.[42]

Before exploring the psychology of identifications, some definitional distinctions must be clarified. First, identifications can be divided into two rough categories. *Ascriptive* identifications pertain to characteristics with which an individual can be described without recourse to knowledge of his or her emotions, attitudes, or actions. Some ascriptive identifications are transitory—such as the state of residence of highly mobile Americans—but many important ascriptive identifications are inborn, permanent, or long-standing—such as ethnicity, gender, religion, nationality, class, and so on. Except in the unusual circumstances of literal ignorance of one's own characteristics (e.g., an individual who is unaware of his or her true ethnicity), the important cognitive question is not whether the individual knows of the characteristic—women know that they are women—but rather how salient the identification is to the individual. Identification statements regarding ascriptive characteristics are best conceived as statements about how important these characteristics are in predisposing toward various sorts of actions in various contexts.

Behavioral/attitudinal identifications pertain to beliefs, discretionary characteristics, and actions. They may refer to political views ("I am a Republican"), policy preferences ("I am an environmentalist"), political actions ("I am a freedom fighter"), and so on. Behavioral/attitudinal identifications are complicated by the flexibility that is often present in how these beliefs, characteristics, and actions are framed. The same behavior may be framed as terrorism or freedom fighting (or both); or as democratic or undemocratic, even when the same definition of democracy is used; or as public spirited or self-serving. Like ascriptive identifications, behavioral/attitudinal identifications vary in salience, and therefore ought to be conceived as cognitions that link identity (e.g., "I am an environmentalist") to predispositions (e.g., "I am an environmentalist to the degree that I will support a pro-environmental measure even though I am also a conservative, and on that basis would be tempted to oppose it").

Within this category of behavioral/attitudinal identifications, there is a narrower category of identifications involving particular individuals. Such a symbolization may expressed as: "I am among the followers of Osama bin Laden" or "I am a follower of Gifford Pinchot's approach to conservation."

It is also important to distinguish between identifications as a category of perspectives and the *processes* of identification. These processes are multiple, and they have impacts not only on identifications but also on demands and expectations. For example, the processes of identification may induce an individual to take on the characteristics or attitudes of another highly optimistic, radical individual. The resulting radical demands, and the optimism that the radical objectives would be achieved, are clearly effects on demands and expectations.

Third, there is a subtle but important distinction between identifications and symbols of identification. Identifications are the outcomes of elaborate processes *by which* individuals ultimately symbolize themselves. The symbols of identification may evoke changes in identifications, but they are "out there" in the broad context. The propagandist may attempt to create and convey identification symbols; these may or may not actually influence the individual's identifications. Moreover, some of the symbols that affect identification may be radically different from the symbols that the individual employs to characterize himself or herself. For example, the symbol of the Middle Eastern terrorist who is perceived as threatening the security of all Americans may reinforce American identity, because "Middle Eastern terrorist" is the "other," and obviously not how Americans symbolize themselves.

Lasswell's analysis of how identifications are formed is remarkably broad. In exploring the multiple ways that identifications can serve the needs of the id, ego, and superego, Lasswell was simply applying the maximization postulate that living creatures tend to act in ways perceived as making them better off. This does not narrow casual factors to internal psychodynamics, because the ego and superego mediate between the individual and the external environment. Thus, being "better off" encompasses the pursuit of greater rewards and good works vis-à-vis the external environment, as well as the strivings for internal emotional comfort and gratification.

Some symbols of identification are appealing because of the instrumental benefit of the resulting identification. People are more prone to identify with effectively contending political parties than with clear losers; club memberships often reinforce social and professional contacts; identifications with popular causes are generally more appealing than are identifications with unpopular causes. There is both an instrumental and emotional gratification of being associated with particular qualities and views.[43] For example, part of the appeal of a strong environmental policy may be the gratification of identifying oneself as an environmentalist. Some Cold Warriors derived satisfaction in being "tough-minded," "hawkish," and "capable of standing up to bullies." Clearly, associating a proposal with compelling value-expressive symbols of this sort can enhance its appeal. Of course, association with particular qualities may also cement associations with particular individuals or groups—a pro-environmental stance associates the individual with other, presumably admired, environmentalists. Lasswell even noted that many of the most common identifications arise simply from personal interaction and the need to have common ground with family, acquaintances, and coworkers.[44] However, Lasswell did not shy away from invoking the dynamics of the unconscious, even in everyday interactions: "This process of becoming emotionally bound is dependent on no conscious process" (1930/1960, p. 185).

More complex dynamics are also involved. Lasswell recognized the psychoanalytic mechanism of identifications formed out of deflected desire. In *Group Psychology and the Analysis of the Ego* (1921/1959), Freud had understood identification as the ego's accommodation to the impossibility of the young child's direct gratification of the sexual impulse. For the young boy, identification is the fallback in the face of the futility of competing with the father for the affections of the mother: The Oedipal complex is resolved through identification with the father (the father is "introjected onto the ego"). Lasswell generalized this pattern. In *Psychopathology and Politics* (1935b/1965), he argued that:

> An emotional attachment occurs when the symbol of the other is taken as one means of gratifying the affectionate (the libidinal) impulses which are not permitted to exhaust themselves in direct and primitive ways upon the object. Strictly speaking, the symbol of the aspect of the self which is taken by the self to be characterized by an 'external' reference secures the libidinal charge. . . . The necessary prerequisite is the presence of aim-inhibited impulses which are available for redirection toward substitute symbols. (p. 28)

"Aim-inhibited impulses" arise either from unacceptable or unattainable desires, or from aggression arising from thwarted desire. The affection that charismatic leaders inspire may lead to sexual attraction that, insofar as this attraction is psychologically threatening, is transformed into strong identification. Lasswell wrote extensively about both repressed and expressed homosexual undercurrents behind Nazi identifications. Identification can also arise out of failed rivalry if the individual has to capitulate to a stronger rival. The appeal of domineering personalities can also be explained this way.

Lasswell was wise not to offer a universal mechanism for the formation of identifications. This was certainly prudent in light of the unsettled and confused understanding of identification processes in psychoanalytic and other psychological theories. Freud lamented in *Group Psychology and the Analysis of the Ego* (1921/1959) that "[w]e are very well aware that we have not exhausted the nature of identification" (p. 53). Laplanche and Pontalis (1967/1974) noted the multiplicity of definitions and dynamics found in psychoanalytic theory and in Freud's theories in particular. These range from the Oedipal resolution mentioned earlier to the more general phenomena of taking on features of another person in order to reduce tension (Hall & Lindzey, 1957).

As mentioned previously, identifications with individuals constitute a variant of attitudinal/behavioral identifications. The potential pull of identifying with particular individuals links the dynamics of individual appeals to the dynamics of policy appeals. A compelling political leader can lend attractiveness to a policy proposal merely by advocating it. The general public (or segments thereof) supports particular leaders in part because of the positions they espouse, and, as a consequence, some policy proposals are attractive because of the leaders with which they are associated. Moreover, the meaning that various segments of the public assign to a particular proposal is influenced by the perceptions of the leaders who are to enact it. For example, the proposal to modernize Iran had a different meaning under the Shah than under a religious cleric such as the Ayatollah Khomeni.

Insofar as policy appeals depend on the allure of particular leaders, the dynamics of leadership-symbol appeals are also relevant. It is rather obvious that an identification shapes attitudes, generally to match the attitudes that the leader is presumed to hold. This does not, however, explain why and how a particular leader becomes the focus of identification. Identification may come if the leader's characteristics evoke admiration, approval, sympathy, or some other positive affect because they are consistent with the id, ego, or superego demands with reference to the self. Straightforward cases would be id-fueled admiration of Slobodan Milosevic for Serbs with highly aggressive feelings toward Croatians and Bosnians; ego-based admiration of Robert McNamara for those who regard him as an analytical and managerial master; and the superego-based admiration for Mahatma Gandhi for those who like to think of themselves as moral and self-sacrificing. The psychological presumption here is that admiration reinforces identification. More complicated cases involving id impulses entail the appeals of ruthless, impulsive, inconsiderate, or violent people, whether Stalin, the late Chicago mayor Richard Daley, Sr., or Bonnie and Clyde. To most people, these characteristics are not in themselves admirable qualities, but the vicarious gratification of imagining oneself as having these qualities may be compelling to many people, all the more so because vicarious gratification is likely to provoke less guilt or shame than is gratification through one's own dark side. Leo Rangell (1980) thus argued that Richard Nixon's appeal was based on his "bad" image as one who was willing to be conniving and vindictive.

Propagandists shape identifications through two strategies: by altering the symbolization of policies or leaders to conform to existing identifications, or by altering the existing identifications to enhance the predisposition of individuals to support the policies or leaders. For the first strategy, characteristics of the policies or leaders are subject to manipulation or even invention. If individuals are disposed to identify strongly as environmentalists, the propagandist may try to cast the policy or leader as environmentalist. If individuals identify themselves as followers of strong authoritarian leaders, the propagandist may advise that leaders fulfill this role. For the second strategy, the associations of the existing identifications are manipulated, emphasized, or downplayed according to whether they enhance or detract from the appeal to particular individuals. If an individual considers himself or herself to be a "democrat," what does this mean? It could mean an ardent advocate of free and competitive elections, but perhaps it could be modified to encompass support for direct democracy or advocacy of egalitarian outcomes. Perhaps the propagandist can encourage these associations by having popular public figures articulate these positions—taking advantage of the existing identification with, or other appeal, of these figures in order to modify the meaning of "democrat." The struggles to redefine identifications are enormously important in determining whether the public will embrace leaders as comrades or regard them as enemies.

Demands

Demand symbols are the essence of political and policy agendas; they are the most direct stimulants to political action. As a category of beliefs expressed through symbolization, demands are analytically distinct from the drives, impulses, and yearnings that arise from the components of personality. Demands—or expressions of desired outcomes—grow out of such impulses, shaped by identifications.

The psychology of demands is, of course, closely linked to the psychology of impulses and needs arising from the personality, as addressed earlier in this chapter. Here it is useful to review the logic of Lasswell's distinctive contribution to the analysis of demands, namely the framework that he developed to inventory the full range of values. His well-known but often misunderstood eight-value framework includes both welfare aspirations (well-being, wealth, skill, and enlightenment values) and deference aspirations (power, respect, rectitude, and affection). This is by no means a theory that these eight categories are fully exhaustive,[45] or that aggregating demands according to these categories has theoretical significance. Rather, the categories were developed to help explore the full range of demands in a given situation, in the vein of heuristics rather than theory. None of these categories is posited as more important in psychodynamics. The utility of the value categories is not in the theories that they can generate, but rather in the completeness of the inventory of the demands that can be identified by investigating the potential relevance of each of the value categories.

This atheoretical treatment of the classification of values and demands reflects significantly on Lasswell's conceptions of psychodynamics. He rejected the reductionist premise that certain types of demands or values are more fundamental or primary than are others, just as he rejected the strategy of theorizing that a minimal degree of satisfaction of certain values is necessary for demands regarding other values to come to the fore. Contrast this with Abraham Maslow's value hierarchy, which posits that certain values associated with survival are more fundamental than are "higher-level" values such as esteem, knowledge, or aesthetic values. Contrast it also with Freud's preoccupation with finding the most primal drives that culminate in complex human behavior. Lasswell's position was that regardless of the primacy of particular drives in early childhood and their later evolution, by adulthood these drives are channeled into idiosyncratic priorities of demands shaped by the specific pattern of deprivations and reinforcements in the individual's personal history.[46] Therefore, no grounds exist for believing that any particular value or value category will *in general* be held more deeply or more fundamentally than any other. It is only on the individual level that the specific associations with other values, symbols, and drives determine the potency of a particular demand. This potency determines the sacrifices of other demands that the individual is willing to endure—including, in some cases, personal survival.

The eight value categories identify dimensions of demands, rather than specific states, that most people would prefer to have more of rather than less. Thus, affection as a value category does not have the specificity of the demand for love from one's mother, but asking whether and to what extent affection may be relevant for a particular individual provides the opportunity to ask whether a mother's love is a specific demand. The eight value categories do not imply that every individual wants more of each value—some people choose to be hermits or to renounce worldly goods, despite the general preference that most of humanity holds for companionship and wealth. Even so, inventorying an individual's demands with the aid of the value categories could still help the analyst to characterize the hermit-pauper as one who renounces these values.

The value categories have an additional virtue: Each category also reflects a dimension of resources that can be employed in the pursuit of demands. Hence, power may be a goal, but it is also a means to achieve wealth or other demands. Personal rectitude can achieve respect.[47] Contrast this with such categories as revenge, self-actualization, or excitement, which may be demands of a sort but do not typically reflect categories of resources that can be used to pursue demands. Each of the value categories has the duality of being *scope* values as demands, and *base* values as resources. The value categories are akin to the input-output tables that economists use to determine production at various stages from raw inputs to final products. The instrumentality of base values is a crucial sign of the flexibility of the Lasswellian system to include—but not be limited to—the means-ends calculations so essential for rational actor models.[48]

Propagandists shape demands by presenting symbols that link with other compelling symbols of demand, with the appropriate identifications to define the groups with which the individual is to cooperate and reinforcing expectations of success. The linkage with other demands can be conveyed through combinations of demands aggregated into manifestos, party platforms, and so on, but they can also be conveyed by separate terms, phrases, references to individuals, and so on that have multiple associations. For example, national flags with crosses, crescents, or the Star of David signify both nation and religion. Demand symbols of multiple associations permit the most compelling components to support the others, as in the case of "democratic centralism," the Communist Party's symbol for party discipline, which ties top-down party discipline (the centralism aspect) with the symbol of democracy. Consider also "the war to end all wars," so frequently invoked to characterize World War I. On the one hand, it denoted the demand for peace, but it also implied the demand for military action to defeat the Axis, while also invoking the expectation that victory in one war would bring a lasting peace. For many, the first demand legitimized the second, and acceptance of the demand components may have strengthened the acceptance of its expectation component, and vice versa.

The use of ideological identifiers accomplishes the same function of signaling linkages. For example, Lyndon Johnson's "Great Society" and the conservative "Compact with America" of the mid-1990s both linked broad programmatic agendas to particular political philosophies and to explicitly partisan political agendas.

Finally, demands are reinforced by "miranda," a special class of identification-demand symbols that represent admirable individuals or accomplishments (Lasswell & Kaplan, 1950). The respect for "honest Abe" Lincoln emphasizes the demand for honesty in politicians, and casts the dishonest in a worse light. The Athenians at Thermopolae and the Allied troops in the invasion of Normandy remind us of the potentiality of great gallantry, and provoke contempt for soldiers or military leaders who shirk battle.

Expectations

Insofar as political action is motivated by means-ends considerations, the expectations of how varieties of actions will produce particular ends are of obvious importance. An expectation statement is an assertion about what "is" rather than what "ought to be," yet clearly expectations will tend to focus on conditions and outcomes that involve demands important to the individual, based on his or her identifications (Lasswell & Kaplan, 1950). By modeling the formation of expectations as part of the dynamic interactions with identifications and demands—as well as within the processes of id, ego, and superego pressures—Lasswell avoided the presumption that expectations simply reflect interpretations of factual information, whether correct or incorrect.

Propagandists shape expectation symbols in order to alter demands and to manipulate the predisposition to action, either to stimulate or stifle action. They invoke futures with riveting possibilities of indulgences or deprivations: America under Communism, chaos if people mobilize themselves, world peace, the classless society, and so on. These futures are often symbolized in terms of gratifications or threats to id, ego, or superego. To increase the power of the expectation symbols, propagandists will also try to associate expectation symbols with identifications and demands. For example, the restoration of Ireland, Kurdistan, Armenia, or any of the other nations that have lost sovereignty in whole or in part and have experienced a diaspora from the national territory will often be symbolized in cultural and nostalgic terms in order to mobilize individuals who no longer reside in the original territory and therefore have little personal stake in the restoration.

Whether to mobilize or to stifle action, expectation symbols are typically exaggerated into utopias or dystopias. However, this presents a challenge to the propagandist: how to lend plausibility to extreme outcomes. Although some extreme expectations will resonate with particular individuals due to compatibility with id, ego, or superego impulses, the plausibility of an expectation symbol often depends on the credibility of the theory presented to account for how events would unfold. Thus, expectation symbolization encompasses not just outcomes, but also beliefs about how the world works, typically on the broad ideological level. For example, "class struggle" implies that politics play out along class lines, and that such politics are conflictual. So defined and understood, "class struggle" gives hope to those who wish to believe in the ultimate victory of the working class. Competing theories, such as the democratic or corporatist visions of interclass harmony, would undermine the plausibility of the "dictatorship of the proletariat."

Lasswell noted the tendency for revolutionary propagandists to present exaggerated outcomes and supporting ideological symbols, and warned that when such propaganda efforts are successful, the resulting identifications with a "master symbol" of a transformed future lead to overoptimism concerning the likelihood of that future. Many Communists embraced Marx's analysis of the inevitability of the classless society. Many current secessionist movements, such as the Basques in Spain or the Armenians in Turkey, are based on confidence of ultimate success. Although this may seem obvious, Lasswell went further to argue that such overoptimism increases the likelihood of violence, because it emboldens efforts to overturn existing regimes and arrangements by force, even in situations in which the objective chances of success are minimal (1935b/1965). Moreover, overoptimism toward master symbols, so long as they elicit strong loyalty, may trigger high-risk behavior, which also makes violence more likely. The relevance of loyalty to this hypothesis is that it turns the overly optimistic individual away from complacency. After all, if the dictatorship of the proletariat is inevitable, why sacrifice for it? This paradox beset the debates among Marxists in Western countries and Latin America for many decades. From a psychological (as opposed to ideological) perspective, the predisposition to activism and violence despite a belief in the inevitability of the outcome rests on the need to express commitment to the vision represented by the master symbol.

SYSTEMATIC EVALUATION OF PROPAGANDA AND SYMBOLIZATION

When Lasswell launched his analysis of World War I propaganda, the state of the art of propaganda studies was still anecdotal, not having become systematically empirical; it was practically bereft of theory and partial rather than holistic in its analysis of political process and psychodynamics. Definitions of propaganda were generally either limited too narrowly to deception by enemies, or were excessively broad in covering all efforts at influence. The literature was largely focused on revealing the distortions of propaganda, presuming that deception—whether by one's enemy or by all warmongers—must necessarily be bad. On the other extreme, the analysis of propaganda as "public relations" or "communications" failed to highlight the distinctive characteristics of deliberate efforts to manipulate through deception, and thus retarded the opportunity to develop theories keyed to the distinctiveness of such manipulation. These problems were interconnected, because theory development was inhibited by both the lack of systematic empirical inquiry and definitions that inhibited the investigation of a significant but not excessively broad phenomenon.

The issue of what constitutes the *analyzable content* of propaganda was fundamental. Rather than appreciating the associative power of the symbols employed by propagandists, much of the literature focused narrowly on the empirical, "news" content of communications deemed propagandistic. Frederick Lumley, although he relied heavily on Lasswell's analysis of propaganda in World War I, took the rather typical position:

> [T]he *content of propaganda* is, not so much facts and soundly marshaled evidences, as it is generalizations or conclusions—and emotionally charged conclusions at that. . . .
>
> The content of propaganda is best described in terms of conclusions, summations and generalizations with an emotional rather than an intellectual backing. . . . Facts . . . are juggled and doctored so that they seem to support the conclusions which the unwary are expected to draw. (Lumley, 1933, pp. 147–148, emphasis in the original)

In short, content was defined as the set of statements (e.g., "The Serbs have massacred 100 noncombatant Bosnians") that are presumed to be intended to arouse positive or negative emotional reactions. This definition of propaganda content recognizes both the possibility of deception and the targeting on the emotional states of the audience, but it neglects the emotive and associative content of the symbols employed by propaganda, and therefore the tactical potential of the manipulation of these symbols.

In fact, some authorities in the emerging field of positivistic psychology held an antipathy toward the analysis of symbols, perhaps because such analysis may have seemed too interpretive and insufficiently quantitative. For example, the Yale University psychologist Leonard Doob, whose own schema on the psychological dynamics of propaganda invoked the associative concept of attitude relatedness, was dismissive of symbolization as the vehicle for establishing these relationships. He devoted only one page to symbols in his 1935 book, *Propaganda: Its Psychology and Technique*, and that reference was largely dismissive.[49] His belittling of symbol analysis, contending that "[s]ocial scientists and others delight in" it as a fad, was reflected in the two examples that he presented—the mundanity of "a plate of baked beans means more than a food [to a New Englander] . . . it symbolizes a local culinary tradition"; and the fuzziness of law: "Law as a mysterious symbol . . . appears to be nothing more than a word which through social conditions has acquired a series of rich, though vague connotations that have grave consequences in practice." (Doob, 1935, p. 50).

Doob's analysis suffered from his failure to address the importance of the content of propaganda symbols and their semantic connectedness. He examined the "psychology of suggestion" created by "stimuli" and "stimulus-situations," but this approach could not connect the semantic texture of symbols with the political strategies of symbol manipulation. He appreciated that "[t]he suggestive power of a word will depend upon its primary and secondary meanings and upon the preexisting attitudes which it arouses . . . this power will vary from one era to another and from culture to culture" (Doob, 1935, p. 60), but the neglect of symbols left Doob's propositions almost bereft of tactical insight. It is well and good to posit that relating one issue to another can relate the affect of one to the other, but the tactics for creating the associations escaped Doob's framework.

Ironically, through Lasswell's work the analysis of symbols became the foundation rather than the obstacle to systematic analysis of propaganda. As Morris Janowitz (1969) noted, Lasswell was the pioneer in trying to create the empirical base for the study of propaganda. This meant not only collating the myriad propaganda studies that had never been organized before (resulting in several bibliographies and overviews, such as Lasswell, Casey, & Smith, 1935; Smith, Lasswell, & Casey, 1946), but also tackling the difficult challenge of meaningfully tracing the development of a propaganda message over time and across contexts. Here, again, the concept of the symbol is crucial. The symbol has power not only as an instrument given strength by its associative power, it is also the marker for tracing the continuity and evolution of propaganda content. Lasswell understood that a sophisticated handling of both changing meanings and associations of symbols is absolutely critical for an empirical content analysis to be relevant. He innovated content analysis techniques for this purpose, developing concordances to track the connections among symbols and thus the evolution of the meaning of any given symbol. Specific terms come and go, as events alter the currency and power of particular symbols; this poses a risk that continuities will be overlooked. An opposite risk is that the same labels change in referent, connotation, or associations; this raises the danger that these changes will be overlooked because of the continuity of the labels.

The concordance initiatives that were inspired by Lasswell adopted his insight that symbols must be categorized in functional categories. Lasswell's functional categories in his earliest work on war propaganda asserted the needs to establish three beliefs: the guilt of the enemy, the enemy's satanic nature, and the likelihood of victory. Some symbols, whether single terms (e.g., "the Hun") or complex stories (e.g., the rape of Belgian nuns) may come or go, but the functions or objectives remain, and may be served by other symbols (Finlay, Holsti, & Fagen, 1967). Alternatively, the original symbol may take on other functions. The Berlin Wall was a symbol of the Cold War and the strength of the Soviet Union; in its fall it has become a symbol of the victory of the West. The challenge of tracking symbols over time, finding the functional equivalents, and learning from these patterns remains a fertile but uncompleted task.

Normative Aspects

It is useful to ask what Lasswell thought of the enterprise of propaganda and symbol manipulation, both descriptively and prescriptively. In normal parlance, "propaganda" has such a negative connotation that one might see Lasswell's "how to" preoccupation with it as an indication of his support for manipulation and antidemocratic practice.

Lasswell viewed propaganda as neither intrinsically good nor bad, but instead as an instrument of persuasion that can be directed to good or bad causes. The breadth of his definition of propaganda, as symbol manipulation to shape opinion, would clearly encompass positive efforts such as civic education, public mobilization for the common good over individual selfishness, or efforts to convince the people of an aggressor nation to abandon an unjust aggression. On the other hand, much of Lasswell's analysis of propaganda was in the vein of unmasking the propaganda techniques of authoritarian governments.

But what of the deception that propaganda entails? In "Propaganda and Mass Insecurity" (1950), Lasswell defined propaganda as "the making of deliberately one-sided statements to a mass audience" (p. 284). If the role of the policy scientist is to bring insight to the public, is deception a legitimate instrument? Lasswell's model of the political psychiatrist as the guide to the public's quest of enlightenment and self-understanding would seem to demonstrate the illegitimacy of propaganda. Yet, Lasswell's pragmatic view was that *if* propaganda can be wielded by a broad range of rivals, it is a matter of balanced advocacy, and better than the lack of efforts to persuade at all. Lasswell made the surprising point that totalitarian regimes actually strive to reduce propaganda in this sense, substituting ritual and threat for argument (Lasswell, 1950). In contrast, democracy depends on multiple actors, within and outside of the state, with the capacity to try to persuade. Lasswell even spoke of "freedom of propaganda"—not "freedom from propaganda" (1950, p. 23). In short, the practice of propaganda, as the effort to change collective attitudes, is consistent with democracy as long as many different would-be propagandists have the right to try to persuade. Open, competitive propagandizing creates an open market place of ideas.

Descriptive Aspects

Analyzing the logic of propaganda and symbol-based appeals may leave the impression that the creation of propaganda is a rational, effective process. However, if we apply the principles of political psychology to the *production* of propaganda, we find a messier, less efficient process. In his first major treatise on propaganda, *Propaganda Technique in the World War* (1927b/1971), Lasswell pointed out that "a formidable list could be drawn up of the propaganda drives which failed or which accomplished their objective after a long period of waiting" (p. 219). Of course, when rivals all resort to propaganda, some will succeed and others will fail. Yet, we can also see propaganda efforts stumbling either because of lack of knowledge of what would work, or because political communication reflects the non-rational personality needs of those who create and deploy propaganda.

In this latter respect, the analysis of the behavior of leaders and propagandists can rely on the same framework as the analysis of the impact of propaganda. Although leaders may wish to put the best face on their actions and policies, their own impulses and psychological needs may be revealed through their mannerisms, the symbols that they intuitively believe would be compelling to their audiences, and their communications in unguarded moments. Symbol streams are only partially subject to strategic manipulation. And, sometimes, the most efficacious symbol manipulations are simply rejected by leaders as inappropriate or even immoral, such as fanning hatred of other groups in order to create in-group solidarity. Thus, id and superego can pull leaders themselves into ineffective propaganda. Often, propaganda is a matter of trial and error, in which those who intuit or stumble on effective symbols survive in the political and policy arena. Given the range of impulses that will be found in many populations, the fact that some people are attracted to a particular propaganda appeal does not mean that the appeal is well designed. This highlights the importance of the capacity of leaders and their propagandists to adapt their symbol output.

Strategies of Propaganda

Thus far we have reviewed and somewhat extended the Lasswellian psychodynamics that account for how propaganda as symbol manipulation engages components of personality and cognition. We have also seen how the propagandist can, at least in principle, fine-tune the symbols of identification, demand, and expectation to resonate with the nuances of personality needs. To demonstrate the depth of the needs to which propaganda appeals can be targeted, Lasswell frequently illustrated the idiosyncratic and partially unconscious origins of such needs through the in-depth assessment of specific individuals. However, this raises an important practical issue for designing a policy or political appeal, or for anticipating the success of such an appeal: Do the propagandists (or, for that matter, observers such as ourselves) know enough about the internal psychodynamics of a sufficient number of individuals to devise effective propaganda or to predict that such propaganda will be effective? This is a fundamental micro-macro issue that Lasswell addressed in two complementary ways.

As indicated earlier, Lasswell often argued that common sociopolitical or economic conditions may predispose large numbers of individuals to particular symbol appeals. Wartime tension, economic distress, rapid change in moral standards, revolution (Lasswell, 1935b/1965), unpunished criminal activity (Lasswell, 1930/1960), and so on heighten particular impulses in many individuals, making the corresponding symbol appeals effective for large portions of the population (1930/1960; 1935b/1965).

Lasswell also emphasized that the *focus of attention* can be influenced through increased "brute force" manipulations of the frequency of specific symbols invoked by propagandists. Rather than try to plumb the depths of personality needs and rely on the subtleties of complex appeal, running the risk of getting it wrong, the propagandist can simply invoke the symbols of the greatest and most obvious positive or negative valence for the broad audience. Consider Lasswell's observation that the appeal of Nazism in Germany was based in no small part of Hitler's *maternal* role as the protector of purity, tapping into deep-seated needs for protection from id impulses.[50] Yet, the leader tempted to replicate the symbolism of maternal preoccupation with purity may find that maternalism and puritanism are taken by the target population to be absurd or threatening. Thus, the propagandist may simply hammer home the known or alleged sexual pecadillos of the rival candidate, or remind the public at every opportunity of the risks of the rival policies.

This approach requires no great sophistication, but rather the persistence and budget to present and re-present the symbols with greater frequency. Of course, this approach can also go wrong, because more complex psychological reactions can make the obvious appeal backfire. For example, the emphasis on a rival's sexual exploits may win the rival admiration and support rather than opprobrium. Nevertheless, Lasswell recognized that the alternative to propaganda based on psychoanalytic theorizing is propaganda based on high frequency of references to positive and negative symbols. The tactical question of how to promote a particular policy may come down to the question of whether to brave the complexities and uncertainties of developing appeals based on possibly arguable psychodynamic insights, or to the simpler application of blatantly positive or negative symbols.

THE STATUS OF LASSWELL'S TREATMENT
OF PROPAGANDA SYMBOLS AND APPEALS
AS A CONTRIBUTION TO POLITICAL
PSYCHOLOGY

Lasswell's treatment of propaganda and the reactions to political and policy appeals is characteristically inclusive of nonpsychodynamic as well as psychodynamic considerations. As with his theories of attitude formation in general, Lasswell's framework for understanding the manipulation of symbols united the psychoanalytical repertoire with the cognitive repertoire of explanation. He saw that identification symbols reflect identity formations arising from thwarted libido, surrogate relationships, or vicarious appreciation for the acting out of id impulses. The appeal of demand symbols arises from id, ego, and superego impulses, often with one dominating in intensity over the other two.

The psychodynamic explanations in Lasswell's repertoire permitted him to address propaganda impacts beyond the full awareness of the target population, including id and superego appeals. Yet, Lasswell never underestimated the importance of nonpsychological factors. He did not dispute that some propaganda appeals, even if intended to manipulate attitudes beyond full awareness of the targeted population, should be perceived for what they are. Nor did he reject the possibility that the individual *might* fully realize the stakes to impulse, reason, and conscience, or that symbols are deliberately manipulated. When the symbol of "Irangate" is generated to forge an association with the presumably negative symbol of "Watergate," the target population may—or may not—be fully aware of the semantic sleight of hand.[51] They may recognize that the symbol "Irangate" was manufactured to highlight the association with the scandal of Watergate, yet nonetheless accept that the connection between "Irangate" and "Watergate" might be valid. In short, Lasswell's framework for analyzing political and policy symbols brings in the realism of conscious appreciation of symbols without precluding the possibility of unconscious psychodynamics.

Those who lose sight of the nonreductionist nature of Lasswell's framework run the risk of misunderstanding the linkages among systemwide aspects, such as prevailing political symbols and the individual psychodynamics. For example, Richard Merelman (1981) found an

> inconsistency between Lasswell's view of state symbolism and his view of the political personality. On the one hand, he portrays political personalities so driven by internal conflicts that their lust for power becomes insatiable. On the other hand, he portrays state symbolism as so deeply embedded in social norms that it smothers the impulse-life of ordinary people. The two portraits cannot both be correct. It is particularly difficult to understand from Lasswell's account how political personalities so driven towards power can be seriously inhibited by "symbols of the whole." The political personality is surely too power-hungry to brook constituted authority or symbolic constraints. At the very least we should expect constant tension between the state and the political personalities who vie to control it, thus creating greater insecurity and conflict than even Lasswell envisages. (p. 480)

The inconsistency that Merelman saw was due to his false presumption concerning the status of Lasswell's theorizing. Merelman incorrectly attributed to Lasswell the position that both of these dynamics must be true in the extreme. Lasswell was trying to trace out the risks of extreme power-centered personalities, but there was no implication in Lasswell's work that all politicians are power centered, nor, for that matter, that all power-centered personalities are extreme. And even those politicians single-mindedly pursuing power may, in particular contexts, recognize the political advantages of observing societal conventions and fostering the attainment of other values. Moreover, Lasswell noted that state symbols are not static, and can be manipulated by leaders (1935b/1965). By taking the power-centered personality as only the polar extreme, Merelman left no room for the interactivity expressed in the following nuanced analysis:

> [I]t is useful to think of the power centered person as one who does not simply assert his will to dominate, but justifies himself by invoking values that are shared with others. The ideology of an established order is a storehouse of symbols on which the politician is able to draw, putting himself forward as the spokesman of party, faction, nation, neighborhood region, religion, or some other group. (Lasswell & McDougal, 1992, p. I-637)

By the same token, Lasswell never posited that state symbols will dominate the norms of all individuals. The importance of prominent political symbols and associated norms is not negated by the possible defiance of the power-hungry, although it may be moderated. The interactions between changes in symbols and the behavior of the power elite are *the* main focus of *World Politics and Personal Insecurity.* Merelman's error was to take each of Lasswell's propositions as an isolated absolute general law, an interpretation that was totally at variance with Lasswell's consistent pragmatist epistemology.

The brilliance of Lasswell's contributions to the study of propaganda and political appeals lies in his conception of symbols as both the key to the dynamics of association and the means for tracing trends in propaganda. He recognized that responsiveness to symbols can be deeply embedded in individual psychological needs and individual cognitive connections, as well as in the associations created by propaganda and other forms of communication. Lasswell's analysis of symbols is a crucial nexus between the micro and the macro.

Chapter 4

Democratic Character

Lasswell's commitment to a broad definition of democracy led him to undertake many studies of the conditions under which democracy can flourish, from his 1935 *World Politics and Personal Insecurity*, exploring how democracy can be shielded from authoritarian reactions to international threats, to his 1966 "Conflict and Leadership," examining the potential for resolving domestic conflicts democratically. Lasswell asked the fundamental questions: What is democracy; how should it be defined so that it is consistent with the ultimate objective of maximizing human dignity? How can democracy be encouraged and preserved?

Of course, numerous questions of political psychology must be addressed to determine how to promote democracy to enhance human dignity. What psychological predispositions and traits underlie the potential for democracy? How dependent is democratic practice on the character of a nation's people? Are antidemocratic predispositions pathological or normal? To what degree are democratic or antidemocratic attitudes subject to change through socialization, civics education, events, or other means? To what degree is democratic practice in public affairs rooted in the orientations toward the microdemocracy of everyday interactions in the family or workplace?

These questions have been debated since ancient Greek times. Lasswell revived Plato's conception of character and constitution, but added psychodynamic functional theory. Now Lasswell's conceptions must be revived, to restore coherence to the bewildering array of findings and theories that have arisen in the contemporary era. The research on leadership, extremism, psychobiography, political culture, authoritarian personality, and related topics has yielded well over 100 conditions, experiences, traits, attitudes, or variables proposed as causes or correlates of democratic or antidemocratic predispositions. The plethora of possible mechanisms and factors has left great confusion over such issues as the essence of democratic character—or even whether there is an essence—and the mutability of democratic predispositions. At the present time, research and theorizing about democratic predispositions seem to be at an impasse, whether

67

because of the intractability of managing the multiplicity of variables, or the confusion over what constitutes democratic character.[52]

Lasswell avoided this morass by creatively adapting the insights of ego psychology.[53] Instead of proliferating the traits and conditions that could be connected with the many components of democratic and antidemocratic predispositions, Lasswell posited the strong, "open" ego as a basic, over-arching attribute that permits the individual to maintain the discipline that democratic practice requires. To link societal factors to democratic predispositions, Lasswell focused on the impact of threats to the "self-estimates"—and particularly self-esteem—emerging from interpersonal interactions, and the adaptations that the individual makes as a result of these interactions.[54] He identified reactions to anxiety as the prime shapers of character, emphasizing the reinforcement of attitudes and behaviors that allow the individual to secure deference, even if that comes at the expense of ignoring the will of others and focusing too narrowly on particular objectives, such as maximizing power to the neglect of the democratic rights.

Should contemporary political psychology, which has largely neglected life history approaches and theories based on deeply embedded psychological needs, go back to Lasswell's psychodynamic approach to understanding democratic character? Our answer is a resounding "yes," but several issues must be addressed for this conclusion to be persuasive. Lasswell relied heavily on the concepts of *psychic energy*, the *energy system*, the *self system*, the *open ego*, and the *id/ego/superego division of the mind*—terms that many political psychologists would find antiquated or too tightly associated with Freudian conceptions. Lasswell also gave enormous importance to the role of anxiety, which today is given a more limited conception and role in psychodynamics.

In this chapter, we show that once the semantic and theoretical equivalents are recognized, Lasswell's conceptions seem far less quaint. More important, Lasswell's conception of democratic character and the mechanisms that he proposed as influencing democratic character remain compelling, accounting for democratic and antidemocratic predispositions by linking the individual psychodynamics to the social process.

CONCEIVING DEMOCRACY
AND DEMOCRATIC CHARACTER

Democratic character consists of the enduring aspects of personality that predispose individuals to support and practice democracy. A conception of democratic character must therefore clarify which aspects of personality are involved, and how *democracy* is to be defined.

Character

For Lasswell, *personality* covered all of the enduring traits manifested in interpersonal relations, encompassing the aptitudes, skills, drives, automatic and unconscious restrictions and compulsions, and ego ideals. Lasswell divided personality into character and aptitudes (Lasswell, 1951).

Character, in turn, is comprised of two elements. The *self-system* consists of the perspectives (identifications, demands, and expectations) related to the individual's basic values. It is labeled the self-system because it establishes the individual's self-conception and orientation toward values and society. The perspectives encompass the cognitions in conscious awareness, including what the individual tells himself or herself about the self and the world. Lasswell's use of the perhaps daunting term *self-system* was in keeping with the usage by the philosopher George Herbert Mead as well as Lasswell's frequent collaborator, the psychiatrist Harry Stack Sullivan (Lasswell, 1951; Sullivan, 1948). This term can be demystified simply by regarding it as the set of perspectives most relevant to values and demands. For example, let us consider a hypothetical statement (whether or not articulated to others) of an individual expressing all three elements of perspectives:

1. "I am an environmentalist" (identification—how the individual symbolizes himself or herself).
2. "I want stronger environmental regulation" (demand).
3. "I believe that the system is such that stronger environmental regulation will be enacted if mass protests occur, including the possibility that if I engage in such protests the chances for stronger regulation will improve" (expectation—both the understandings of how conditioning factors operate and predictions of future states under various contingencies).

Second, the *intensity system* consists of the factors that determine value priorities and the intensity of motivations for action with respect to the individual's demands (Lasswell & McDougal, 1992). Perspectives alone do not determine predispositions or stress toward action. Something other than cognitions must establish whether the individual has both the impetus and capacity to overcome obstacles to achieve demands (Lasswell & McDougal, 1992). Lasswell (1951) posited that this component of character constitutes the "degree of support, opposition or non-support received from the unconscious parts of the personality" (p. 482).

Lasswell labeled this the "energy system" in his earlier works, but changed the term because the "rather precise meaning [of energy] in physics" differs from some of the implications of "intensity," such as the connectedness of particular intensities to particular symbols and actions (Lasswell & McDougal, 1992, p. 598). The aggregative nature of energy is not shared by intensity, which is more contextually fixed and determined. Freud posited the fixed nature of total psychic energy, but Lasswell understood that total intensity is not necessarily fixed over time. Intensity can shift from one focus to another, and changes in intensity with respect to one focus may affect the intensity with respect to another.

Thus "character," as Lasswell understood it, is comprised of the aspects of personality that account for the predispositions to act, as well as the cognitions relevant to these predispositions. Character does not include the aptitudes and habits of thought that round out the concept of personality, except insofar as these additional aspects shape the content and intensity of identifications, demands, and expectations (1951, p. 513).

Democracy

Even within the conventional definitions of *democracy*, the commitment and capacity to engage in and defend democratic practices have multiple meanings. Democracy can be defined narrowly or broadly along at least two axes: the aspects of democratic practice, and the range of arenas or venues.

Practices. Democratic practices include aspects of restraint: permitting those with competing preferences to enjoy the legal rights of participation and to participate free of disrespect or harassment. They also encompass dimensions of participation: to increase the rewards for the individual or his or her identification groups and for other groups. Finally, practices can be extended to defending democratic practices against threats from others.

The distinction between practices requiring restraint and the proactive practices is especially important. Permitting competitors to take advantage of democratic freedoms requires the discipline to resist the anxieties triggered by threats. Democratic practice requires forbearance, restraint, balance, and tolerance. This is, of course, particularly relevant in times of crisis. As Lasswell (1951) noted, "When we speak of democratic character, of course, we have in mind the development of self and energy systems which withstand adversity on behalf of patterns of value and practice" (p. 513).

Under differing circumstances, democratic attitudes would require different levels of intensity of commitment. For example, defending democratic practices in which formal democratic institutions do not exist or are under attack may run the risk of severe reprisals. The broad question, therefore, is not whether a population is simply democratic or anti-democratic, but rather whether it is democratic in a range of situations varying in terms of how threatening they are to the population's other values. Over time, the level of threat may vary. Therefore, democratic predispositions can be viewed in terms of the thresholds at which a population would embrace, or fail to oppose, antidemocratic practices.

Scope of Arenas or Venues. The second dimension of democratic practice addresses whether the focus of attention should be limited to public affairs and government as conventionally defined, or extended to interpersonal interactions at other levels and in other areas. Democracy in the family, the workplace, religious institutions, voluntary organizations, and other institutions has its intrinsic limits. Yet, the tolerance for all voices to be heard, and the commitment to share benefits broadly, are parallel to the standard conception of democracy pertaining to public affairs and government.

Lasswell's conception of democratic practice was derived from his higher commitment to maximizing human dignity. In "Democratic Character," Lasswell wrote that a "democratic community is one in which human dignity is realized in theory and fact. It is characterized by wide rather than narrow participation in the shaping and sharing of values" (Lasswell, 1951, pp. 473–474). Rather than confining democratic practice to the affairs of government and public policy, Lasswell conceived of democratic practice as running throughout everyday life, from the family to the workplace as well as in relation to the affairs of state. Human dignity is enhanced or deprived at all of these levels, and the participation in the shaping and sharing of values ranges across the whole spectrum of human interactions.

The combination of "shaping and sharing of values" signals the dual nature of democratic practice: it not only permits a broad range of individuals to participate in establishing what the collectivity will pursue ("shaping the values"), but also permits a broad—fair—allocation of the fruits of these pursuits (the "sharing of values"). Democracy is more than participation (sharing power); it is also equity in the distribution of nonpower benefits, whether material (e.g., wealth) or deferential (e.g., respect or affection). Lasswell thus defined democracy in terms of willingness to share power and other values fairly in all social interactions. As long as other people suffer deprivations, participation on behalf of others is an imperative of democratic practice. The only aspect of practice that is not a requirement of the democratic character is self-aggrandizing participation.

This conception reflects an important tenet of Lasswell's theory of democratic character: The traits associated with democratic practice tend to generalize across different types and levels of social interactions. The individual with the combination of self-discipline, flexibility, openness, and optimism that is conducive of democratic commitment with respect to family, workplace, and professional organizations is likely to have the same characteristics with respect to public affairs, his or her religious institutions, and so on. Lasswell recognized that this is not to be regarded as a general law, and in fact his displacement hypothesis proposed that orientations on the public level may, in some cases, absorb hostilities and other negative impulses in order to remove these impulses from the foci that are closer to home (1930/1960). Despite the possibility that displacement mechanisms are at play in some individuals, we would expect that, for the general population, democratic predispositions in proximate interpersonal relations will be positively correlated with such predispositions in public affairs.

THE THEORETICAL CHALLENGES

A complete psychological theory of democratic character would have to link inborn tendencies or developmental patterns to psychological traits or mechanisms, which in turn result in predispositions that either encourage or suppress democratic attitudes and behavior. An even more complete psychosocial theory would include social interactions and sociopolitical conditions as part of the developmental patterns and as the context in which these predispositions are expressed.

Most psychological theories have focused heavily on traits, either as explanatory variables or as links in a causal chain from social conditions or developmental patterns to predispositions. The first challenge to such a theoretical approach is the huge number of possible traits that can plausibly be linked to democratic predispositions: capacity to feel concern,[55] empathy, emotional warmth, compassion, egalitarianism, optimism regarding long-term improvements, optimism regarding human perfectibility, tolerance of difference, tolerance of ambivalence, tolerance of ambiguity, belief in justice, capacity to delay gratification, capacity to forgive past injuries, capacity to engage in give and take, respect for process, value balance, sociability, need for affiliation, willingness to take moderate risks, respect for rights of others, capacity for self-criticism, capacity to accept defeat, cooperativeness with partially opposing groups and individuals, ego strength or self-control, and conscientiousness.

In their analysis of the authoritarian personality, Adorno, Levinson, Sanford, and Frenkel-Brunswik (1950) suggested that the following traits are associated with antidemocratic predispositions: submissiveness, need for rigid hierarchy, need for power and toughness, conventionalism, anti-intraception,[56] emotional coldness, intolerance for deviance, destructiveness, cynicism and pessimism toward people, projectivity,[57] tendency to stereotypy, need for dominance over subordinates, submissiveness to authority, ethnocentrism, authoritarian aggressiveness, superstitiousness, preoccupation with sex, preoccupation with power, strong conventionality, dependency, fear of being weak, self-rationalization, projection of negative impulses onto others, and resentment. Or, alternatively, one could list the traits and attitudes that may be antithetical to democratic beliefs and practices: perception of relative deprivation, absolute deprivation, tough-mindedness, envy, bigotry, xenophobia, capacity to hate, anxiety, insecurity, suspiciousness, paranoia, inferiority feelings, self-centeredness, elitism, intolerance, strong risk aversion, impulsivity, low self-insight, need for closure, and sadism.

Some of these characteristics are simply facets of what is meant by democratic or antidemocratic predispositions (e.g., need for dominance); others are characteristics of temperament and personality that might induce such predispositions. Yet, the efforts to relate these characteristics to democratic attitudes or behaviors typically yield only modest or inconsistent correlations, without providing an organizing principle related to causation or the hierarchy of importance.[58] Moreover, the trait analysis approach does not yield insights into what interventions, if any, could make a population more democratically oriented.

The second theoretical issue is whether democratic predispositions are "normal" from a psychological perspective. For most of human history, most institutions have not been democratic in any meaningful sense of fairness in the shaping and sharing of values. Therefore, to accept that antidemocratic predispositions reflect some form of psychopathology in the generic case of human interaction is to label the bulk of human experience as pathological.

The third theoretical issue is whether the predispositions of the several aspects of democratic practice can be covered by the same psychological explanations. Although the broad definition of democratic practice calls for both active participation and restraint, it is possible that these predispositions arise from different or even opposite psychological characteristics and dynamics. For example, restraint may reflect apathy.

The fourth theoretical issue is whether psychosocial explanations, linking societal characteristics and practices to democratic predispositions, are even relevant. One alternative conception, a nature rather than nurture model, is that neurological and random developmental variation, quite apart from practices that influence development, produces a range of personality types in any society; some individuals will be democratically oriented, some will be prone to disruption and violence, some will be intolerant of conflicting views, and so on.[59] Whether or not democracy emerges in any given society would thus depend on how institutions capitalize on the prodemocratic predispositions and neutralize the impact of antidemocratic tendencies of the general population or of particularly antidemocratic individuals. Obviously, democratic practice is more prevalent in some contexts than others, but this does not necessarily mean that the psychological characteristics associated with democratic predispositions are more prevalent, given the alternative explanation that social and political structures and norms may simply hold antidemocratic predispositions in check. Another alternative model is that the variations in psychological predispositions are minor compared to the variations in the levels of threat that could challenge democratic practice. Rather than looking at whether Germans in the interwar period were somehow less democratically predisposed than were other peoples, we might ask whether any nation, confronted with the material hardships and humiliations following WWI, could have maintained democratic attitudes and behavior.

LASSWELL'S THEORY OF DEMOCRATIC CHARACTER

Lasswell began by asking whether the highly generalized orientation of fairness in the shaping and sharing of values corresponds to one or more psychological characteristics. He noted that such fairness depends on three elements: being positively disposed toward other people, a degree of balance in the values that the individual seeks, and the capacity to control selfish, hostile, or punitive impulses. Lasswell's answer was to combine the notion of the open ego with the concept of ego strength. This combination consists of:

• *Identifications* that are warm, inclusive, expanding, and capable of broad friendship.[60] Lasswell pointed out that the open ego is not the same as the capacity to form sentimental bonds. Indeed, intense and all-embracing bonds often "represent a socialization of fears and hostilities directed against other human beings" (1951, p. 496).

• *Demands* that display breadth across the values (Lasswell, 1951). Narrow demands, especially the obsession with a single value, jeopardize the balance required for democratic practice. The ideal is the individual who, in valuing respect, rectitude, and affection, is motivated to behave respectably, righteously, and cordially. The particular concern is with the power-centered personality who is so intent on maximizing power that democratic self-restraint is abandoned.

• *Expectations* that reflect confidence in human potentialities. Expectations involve not simply a matter of political trust, although this is crucially important in the give and take of politics; expectations are also key to the potential for inclusive identifications and capacity to withstand adverse circumstances (Lasswell, 1951).[61]

• *Freedom from anxiety*, to ensure high-level functioning (Lasswell, 1951). This should not be taken to mean that a democratic character could be expected to be totally free of anxiety.[62] The question is whether anxiety can be kept under control without significant impairment. This impairment is relevant to the final point.

• *Capacity to control the eruption of antidemocratic impulses* (Lasswell, 1951). Even when reason and conscience call for democratic practice, raw impulses of a selfish, hostile, and aggressive nature may emerge if ego strength or, to use a more contemporary term, impulse control is deficient. This eruption is more likely in times of crisis, when stress and anxiety are high (see chap. 6).

The first three elements reflect key perspectives of the self-system; the last two are aspects of the intensity (or energy) system. The perspectives provide the reasons to be predisposed to support broad participation in shaping and sharing values. The demands on the self are obviously the most proximate connection to democratic predisposition: Individuals must place demands on themselves to share power and other benefits. Broad identifications help to turn demands away from self-aggrandizement and toward the community. Optimistic expectations justify the belief that sharing power and other rewards will benefit all, including the individual and the inner circle of family and friends.

Identifications ⎱ Demands (including self-demands) → Democratic/
Expectations ⎰   antidemocratic predispositions

Factors involving ego strength are also interconnected. For Lasswell, anxiety prompts action—often, but not always, relieved through discharge that is aggressive or punitive. Together, they address whether the ego can prevent anxiety from diverting the individual away from democratic predispositions into narrowly self-protective attitudes and behavior.

A key point here is that Lasswell's conception of the democratic character does not invoke five separate traits, but rather a single, coherent consolidation or crystallization of components of the self-system and the intensity system. The perspectives are nearly coterminous with prodemocratic attitudes, whereas the capacity to minimize anxiety and the eruption of antidemocratic impulses is crucial for maintaining these perspectives in thought and action.

If this constellation of characteristics is the essence of democratic character, how does it come about? Lasswell's theory can be summarized in eight propositions.

1. Individuals have what we might call "primary impulses" that normally span the range of desires for affection, control, material goods, safety, and so on. Generally speaking, individuals want many things, whether these things fall into the categories of "deference" (i.e., power, affection, respect, or rectitude) or "welfare" (physical well-being, wealth, skill, or enlightenment). When such impulses are not satisfied, anxiety ensues.

2. Individuals who experienced earlier deprivations that were overcome to a greater or lesser degree by resorting to the use of a particular resource ("base value") will come to value that resource as an end in itself, and will tend to narrow their desires to the maximization of that value. In other words, these secondary impulses arise from the reinforcement of behaviors that satisfy primary impulses but supplant other impulses in attracting the greatest intensity toward thought and action. For example, an obsession with wealth may stem from earlier deprivations of respect, which were at least partially overcome by impressing others with a display of wealth. Something that begins as instrument becomes an end in itself, through a process of goal substitution.

These secondary impulses tend to reflect a narrowing range of values held by the individual, as certain behaviors are selected over others and become more central in defining the individual's character. In his essay on democratic character, Lasswell (1951) wrote, "The characteristics of democratic character have often been cast into relief by the study of individuals who are infatuated with the pursuit of one value to such a point that the integrity of the common life is imperiled thereby" (p. 498). For example, if wealth is found to secure respect, power, and affection, then wealth will increasingly become an end in itself, *beyond* the material goods that it can provide. Or a child, in overcoming loneliness and physical insecurity through intense affection with one individual, whether a parent or sibling, may come to regard the love of that individual as the overwhelmingly important goal.

In terms of democratic character, Lasswell was particularly concerned about power becoming an end in itself, because of its obvious implications for denying the political rights of others. He noted, "Power is expected to overcome low estimates of the self, by changing either the traits of the self or the environment in which it functions" (Lasswell, 1948b, p. 39). When the need for power is excessive, it encroaches on the respect for the power of others:

> [T]he human being who is fascinated by power is out of harmony with our basic concept of human dignity. . . . To the power-centered person all human beings and all contacts with others are opportunities for imposing his will, or for enlisting the other person in some manner that contributes to the imposition of his own will in some future situation. Hence he imposes a wall of insulation and isolation between himself and others, with the result that a growing sense of alienation from mankind becomes one of the recurring complaints of those who attain power, or only aspire with all the intensity of their being to acquire it. (1951, p. 498).

3. Deprivations of deference are especially likely to generate anxiety that leads to this narrowing of values as well as to changes in character. Lassweel (1951) wrote, "[F]ailure to develop democratic character is a function of interpersonal relations in which low estimates of the self are permitted to develop" (p. 521).

4. Among the deprivations of deference, those that threaten self-esteem have the greatest distortive and disruptive impact. Although low self-estimates involving other values such as power or wealth can undermine democratic predispositions, self-respect holds a special place: "[T]he causes of destructive impulses have been painstakingly explored, and the upshot is to emphasize anew the pathogenic importance of insufficient self-respect" (Lasswell, 1948a, p. 15). Lasswell (1948b) also noted, "Social anxiety . . . is acute concern for the *deference* responses of others, and includes the incorporation and application to the self of deprivational appraisals. . . . According to the social-anxiety hypothesis democratic character develops only in those who esteem themselves enough to esteem others (to use of phrase of Harry Stack Sullivan's)" (p. 162).

5. *Intermittent* deference rewards and deprivations from individuals of higher status in terms of power or respect are especially important in arousing anxiety and shaping the perspectives of the individual. Respect from the powerful is pivotal, and the leader who keeps the deference-dependent guessing about their status is likely to have the greatest impact. Although Lasswell's framework was very different from the simple stimulus–response approach of B. F. Skinner, in this one respect they agreed on the efficacy of variable reinforcement (Ferster & Skinner, 1957).

6. Individuals continually face the challenge of fending off negative impulses, whether primary or secondary, so that they do not reach expression through action. These impulses may be directed against the self as well as against others.

7. Impulses are dealt with differently, depending on their consistency or inconsistency with reason and conscience and the individual's "ego strength."[63] Six outcomes may be expected:

A. Antidemocratic impulses may be expressed without any conflict with reason or conscience, if societal norms are congruent with these impulses. In his essay "Democratic Character" (1951), Lasswell concurred with Plato and Aristotle that democratic character is not to be expected in cultures that have not endorsed democratic practices. Here he addressed the question of whether antidemocratic character is pathological in nondemocratic societies, and answered "No." Even in democracies we can point to institutions and subcultures in which expectations of democratic practice are low, and therefore authoritarian attitudes and practices may not be correlated with psychological conflict. Davids (1957) and Redl (1971) found that authoritarians among military personnel do not exhibit greater indications of psychological conflict, such as neuroticism.

B. Impulses may simply be expressed, without anxiety, even if they do clash with society's standards of reason or conscience. In the extreme, this is the profile of the sociopath—the individual who robs a bank on a whim, the remorseless murderer, or the totally unscrupulous businessperson. Such a person may experience no anxiety, because conscience (superego) is so underdeveloped that no internal conflict arises to generate anxiety.[64] The prospects and approaches to prevent or treat these sociopathic personalities are uncertain, because contemporary research has revealed a host of subtypes and etiologies of individuals with minimal or defective consciences (Lykken, 1995). Lasswell (1951) maintained that the potential for superego is present in every individual, barring brain abnormalities; yet the superego can be stifled. Proper socialization is crucial for avoiding the atrophy of conscience.

C. Impulses may be suppressed, but with some effort that impairs the capacity to concentrate on and execute other mental activities or physical actions. Reason or conscience—or both—deter the individual from acting on the impulse, yet the psychological cost is anxiety, which is not only painful but also to some degree incapacitating. This impairment is typically manifested as rigidity, apathy, resistance to new information and thinking, low tolerance for ambiguity, inability to sustain activity, and difficulty in suppressing other unsocialized impulses (Lasswell, 1951). Sometimes the impulse will be expressed despite the individual's realization that it is inappropriate, reflecting low impulse control. Particularly in times of great stress, the impaired individual is likely to succumb to negative impulses (see chap. 6).

D. The impulses may be displaced so as to reduce the conflict and anxiety. They may be transformed into more socially acceptable impulses, through sublimation or reaction formation, even if the resulting attitudes still permit the expression of aggressiveness and hostility.[65] Lasswell (1951) wrote, "May not destructive tendencies contribute positively to the formation of a self-system and to the effective energies available to the democratic character? . . . [I]t is apparent that the destructive energies of a person may be directed against enemies of the democratic community. Indeed, any other behavior would betray the opportunities and responsibilities of democratic citizenship" (pp. 506–507). This insight helps to understand support of the virulent McCarthyite anticommunist witch hunts as well as strong hostility toward particular authoritarian regimes of Saddam Hussein and Mouammar Khaddafi.

E. The impulses may initially conflict with preexisting perspectives, but the perspectives themselves change, leading to a lessening of the conflict and therefore the anxiety. The individual's demand for fair treatment of other groups may diminish if it stands in the way of personal economic advantage. Racist identifications (i.e., the narrowing of identifications from "all people" or "all citizens" to "African-American" or "Arab" citizens), demands, and expectations will reduce the guilt and anxiety of racist actions, whether for economic, social, or political reasons. Lasswell's account of such dissonance reduction anticipated, with greater generality, the theories of cognitive dissonance and cognitive consistency of more recent psychology. Some sociopaths may constitute a subcase of this pattern, although it is also possible that extremely pathological individuals, presumably because of idiosyncratic experiences and distorted reactions to these experiences, may never experience qualms concerning antidemocratic or otherwise antisocial behavior.

F. The impulses may be suppressed rather easily with little conflict or anxiety. This is the outcome when ego strength is high. The strong can deal with the unsocialized impulses that arise to a greater or lesser degree in any individual.

8. Democratic character, in social and political systems in which democratic norms are accepted, will predominate insofar as this sixth mode of reacting to antidemocratic impulses prevails. Otherwise, antidemocratic impulses, narrow agendas, power mania, and antidemocratic perspectives will emerge. The sublimation or reaction formations, if also expressed through hostile predispositions, can undermine democratic practice.[66] The net result is that democratic character, where democratic norms are accepted, depends on the successful suppression of antidemocratic impulses, but the capacity to suppress these impulses is moot if the perspectives are already so distorted that antidemocratic impulses do not clash with reason or conscience.

Although these reactions are individual, the sociopolitical challenge is to identify the prevalent cultural, economic, or political patterns of interpersonal relationships that could account for the eruption or suppression of antidemocratic impulses in large segments of society. Beyond the obvious case of the society in which democratic norms simply have not been embraced, Lasswell, like so many theorists from Plato on, pointed to childrearing practices and the treatment of young adults. In his essay on "Democratic Character" (1951), Lasswell wrote:

There is reason to believe that in some cultures the possibility of developing an outgoing democratic character is excluded at an early period. The prevailing patterns of child care appear to induce early despair that profound gratifications can emanate from other human beings; yet they prevent this despair from putting a stop to all externalized activity. Indulgences are wrested from the hostile, reluctant universe by a variety of sly maneuvers. (p. 497)

However, Lasswell also focused on early career experiences, anticipating by several decades the theories of James David Barber (1972). In some societies, rewards come consistently from diligence and performance; elders and other reward-bestowers are fair and consistent; individuals are rewarded for the breadth of their integrity and accomplishments. In other societies, rewards come from extremely narrow accomplishment, or from political connections, factional battles, or chance; economic gains cannot be ensured by steady hard work, or they can be lost in an instant; love is bestowed or withdrawn capriciously; and so on. Viewed this way, it is not difficult to imagine broad reward structures that differentiate the society that nurtures the open ego from the society that does not.

Lasswell's conceptions and explanations of the open ego and ego strength are closely related to the work of Adorno, Frenkel-Brunswik, Levinson, and Sanford on the authoritarian personality, although without the methodological issues that have made these studies so controversial (Stone, Lederer, & Christie, 1993). The authoritarian personality model links ego-weakness to conventionalism and authoritarianism, superstition and stereotypy; and lack of awareness of unacceptable tendencies and impulses in the self and tendency to project negative impulses onto others (Adorno et al., 1950). The preoccupation with power and toughness (what Lasswell would term the "power-centered personality") is attributed in the authoritarian personality model to "overemphasis upon the conventionalized attributes of the ego. The underlying hypothesis is that overdisplay of toughness may reflect not only the weakness of the ego but also the magnitude of the task it has to perform, that is to say, the strength of certain kinds of needs which are proscribed in the subject's culture" (Sanford, Adorno, Frenkel-Brunswik, & Levinson, 1950, p. 237).

It is also important to see that anxiety has two roots in this model: One is the failure to achieve remaining objectives, the other is the clash between impulses and the logic or morality that condemns their expression. The two-edged sword of anxiety makes the control of anxiety levels one of the central issues in the creation and maintenance of democratic practice.

STRATEGIES OF INTERVENTION

Thus, three types of undemocratic individuals can be found: the benighted, the character deformed, and the anxiety plagued. The benighted grow up in societies in which they are not exposed to democratic norms. The character deformed have reconciled the anxiety of clashing impulses, reason, and conscience by focusing on a narrow set of values at the expense of those attitudes that reinforce democratic practices. The anxiety plagued have not succumbed to such deformations in shaping their perspectives, but the continuing struggle leaves them so impaired that either antidemocratic impulses erupt in them under conditions of stress and crisis, or their participation in political life is ineffective or absent. These distinctions are crucial for devising prodemocratic strategies.

Consider first the benighted. The obvious strategy for the advocate of democracy is to establish democratic norms as the appropriate standards of morality. Civics education and socialization are employed; past sacrifices for democracy and equity are emphasized. Admired symbols (what Lasswell and Kaplan, 1950, termed "miranda") can be invoked (e.g., George Washington refusing to be crowned, or the life of "honest Abe Lincoln"); sometimes these miranda symbols can simply be created.

Yet, the equally obvious challenge is the conflict between democratic norms and the preexisting norms that still have potency. For example, many nondemocratic societies are strongly patriarchal, or intolerant of open conflict. The strategy, then, must be to exploit linkages between the traditional and democratic symbols and norms. Some nations have been led into democratic practice by strong, patriarchal leaders, such as Lech Walesa and Boris Yeltsin. Konrad Adenauer led Germany into sustainable democracy as a 73-year-old chancellor of unimpeachable integrity, serving for 14 years. In Afghanistan, the *loya jirga* ("grand council") was convened in 2002 to legitimize the nascent Afghan democracy by linking it to this traditional assembly, which some authorities claim dates back two millennia (Roashan, 2001). In South Korea, democratic forces countered the authoritarian government's appeal for a strong, authoritarian government to oppose the North Korean menace (e.g., the garrison-state appeal) with the symbolism of moral superiority over the totalitarian North Korea: South Korea could tolerate political competition that democracy requires.

In addition, the miranda of the old norms must be undermined. In occupied Japan, the war was interpreted as the folly of militaristic military leaders (but not the Emperor); in postcommunist Russia, the communists are cast as self-aggrandizing thugs rather than as champions of the working class. Of course, the credibility of these strategies is often strengthened by the reality of the depiction.

Consider next the character deformed, whose challenge to the advocate of democracy is their lack of anxiety. Their perspectives allow undemocratic impulses to be expressed without clashing with a conscience that is, in terms of democratic objectives, underdeveloped. The short-term strategy must be to create a degree of anxiety by emphasizing whatever discrepancies exist between the practices and the values that are publicly espoused. Presenting new identities may be necessary to highlight the salient discrepancies between practice and democratic norms. Role models of democratic character ought to be highlighted to present alternative identifications—for example, Gandhi as one whose willingness to share extended beyond Hindus to Muslims, whose personal sacrifice was willingly given.

The participation of White activists in the civil rights movement in the U.S. South and in South Africa's anti-apartheid movement—like the engagement of upper- and middle-class youth in the revolutionary movements in Latin American countries such as Argentina and Uruguay—aroused strong anxiety among the privileged. For some, this anxiety heightened their resistance to democratic change, but to others, it was the impetus for changes in self-demands. Of course, plausible expectations must exist that outcomes will not be so threatening as to push anxiety levels to intolerable levels.

The long-term strategy for the character deformed is more daunting. The key, according to Lasswell (1951), is "the development of self and energy systems which withstand adversity on behalf of democratic patterns of value and practice" (p. 513). But what does this entail? Lasswell (1951) warned that:

> The task is nothing less than the drastic and continuing reconstruction of our own civilization, and most of the cultures of which we have any knowledge. Since the basic postulate of behavior is the maximization of indulgences over deprivations, our task is to consolidate democratic conduct by directing the indulgences toward those who act democratically, and the deprivations toward those who do not. This calls for a reconsideration of adult-to-adult and adult-to-pre-adult relationships for the purpose of achieving a pattern of adult conduct that, in accordance with the maximization principle, gives differential rewards to democratic practice, and thereby provides continuing support for democratic performance, and aids in the development of character systems which are capable of acting democratically in the race of adverse conditions. The aim is to bring into being a democratic equilibrium in societal relations in which deviations are promptly rectified. If we were designing a machine, it would be possible to 'build in' a set of servo-mechanisms which perform this re-stabilizing/operation. Since human relations are not mechanized, our task of creating and sustaining a democratic equilibrium is more complex. And the complexity is augmented by the prevailing anarchy in the world community, which keeps alive the expectation and the application of violence in the arena of world affairs, and also in the civic arena of police states. Hence the tremendous task of reconstruction must proceed in the face of adverse contemporary conditions and of anti-democratic inheritances from the past. (pp. 513–514)

This model presumes that democratic behavior cannot simply be "taught" in the narrow and conventional sense of educating youth via civics courses or other words or exhortation. Rather, democratic predispositions arise from the rewarding of democratic behavior over undemocratic behavior. The prosperity and stability of West Germany is a clear example. Chile may be the clearest contemporary example. Despite the authoritarian nature of the military government that ruled Chile from 1973 to 1990, economic and social reforms, as well as the recognition that unrestrained conflict had brought on the military dictatorship, fundamentally reconfigured the expectations of the country's political and economic groups. One might have thought that the brutality of the executions and tortures would have radicalized the affected population for many decades, or that the crushing of the Left would be taken by the Right as an opportunity for long-term domination. Yet, the politically and economically significant groups no longer expected that they could win all or lose all in terms of economic policy, political power, or other rewards (Constable & Valenzuela, 1989/1990; Hite, 2000; Valenzuela & Constable, 1991). Radicalism, from the Right or the Left, came to be seen as holding much greater risk than reward. Democracy was restored with agonizing slowness, but the hard-won democratic victories, and the stabilization of rule of law, established a remarkably strong appreciation for democratic process and suspicion of nondemocratic movements and practices.

Finally, consider the anxiety plagued. When anxiety levels are uncomfortably high, two strategies—again differentiated between short term and long term—are available. The short-term strategy, taking existing perspectives as given, is to train people to cope more effectively with anxiety. Lasswell (1941a/1948) remarked, "The task of reducing human destructiveness is to discover and to spread proper methods of controlling destructive impulses, once aroused, and of reducing the occasions that prod them into concentrated life" (pp. 251–252). Part of such training is to provide insight into the particular sources of insecurity; another aspect is to recognize the signs of anxiety so as to know when to seek help. Finally, the individual must be trained to know how to identify and approach qualified experts to gain insight and coping skills through them (Lasswell, 1941a/1948). These steps, unsurprisingly, are parallel to those required to seek competent psychiatric help. To address these problems on a wholesale basis, Lasswell recommended using mass communications. In fact, he acted on his own theory and pioneered in the production of radio programs in the pre-WWII period and thereafter to control the anxieties arising out of the emerging crisis as well as to counter propaganda aimed at generating anxiety. For example, a 1943 program with Peter Drucker and Walter Johnson conveyed the reassuring message that WWII was providing opportunities to strengthen the U.S. middle class, which in turn would strengthen American freedom and democracy.[67]

The longer-term approach is to present novel models of identification to activate alterations in self-demands. Changes in identifications can be structured to relieve (as well as redirect) anxiety by reconciling preexisting conflicts between actions and conscience. The sinner-to-saint model epitomized by St. Augustine is parallel to the transformation of segregationists into integrationists (e.g., George Wallace), cut-throat businesspeople into humanitarians, or hawks into pacifists. Presumably, when these transformations occur, the new configuration of identifications, demands, and expectations reduce guilt-induced anxiety. Democratic identifications that arouse id and superego can reduce anxiety by providing an outlet for impulse that is consistent with morality (Lasswell, 1932). For example, part of the allure of the civil rights movement in the U.S. South to social activists was the risk taking and flaunting of convention. Part of the attraction of philanthropy is, in some cases, the feeling of superiority over the less generous.

The new identifications and related demands may generate other anxieties. For example, anxiety may arise from the difficulties of accomplishing a new mission, as well as from the struggle against the remaining archaic impulses and new demands. A certain level of anxiety is necessary to avoid complacency and inaction, yet presumably the overall level of anxiety from new perspectives will be lower, or their attractiveness will not materialize.

It must be emphasized that, according to Lasswell (1951), these changes do not come easily. The key is "the development of self and energy systems which withstand adversity on behalf of democratic patterns of value and practice," but this entails major changes in fundamental sociopolitical arrangements—as mentioned earlier, it requires the "drastic and continuing reconstruction of our own civilization" (p. 513).

THE IMPORTANCE OF DEMOCRATIC CHARACTER FOR DEMOCRATIC PRACTICE

Returning to some questions concerning the status of democratic character within democratic theory, we need to ask: How deeply embedded is democratic (or antidemocratic) character within any given social structure and ideological matrix? When highly anxiety-provoking situations occur, will strongly entrenched democratic character still prevail? Can democracy be sustained in a society in which democratic character is not well established, or are the efforts to democratize such countries as Russia or Afghanistan doomed at the outset without fundamental changes in personality and the social structures that form personality? Is the character of the elite or the general population more important in supporting and safeguarding democratic practice?

The answers to these questions depend in part on the relative importance of democratic character, compared to the many other factors that arguably may impinge on democratic practice. Lasswell (1951) noted that mainstream Marxists ignore the fundamental importance of personality factors in favor of material conditions. Yet, outcomes also depend on the stability of character in the face of changing conditions.[68] In keeping with his commitment to the importance of contextual variation, Lasswell cast his propositions about democratic character and its origins in terms of provisional hypotheses of potential but not unvarying applicability. Basic patterns can be overturned by unusual conditions or events; equilibrium patterns and "developmental" patterns of change interact in complicated and varying ways. This epistemological position led Lasswell to an intermediate position in addressing all of these questions.

Is Democratic Character Fixed?

Clearly, Lasswell's short- and long-term recommendations to manage anxieties and prevent the narrowing of values imply that although character is shaped in childhood and adolescence, it is not totally fixed. Individuals can develop; so too can societies. Within a generation, democratic character can be altered; indeed, it can change still more dramatically from generation to generation. Of course, if sociopolitical structures remain unchanged, the socialization will replicate similar patterns of character.

The hope for hitherto nondemocratic countries lies in the possibility that major reconfigurations will occur. With great admiration, Lasswell (1951) cited Plato's analysis of swings in personality from generation to generation and the consequent implications for changing commitments to particular constitutions, including democracy. Lasswell (1951) also took approving note of the argument of the social psychologist Gustav Ichheiser that psychologists exaggerate the continuity of personality, as well as David Reisman's speculation that modernity brings other-directedness, lessening the hold of character, undemocratic or democratic.

Is Democratic Character Sufficient for Democracy?

Answering this question requires us to recognize that democratic character, the commitment to behave democratically and to defend democracy, and democratic practice are not all-or-nothing constructs. Each component of the perspectives and intensity dimensions of democratic character is a continuum. Democratic commitment, such as the willingness to share power and other benefits, is a matter of degree, influenced by the extent of sacrifice and risk that one would have to endure to fulfill the commitment. And "democracy" is not exclusively a question of whether national governments are freely elected, but rather consists of a host of practices at many different levels involving the whole range of valued outcomes. Although character is a crucial connection between basic interpersonal social structure and politics, the presence or absence of democratic character does not guarantee democratic practice under all circumstances. Lasswell was not naïve about the potential of democratic character to save democracy from extreme provocations. In his essays on political mood and climate, he chronicled how some provocations can bring out the antidemocratic impulses even in the populations of long-standing democracies.[69] His famous "developmental construct" of "The Garrison State Hypothesis" envisioned the possibility that anxiety over security could drive even the most ostensibly democratically committed nations, including the United States, to place more and more responsibility into the hands of the "specialists in violence," to the detriment of civil liberties (Lasswell, 1937, 1941, 1962; Lasswell & Stanley, 1997).

One implication of Lasswell's conception of continuum is that the impact of democratic character on democratic practice should be conceived in terms of thresholds. High levels of anxiety may overwhelm the capacity to withstand antidemocratic impulses. We think of this primarily in terms of threats. Yet, situations of seemingly enormous opportunity may also swamp inhibitions. Lasswell noted that "[so] potent is the urge for individualization in prosperity that orthodox symbols and practices are neglected for the sake of a steadily increasing myriad of individual demands. New operations collide with old restrictions. Lured by new hope of tangible advantage, enterprisers view delay with impatience, often facilitating by bribery, if necessary, the readjustment of ancient rules to emerging conveniences" (1935b/1965, p. 117). Sometimes the opportunities for rapacious gain that arise during major economic or political transitions (e.g., in the transitional countries of Eastern Europe and the former Soviet Union) are irresistible to many people who would have been able to maintain their integrity if the temptations were more moderate. Thus, the societies of strong or weak democratic character can be classified in terms of how extreme the threats or opportunities would be to overcome democratic discipline.

Can Democracy Be Sustained in a Society Without Strong Democratic Character?

The *necessity* of democratic character depends on two factors: whether the threats and opportunities are moderate enough to negate the need for the discipline that democratic character provides, and whether antidemocratic impulses can be turned against threats to democracy. Lasswell's answer was that both are possible in principle, but neither is sustainable. Except for the society that is totally static economically and politically, the tensions that drive aggressive impulses cannot be avoided, because both the highs and the lows trigger actions or reactions that entail opportunities and threats to various segments of the population. Regarding the levels of threat or opportunity from economic conditions, Lasswell pointed out that neither prosperity nor depression necessarily reduces levels of tension. Economic depression poses its obvious insecurities. However, Lasswell also noted that in times of prosperity, the self-confidence, individuality, and differentiation that flourish for those taking advantage of emerging opportunities pose serious threats to those adhering to conventional rules and criteria of privilege (1935b/1965).

Regarding the possibilities of marshalling aggressive impulses to support democracy, we have already cited Lasswell's questioning the sustainability of the accommodation of channeling "destructive tendencies . . . against enemies of the democratic community. . . . The characters which are achieved by a complex process of balanced defense are viewed as constituting less enduring formations than those which evolve more directly" (1951, pp. 506–507). In short, whenever highly aggressive and authoritarian impulses are directed to defend democratic practice, there is a high risk that they might culminate in undermining democracy. Authoritarian rule that invokes democracy is not simply hypocrisy; it may also represent the paradox of "destroying democracy in order to save it."

Does the Character of the Elite or the Masses Determine the Strength of Democracy?

A closely related question is whether an elite committed to the democracy can transcend the antidemocratic character of the general population. Both

Edward Shils and Robert Dahl claimed that the personalities of leaders are more important than are those of followers.[70] Yet, Lasswell's framework and theory expose the severe limitations of posing this issue as if the character of elite and masses are not intimately interconnected. Certainly, through the strategies outlined previously, democratic leadership can influence the behavior of the public. However, there is no reason to assume that this is solely a one-way relationship, nor that modeling the relationship this way would be a fruitful exercise. Lasswell's great insight, often overlooked by those preoccupied with establishing simple frameworks of necessary and/or sufficient conditions, is the "incessant interplay of predisposition and environment" (1951, p. 489). Leadership patterns are part of the environment for the public's evolving predispositions; in parallel fashion, the public's distribution of character traits is part of the environment for leaders (see chap. 6).

The most fundamental complication in considering the question of the primacy of elites is in the fact that potential leaders span a broad range of character types; thus, insofar as some public support is necessary for a leader to rise and survive, the public chooses leaders whose character fills the needs of the public. Lasswell (1948b) wrote that the "appearance of a tyrant is an extreme sign of mass demands for the devalued self to depend upon someone else. So long as these dependency demands are generated in the lives of men, the masses will force themselves upon potential tyrants, even though at first glance it looks as though the tyrants were forcing themselves on the masses" (p. 163). By the same token, except in times of crisis, elites evincing an antidemocratic character are unlikely to find support to sustain their rule among masses of democratic character. Another connection comes from the influence of leaders on the capacity of the public to resist antidemocratic impulses. Leaders whose strategy of rule is to manufacture crises will raise anxiety levels and signal that aggressive action and power grabbing are necessary; malignant leaders reduce the faith in the potential benevolence of humankind.

The second complication is again the issue that the democratic character and democratic practice are matters of degree and exist on multiple levels. To say categorically that leaders of an antidemocratic character would undermine democratic practice or the democratic character of the general population ignores the obvious possibility that mildly antidemocratic leadership (obviously a quite common phenomenon) is an utterly different situation than that of leaders exercising state terror. Similarly, because the breadth of democratic practice ranges from family relationships to national and even international politics, there are myriad relationships that would have to be analyzed through detailed contextual analysis.

Lasswell believed that the determinism reflected in the assumptions that democratic character is determined by the behavior of the elite or established through deeper cultural practices should not be accepted as doctrine, but rather should be subjected to empirical inquiry. In his 1951 discussion of the empirical methods for studying democratic character, he wrote:

The following questions are among those whose relevance will not diminish: "To what extent is it possible to achieve democratic conduct in adult life without forming democratic character in early life? To what extent can democratic character formed in early life persist against anti-democratic environments in later life? In what measure can democratic conduct in later life form democratic character among adults (and the pre-adults influenced by them)?" (p. 523)

Lasswell did not maintain that empirical research would soon or ever resolve these issues and arrive at a universal, general law. The multiplicity of facets of democratic conduct—and the complexity of the interactions between environment and psyche—make a definitive *general* answer to these questions impossible.

ANXIETY AND PSYCHIC ENERGY

Two of the psychological concepts prominently employed by Lasswell in his theory of democratic character raise the question of the obsolescence of his views. First, Lasswell's stress on anxiety seems excessive to many today; although anxiety is still a central concept in psychology and psychiatry, the narrowing of the definition to make it more amenable to empirical measurement has shorn it of its theoretical breadth. This narrower conception conflicts with Lasswell's argument that anxiety "performs a function of such enormous importance in the lives of people and in the social process as a whole that it deserves more extended comment" (Lasswell & McDougal, 1992, p. 617); or that "[p]ersonality warping begins in the use of various defenses of the conscious life against the shattering dysphoria of anxiety" (Lasswell & McDougal, 1992, p. 690). Second, Lasswell's frequent reliance on the concept of psychic energy might strike some as both quaint and theoretically objectionable, because this concept has been strongly challenged in psychological and even psychoanalytic circles for many years (Applegarth, 1971; Germine, 1998; Swanson, 1977). These objections to the continuing relevance of Lasswell's formulations must be examined.

The Meaning of Anxiety

To assess the legacy of Lasswell's emphasis on anxiety, we must be sensitive to the shifting meanings of the concept. *Anxiety* has undergone a progressive narrowing of meaning from Freud to the present. For Freud, anxiety (*Angst*) was an umbrella concept that encompassed the whole range of unpleasurable affects that impel action, as distinguished from such other unpleasurable states as grief or sorrow, by excitation that would then be discharged.[71] As a primal source of physical and mental activity—in some of Otto Rank's and Freud's formulations originating in the trauma of birth[72]—anxiety provokes personality impacts of enormous scope. Considerable debate and confusion arose over the definition of anxiety as an affect in the context of other labels denoting negative affects, such as fear.[73] This was exacerbated by the ambiguity as to whether the definition is to be considered as a particular affect or condition, or as a metapsychological concept to account for the origin and form of psychic energy.

The underlying theme of Freud's many and varying formulations of the role of anxiety is that potential psychic energy is mobilized by anxiety; however, the energy available to the individual may or may not be up to the task of addressing the anxiety-producing issues in a constructive way. Thus, for psychoanalytic theory, anxiety is a crucial and extremely complicated phenomenon: an adaptive reaction to danger. Freud (1926/1977) noted that the heightened heart and respiration rates associated with anxiety reflected the evolutionary advantage of priming the individual for flight or fight, but also were a potentially crippling burden.

Hence, psychoanalytic theorizing about anxiety—the main focus of several of Freud's monographs—was preoccupied with discovering the origins and transformations of anxiety as a particular affective state with a peculiarly important role in psychological development. The transformations of anxiety from one form or focus to another over the life history of the individual were invoked to account for the emergence of the ego. The particular transformations of anxiety from one form to another—the very early physical deprivations of hunger or pain become transformed into fear of loss of love, or into castration anxiety, among many other specific anxiety states—signal the special role of the concept of anxiety.

The debate within psychoanalysis over whether anxiety in adolescents and adults arises strictly from social interactions, as proposed by Lasswell's long-time collaborator Harry Stack Sullivan,[74] further complicates the theory of anxiety. Sullivan proposed that the peculiar symptoms of anxiety—the "uncanny feeling"[75] of dread, awe, and horror—arise exclusively from interpersonal relationships. According to Sullivan (1948), straightforward fears regarding physical threats, such as falling, do not have the symptoms that he placed under the rubric of anxiety. Sullivan's theory was in keeping with some of Freud's later speculations on anxiety, which emphasized that although anxiety may have its roots in evolutionarily adaptive physiological reactions to the dangers of the withdrawal of needs and comforts for the newborn, it transmutes over the course of the child's development into social anxiety that is a danger signal to the ego of the superego's disapproval (Freud, 1926/1959).

In contrast, for contemporary psychology and non-Freudian psychiatry, anxiety, although an important clinical phenomenon, is largely conceived as a condition or indicator of pathology, or even as a chemical imbalance. Contemporary psychiatry often glosses over the distinctions among anxiety, fear, dread, panic and other severely negative mental states. For example, the most recent version of the *Diagnostic and Statistical Manual of Mental Disorders* used these terms in its section of "Social Phobia (Social Anxiety Disorder)" in virtually interchangeable fashion (American Psychiatric Association, 2000). The defining characteristic is acute discomfort, not the theoretical concept that for Freud and Lasswell combined negative affect *and* the notion of impulse toward action. No concept in contemporary psychology has the equivalent breadth. Moreover, fear, dread, and panic are likely to have different implications for the political psychologist, if not to the clinical practitioner.

Lasswell was very much in the Freudian tradition in according anxiety a crucial role. He also defined anxiety essentially as the entire set of unpleasurable affects that impel action.[76] Lasswell (1948) extolled the virtues of a broad definition of anxiety, because a broad definition allows the observer "to approach the task of exploring the entire social process for the sake of discovering pathological sequences" (p. 117).

But why give anxiety such a prominent role? Anxiety plays a key role in the development of character, both in the wrenching personality deformations caused by highly traumatic events and by the adaptations built up gradually to cope with anxiety.[77] Rather than assuming that suffering from anxiety is an unusual or pathological condition, Lasswell's (1948b) point of departure was to recognize that some "psychiatrists . . . regard the task of coping with anxiety as fundamental to the development of every person" (p. 117). Lasswell accepted the psychoanalytic proposition that anxiety is pivotal in deforming personality. He wrote in his essay on "Democratic Character" (1951) that the "theory of anxiety is the most fundamental feature of psychiatric theory, since the disorders with which the psychiatrist is concerned are seen as unsuccessful modes of defending the ego against anxiety" (p. 509).

Second, anxiety impels both constructive and destructive action. In contrast to other unpleasant affective states, such as sorrow or mourning, anxiety leads to either expression vis-à-vis the external world or internal psychological changes so as to reduce the anxiety level. Hence, a theory that tries to account for the eruption or containment of antidemocratic actions quite naturally concentrates on the negative affects that create tension to act. Lasswell embraced Freud's insight that although anxiety can have the obvious negative impacts of provoking either overtly antidemocratic actions or apathy and withdrawal, it can also be the danger signal of unreasonable or unconscionable impulses that in many instances inhibits inappropriate behavior.

Third, for Lasswell anxiety was the regulator for the flow of intensity from one focus to another. Anxiety is produced by both the conflicts between raw impulse and reason, and those between conscience and reason.[78] Lasswell and McDougal argued:

> Anxiety performs a function of such enormous importance in the lives of people and in the social process as a whole that it deserves more extended comment. We referred . . . to the role of anxiety in the resolution of conflicting impulses. It will be recalled that repression occurs when a state of acute anxiety exists; more specifically, when colliding impulses induce a state of intolerable discomfort, stress and strain. Attempting to escape from dysphoria, the individual may meet the crisis by prohibiting the completion of one impulse, and by giving priority to the other. Moreover, defenses are erected against facing the internal crisis again (resistance). If

repression is completely successful, the intensities of the repressed impulse are automatically routed to the channels of expression appropriate to the successful act. If the repression is somewhat less than successful other defenses are adopted, consisting in the main of substitute channels that at least prevent the repressed impulse from appearing openly with full intensity at the focus of waking awareness. (1991: 617–18)

The Role of Psychic Energy

Psychic energy has been one of the most contested concepts of psychoanalytic theory.[79] Lasswell used the concept of psychic energy to explain the intensity of the impetus to action (the basic formula is that impulse gives rise to subjectivity, which gives rise to expression), the impairment resulting from the focusing of energy to address anxiety-generating conflicts (Lasswell, 1930/1965), and the force of displacement when the original impulse is blocked from expression. Lasswell's use of the concept may make his psychology seem archaic.

However, for Lasswell's purposes, the concept of psychic energy can be considered equivalent to intensity or impetus toward action. This is why he and McDougal were able to change the label of the "energy system" to the "intensity system" without altering any theoretical propositions. Assume that individuals act on a limited number of the available opportunities to obtain rewards or avoid deprivations, and therefore that some mechanism of selectivity must be at work. Then intensity, or energy, is the marker for the fact of selectivity. Political psychologists do not have to know the physiological bases of psychic energy or intensity, but rather agree with the obvious proposition that different aims are pursued with different levels of intensity, and that these intensity levels are interrelated. To accept Lasswell's approach it is sufficient to accept three premises: (a) for a given individual at a given point in time, certain foci have greater intensity than others; (b) the intensity of one focus may influence the intensity of others; and (c) a reduction of the intensity associated with one focus may result in the increase in the intensity of others, whereas an increase in the intensity of one may result in the reduction of the intensity of others.

Of these propositions, only the third is controversial. It is a weak version of the economic or conservation principle that Freud expressed in terms of a closed system of energy. Freud's strongest version was that the total quantum of psychic energy is fixed; it will be allocated ("cathected") across a range of objects and different agencies within the personality; and, owing to the fixed nature of this quantum, the reduction of energy associated with one focus must result in an addition of the same amount of energy associated with other foci (Applegarth, 1971; Freud, 1924/1961). Lasswell's formulations did not require the fixed-quantum premise, although the premise is consistent with any of the dynamics that Lasswell proposed.

Therefore, to justify Lasswell's use of the energy metaphor, we only have to demonstrate the validity of the third premise of the interconnect-

edness of intensities. Lasswell's own efforts to demonstrate this intercon-
nectedness relied on clinical and historical evidence of displacement and
impairment. In *Psychopathology and Politics* (1930/1960), he relied on the
life histories of former politicians who had suffered serious enough mental
problems to be hospitalized in a mental institution, chronicling seemingly
obvious cases of displacement and rationalizations of these displacements.
In *World Politics and Personal Insecurity* (1935b/1965), he presented historical episodes of impairment. Lasswell was not positing that the transfer
of intensity always occurs, nor that it occurs with any given level of frequency. Instead, he simply provided convincing instances to demonstrate
the possibility and nature of such transfers.

WHY HAS CONTEMPORARY
POLITICAL PSYCHOLOGY DIVERGED
FROM LASSWELL'S POSITION IN THE ANALYSIS
OF DEMOCRATIC CHARACTER?

As mentioned earlier, political psychology since Lasswell's pioneering
work has tried to account for democratic predispositions by finding the
empirical correlations among conditions, personality traits, and behaviors
or attitudes. Lasswell himself strongly encouraged empirical studies, and
indeed wrote many articles on how to gather systematic empirical information on perspectives, life histories, and so on.[80]

The analysis of sociocultural factors, often labeled "political culture" or
"national character" research, has typically focused on defining the cluster
of predispositions posited as modal for a particular political culture; it
then attempts to correlate this cluster with political behavior.[81] Yet, even if
such a cluster can be related to political behavior, the question remains as
to how and why particular political cultures develop. Thus, the second and
related focus of research on political predispositions has concentrated on
how individuals develop their political beliefs, either from defining events
(e.g., wars, genocides, economic depressions) or from the transmission of
beliefs from particular actors (parents, teachers, peers, political figures).
This is the province of political socialization research, which has had a
generic focus on how events and conditions shape political attitudes, but
with a large volume of research on how other actors inculcate political
values. In this regard, the political socialization research, and efforts to
account for political culture, have essentially been theories of learning. Its
theoretical pretensions have often been confined to the dubious question
of the relative weights of the influence of different actors (e.g., parents vs.
peers vs. teachers)—a problematic question because different outcomes
are likely depending on details of the context.

The crisis in political socialization research was dramatic, although
recent signs of recovery are promising. By the 1980s, political socialization literature seemed stalled. In 1985 and again in 1989, Timothy Cook
noted the collapse in the publication of political socialization research in

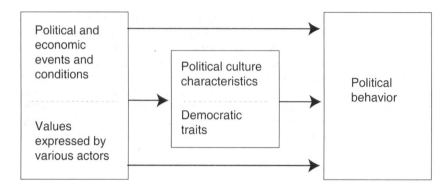

Standard framework of socialization and political culture theories.

the major U.S. political science journals.[82] Shawn Rosenberg (1985) concluded that this stagnation was due to the dominance of easily testable
sociological hypotheses at the expense of more complex modeling of the
dynamics of psychological mechanisms. More recently, however, students
of political socialization have rediscovered the virtues of broader models
that focus more on the interactions among socializers and the potentially
socialized, even though these models are much more challenging to test
with conventional measures. Judith Torney-Purta (2000) noted that the
"models used in many of the older political socialization studies are called
into question by these new approaches. Resistance as well as inculcation
has become important, and that resistance is not always in a form measured by the instruments frequently used" (p. 94). The prospect of robust
and consistent correlations, the sine qua non of the standard approach,
has largely failed to materialize.

We can see the limitations of the standard framework of socialization
and political culture theories in the accompanying figure by comparing
it to Lasswell's model, which also incorporates dynamics of learning, but
with far greater theoretical content and texture. For Lasswell, individuals
"learn" not only in the conventional sense by adopting the beliefs expressed
by others, or by drawing inferences from their own observations, but also
by taking on attitudes and overt behaviors that are positively reinforced.
Such learning includes the adoption of coping mechanisms to reduce anxiety, address low estimates of the self, and so on.

Why did this narrowing occur? The central problem is that the project
of correlating external factors (events and conditions or values held by
others) directly to traits, and then correlating traits to political behaviors,
ignores the internal psychological mechanisms that Lasswell's framework insists that we must take into account. These mechanisms not only
give meaning to the external world, but also determine whether a given
external cue will be transferred directly into the perspectives of the individual or, alternatively, will be inverted. As Lasswell (1951) insisted, many
"democrats appear to develop in opposition to anti-democratic parents"

(p. 507). With individuals reacting differently to the same external conditions as a result of different psychological needs and processing, it is no wonder that the flat correlational exercises have not yielded robust or consistent results. In contrast, what Lasswell always had in mind was to marshal empirical information in order to examine *configurations* of factors in particular types of contexts.

The difference can be illustrated by examining one of the few studies that tried to test Lasswell's proposition that power seeking in some power-centered personalities stems from the psychodynamics of overcoming low self-esteem. Clarke and Donovan (1980) analyzed interviews with 25 Arizona politicians to try to correlate self-esteem with the attractiveness of exercising political power. They found that individuals with high levels of self-esteem, as they reported and as judged by those analyzing the interviews, enjoyed the exercise of power, whereas those with low levels of self-esteem had negative or ambivalent stances toward the exercise of power. Thus, Clarke and Donovan concluded that there is no support for Lasswell's hypothesis.

However, the measurement of contemporaneous self-esteem and attraction to power misses the whole point of the life history relationship that Lasswell posited. Lasswell's hypothesis in *Psychopathology and Politics* (1930/1960) was that *some* (but not all) individuals *succeed* in overcoming deprivations in deference and self-esteem by exercising power; the reinforcement of overcoming low self-esteem leads them to enjoy exercising power. Lasswell never posited that the exercise of power always gains the rewards of greater deference and higher self-esteem. Presumably, individuals who at mid-career still suffer from low self-esteem have not overcome deprivations of deference through the exercise of power, whereas the individuals

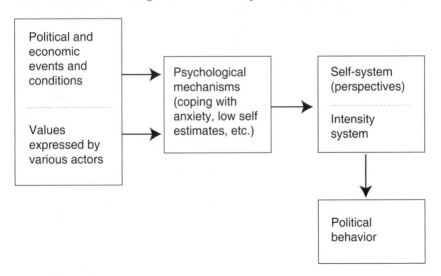

Lasswell's Framework.

who enjoy the exercise of power may have gone through the pattern of positive reinforcement that Lasswell proposed. Of course, the fact that high self-esteem individuals enjoy power does not necessarily mean that they all suffered from low self-esteem at earlier stages. For that matter, Lasswell's theory of "political man" did not presume that the individual driven to a preoccupation with power would enjoy its exercise. One might even question Clarke and Donovan's premise that those enjoying the exercise of power are more power centered; after all, the real surprise is that the low self-esteem individuals remain in politics even though they dislike it. The point here is that contemporaneous correlation of traits, without life history analysis, simply cannot test the psychodynamic mechanisms that Lasswell proposed.

The obvious next question is why the internal dynamics have been neglected. Certainly, a large part of the answer is that many researchers have taken the easy path of correlating the easily measurable, while still holding the aspiration of contributing to general theory. With some notable exceptions, such as the Q-technique,[83] political psychologists have not gone very far in following Lasswell's recommendation to find ways to measure subjectivity reliably and systematically. Cook (1985) argued that political socialization research went astray because of its overreliance on conventional survey techniques, which are particularly unreliable for studying children; such studies also disregard the connections to cognitive development and psychodynamics. Therefore, the variables that intervene between the external world and the formation of political character, ranging from total anxiety levels to defense mechanisms, have hardly been explored. Lasswell's insights point the way to a new frontier for the field.

Chapter 5

Political Psychology and the Risks of Leadership

Harold Lasswell contributed to leadership studies both through his work on the political psychology of leaders and followers, and also in his analysis of how the skills and resources of political elites enable some leaders to rise over others. Although his work was more often termed "elite studies," he addressed the issues that still preoccupy the field of leadership studies. Writing in the dark years of the Depression, the radicalization of interwar Europe, and the emergence of the Cold War, Lasswell was particularly sensitive to the risks of various leadership trajectories. Although his classification of leadership styles differs from the categories that are in vogue today, his analysis provides important insight into the risks of contemporary prescriptive models of leadership, and can help to advance the study of leadership in the 21st century. In order to go forward, we can go back to Lasswell's conception of the risks of leadership.

Any reading of the contemporary discoveries in leadership studies would show that Lasswell was far ahead of his time in both outlining the framework for studying leadership and developing psychological theory for it. As early as the 1930s, Lasswell conceived of leadership as encompassing the leader–follower relationship, which is now known under the trendy acronym of LMX—"leadership–member exchange." As early as the 1920s, in his work on political and policy appeals, Lasswell examined the emotional and symbolic bonds that form between leaders and followers (Lasswell, 1927a, 1927b/1971, 1932). In his voluminous work on political elites, also predating the bulk of leadership studies, Lasswell highlighted the skills that permit certain leaders to rise above others in varying circumstances. Indeed, as we show in this chapter, Lasswell's insistence that every leader–follower relationship entails one sort of exchange, whether material or emotional, is the key to clarifying the current confusion with respect to so-called transactional and transformational leadership.

For Lasswell, the characteristics and needs of followers were as relevant as the characteristics and needs of the leaders. For example, Lasswell (1948b) wrote that the "appearance of a tyrant is an extreme sign of mass demands for the devalued self to depend upon someone else. So long as these dependency demands are generated in the lives of men, the masses will force themselves upon potential tyrants, even though at first glance it looks as though the tyrants were forcing themselves on the masses" (p. 163). His analysis of leaders' manipulations of symbols to shape relations with followers tied leadership strategies to propaganda tactics. His insights on the nature of the relationship between charismatic leaders and their followers anticipated the alarms that the more thoughtful leadership studies experts are starting to sound (Conger, 1988, 1989; Gibson, Hannon, & Blackwell, 1998).

Lasswell's functional conception of roles also cut through the current, essentially trivial debate over whether particular relationships or behaviors ought to distinguish "leaders" from "managers" (Frame, 1995; Zaleznik, 1977/1992). By defining roles functionally rather than conventionally, Lasswell specified the leadership role in terms of providing *orientation*. Thus, the "fundamental characteristic of leader–follower relation appears to be the giving and receiving of orientation" (1966, p. 211). Managers oversee various activities within organizations; insofar as they *also* provide orientation—that is, influence the foci of attention, norms, or perspectives or those whom they manage—they are performing as leaders as well.

Lasswell's theoretical contributions to leadership began with his definitive work on the triple-appeal principle, which laid the groundwork for understanding the attractions of leaders who project different images that may or may not resonate with potential followers. His characterization of "democratic character" in relation to democratic leaders corresponds closely with the characteristics that comprise the ideal leaders prescribed by the dominant leadership models: the capacity to share, freedom from internal conflict, optimism and confidence about the future, and the potential goodness of people (Kets de Vries, 1979; Lasswell, 1948b).

This chapter is not dedicated simply to justifying Lasswell's place in the pantheon of leadership theorists. It is more important to use Lasswell's rich theoretical heritage to understand the challenges facing contemporary leadership studies.

Certainly, in order to further contemporary studies, we need to examine Lasswell's rich analysis of the psychodynamics of democratic and antidemocratic predispositions. Lasswell's contributions encompass the psychological origins of charisma and its impact on the accountability dimension of leader–follower relations, as well as the phenomenon of impostorship.

What is more, Lasswell's broad framework of perspectives and values permits us to assess what can remain of the distinction between transactional and transformational leadership. We should take seriously James MacGregor Burns' insistence that transactional leadership can go far beyond the exchange of benefits serving narrow self-interest. Burns wrote that it "is possible that transactional opinion leaders will appeal to fundamental, enduring, and authentic wants, to deeply seated latent needs, and even to followers' convictions about morality and justice" (1978, p. 258). However, if transactional leadership can entail such higher-order commitment as followers' self-sacrifice in exchange for the approval from the admired leader, transformational leadership cannot simply be distinguished by its monopoly over transcendent values.

Lasswell's application of psychoanalytic principles to leadership studies can lead to better understanding of the risks and benefits of the leadership styles. Instead of *defining* transformational and charismatic leadership as good, we ask whether these styles are functionally appropriate in various types of circumstances.

Finally, in this chapter we examine these contributions at greater length in order to understand the correspondence of Lasswell's own categorization of leadership styles with the models of contemporary importance. Insofar as these contemporary models share elements with Lasswell's classification of leadership styles ("agitator," "administrator," and "theorist"), Lasswell's insights into their psychodynamics can help to illuminate the underlying patterns of contemporary models.

CONFRONTING THE OPPORTUNITIES AND RISKS OF POLITICAL LEADERSHIP

The Dilemma: Balancing Transformational Potential and Responsibility

A major preoccupation of today's leadership research is to determine how to select and empower leaders committed to inspiring their followers, instilling their followers with the motivation to be self-activating, and transforming their institutions. Many scholarly treatises on leadership explicitly or implicitly endorse transformational, status quo-challenging, charismatic leadership models. The leadership movement takes transformation as virtually an article of faith. The mass-audience publications on leadership, usually targeted at business and nonprofit organizations, are positively exuberant about the benefits of transformational leadership; transformational leaders are typically depicted as not only capable of bringing aan organization out of its ruts of traditional practice to a new and visionary aim, but also are presumed to be more caring and more self-sacrificing concerning the organization's followers.

The attraction of a prescriptive model along these lines gives rise to efforts to design organizations, recruitment structures, and training to select and groom leaders with the mandate to be transformational, thus minimizing the value of the institutional constraints on leaders' discretion. Yet, ever since the 1930 publication of Harold Lasswell's *Psychopathology and Politics*, political psychology has been grappling with Lasswell's profound insight that the impulses to leadership, as well as the reactions of potential followers, are often rooted in problematic psychological dynamics. Myriad organizational analyses and individual psychobiographies depict troubled leaders as compensating for insecurities, projecting personal issues onto policy issues, pursuing quixotic goals, gratuitously antagonizing potential allies, and losing sight of the need for balanced objectives. Will leaders with the desire and capabilities to overturn existing patterns do so responsibly or irresponsibly? If the drive to leadership rests on such dynamics, how can an institution or a nation embrace highly assertive, transformational leaders and emerge with effective and responsible leadership?

The Centrality of Leadership Styles

Contemporary studies of leadership largely approach the issue of effective and responsible leadership by focusing on leadership styles, encompassing leaders' traits, priorities, and relationships with followers and other leaders in varying contexts. This now vast leadership literature[84] addresses the advantages and risks of various leadership styles by classifying different leadership styles, assessing which styles are most suitable for various circumstances and objectives, developing techniques for determining whether particular individuals have such styles (to assist in the selection process), and determining how to promote suitable leadership styles, through recruitment and selection processes, training, incentive systems, or other means.

Three approaches are most suitable for shaping leadership styles. First, insofar as preexisting personality types are differentially predisposed to particular leadership styles, these types can be encouraged or filtered out by recruitment, selection, incentive, and advancement mechanisms. Therefore, it is essential to see whether personality types coincide with predispositions to particular leadership characteristics. Only with these correlations can we direct the analysis and design of mechanisms to encourage the emergence of particular leadership characteristics.

Another approach is to shape the institutions that have the potential to influence the styles and relationships of those individuals who already have assumed leadership roles. The two major tools examined by leadership studies have been training and incentive systems. This raises the metaquestion of whether, and to what degree, individuals can be trained or influenced by incentives, with respect to leadership styles and relationships. If reform is needed to change leadership styles and relationships, are there promising alternatives for training and incentive restructuring?

Perhaps the relationship between preexisting personality types and leadership styles is not so tight, and incentives can induce individuals with particular personality traits to adopt different leadership styles. For example, if individuals with extremely power-centered personalities find that the system blocks leadership advancement of authoritarian leaders, one possible outcome is that they would reconcile themselves to more democratic styles; on the "compromise formation" accommodation that some power is better than no power. The obvious problem with regard to compromise in such leaders is that power hunger will reassert itself once the leader reaches a particular level of authority. Another example is the highly flamboyant individual with charismatic potential who is thrust into a leadership position that requires an instrumental, mundane, tit-for-tat transactional managerial style. Would the potentially charismatic leader be able to tone down his or her flamboyance if the incentive structure punishes flamboyance? These two examples should make it clear that there is no reason to assume a priori that the same conclusion would hold for different leadership styles. Thus, the issue of the strength of the linkage between personality and leadership style is again engaged.

The third approach is to change the degree to which leadership selection is controlled by peers, higher-level co-opters, or followers. The relevance of this consideration to leadership style is that potential leaders are more or less attractive to those who choose them according to the personality traits and leadership styles that selectors perceive, and according to how well particular leaders' apparent personality types fulfill the followers' emotional needs. What political structures or conditions permit or facilitate the selection of leaders with personalities predisposed to appropriate leadership styles?

There is great variety in the selection roles of peers, co-opters, and followers, and in the capacity of selectors to know or to act on the knowledge of potential leaders' personalities. Even for elected officials, some campaign and electoral structures—such as single-party-dominated systems where political leaders advance through governmental or party bureaucracies—make it difficult for voters to glimpse the personalities of candidates, let alone participate meaningfully in their selection. For example, prior to the 1990s the dominant Mexican political party, the PRI, nominated its presidential candidate through secretive consultations among party and governmental leaders. Because of a combination of voter loyalty and PRI control of the election process, the PRI candidate was certain to win. The voting public thus had no direct role in filtering the personality types (or leadership styles) of the individuals who emerged as presidents. Many Mexican presidents had advanced up the bureaucracy due to possession of insider skills and traits that ensured bureaucratic survival.

In other circumstances, the rise to power through more competitive election or through populist movements makes the leader's appeal to existing and potential followers an important aspect of recruitment and selection. Complicating the picture even further is the fact that followers, even if they do not have a direct role in the selection of leaders, may play a crucial indirect role. In the military, for example, selection by higher officers means that "followers"—enlisted personnel and lower-level officers—do not choose their leaders, but although this may render leaders' appeals to followers unimportant in some circumstances (e.g., if clique politics among the higher officers, rather than past performance as a commander, dominates the selection), in other circumstances the rising officers' ability to win the respect and enthusiasm of their troops contributes to the successes that make them competitively attractive for promotion.

As important as these questions are, the contemporary leadership literature is strangely quiet about the personal psychodynamics that underlie both the motivations of the leader and the appeal to potential followers. Without theories of how individual psychological needs influence personality, and how personality in turn shapes leadership styles, it is difficult to address the task of promoting particular leadership styles. Equally important, it is difficult to assess the potential risks of unleashing leadership that overturns existing conventions and structures. This vacuum in contemporary leadership studies is perhaps attributable to the current preference for measurable correlations over complex psychological theories that try to account for the emergence of personality types and their linkages with leadership styles. As we see next, going back to Lasswell's contributions can deepen and revitalize the study of these relationships and therefore help us to understand the dilemmas of transformational potential and responsibility.

Relevant Dimensions of Leadership Styles

We focus on how Lasswell's contributions illuminate the dimensions of leadership style that are most directly relevant to the advantages and disadvantages of strongly empowering leaders and their followers to transcend tradition and institutional constraints. Because the categories of leadership styles invoked by contemporary research are far too numerous for us to assess all their connections, we confine our analysis to four dimensions. These are democratic versus authoritarian, transformational versus transactional, task oriented versus human relations oriented, and charismatic versus noncharismatic. These four dichotomies certainly do not capture all aspects of leadership styles, but both the volume of research and writing on each and the formal or informal factor analyses of underlying dimensions instill confidence that the four do capture many of the relevant distinctions (Bass, 1990; Gordon, 2002)

Democratic Versus Authoritarian Leadership.   First, how do we account for democratic leadership styles? Basing their analysis on a host of concepts and distinctions in the leadership studies literature, Bass and Stodgill (1990) argued that the bulk of these characteristics fall on one side or the other of the democratic-authoritarian dimension. Bass and Stodgill called these the "two overarching clusters of leadership styles" (p. 419). Thus, if we can account for how and why some leaders are disposed to behave democratically, we can address a significant part of the differentiations among leadership styles. This bolsters the importance of Lasswell's preoccupation with the development of the optimism, sense of fair play, and willingness to share that characterizes democratic character. His classic 1951 "Democratic Character" essay is as relevant to political leadership as it is to the responsible behavior of the body politic reviewed in chapter 4 of this text.

Transformational Versus Transactional Leadership.   The remarkable work of James MacGregor Burns (1978) posed the prescriptive model of leadership that transforms relationships within the institution in order to orient followers to "higher" objectives that transcend their personal interests.[85] The leader's sensitivity to followers, and willingness to empower followers, are key to bringing followers to higher objectives. The large volume of research on transformational leadership has focused predominantly on how to encourage this form of leadership. It casts transactional leadership, in which the leader–follower relationship is essentially defined in terms of exchange, as less attractive because neither leaders nor followers are elevated to higher concerns, even if the original concerns or objectives may be altruistic. However, there is obviously no guarantee that the transcendent goals pursued through transformational leadership are feasible, responsible, or even ethical. The early Jesuits exhibited considerable transformational leadership, but that did not make their participation in the Spanish Inquisition a moral act. One might try to avoid this problem by defining transformational leadership as leadership that orients followers to only laudable goals, but this begs the question of whether, and under what circumstances, efforts to transform goals lead to positive or negative outcomes. If we explore the personality correlates of transformational leadership versus transactional leadership, we can get a deeper understanding of the potential pitfalls as well as the advantages of such assertive leadership.

Task Versus Human Relations Orientations.   The distinction between *task-oriented* and *human relations-oriented* leadership is of interest because of its partial overlap with the transformational-transactional leadership dimension. This distinction has been less frequently subjected to the assumption that one pole of the dichotomy is generally preferable to the other. Fred Fiedler (1967) noted "that both directive, task-oriented leaders and non-directive, human relations-oriented leaders are successful under some conditions" (p. 180). The obvious question is whether we can identify the situations in which one form of leadership is more effective than the other. We can find situations in organizations or whole polities in which accomplishing particular tasks is more compelling than is tending to personal relations; in other circumstances, higher interests are sacrificed for personal relations. The relationship between this dimension and transformational leadership is very complicated. Although different leaders undoubtedly assign different priorities to interactions with followers and the accomplishment of tasks, the transformational prescription argues for high levels of both: The sensitivity to coworkers or followers is valued in itself and is an instrument for accomplishing tasks effectively. In short, a high level of task orientation does not necessarily mean a low level of human relations orientation, or vice versa.

Charismatic Versus Noncharismatic Leadership.   Finally, the nature and correlates of charismatic leadership have attracted enormous attention in leadership studies, because of the dramatic agendas that charismatic leaders can pursue, the common view that charisma is an extraordinary leadership asset, and the fascination with leadership based on the nearly indescribable appeal of having a "special gift." As an analytical category, charismatic leadership should be defined simply as leadership by individuals with charisma, not as a prescriptive model that presumes charisma will be used well. Otherwise, charismatic leadership becomes the special case of transformational leadership assisted by the asset of charisma, with the same outcomes preferred by the prescriber: follower participation, sensitivity to followers, inspiration, and so on. This explains why studies of transformational leadership and charismatic leadership often seem to yield the same results. Shamir, House, and Arthur (1992) noted the "considerable convergence of the findings from studies concerned with charismatic leadership and those concerned with transformational and visionary leadership" (p. 8). This would imply that the psychology of charismatic leadership is simply the psychology of transformational leadership, despite what seems to be the distinctiveness of the asset of charisma.[86]

However, there are good reasons to distinguish charismatic leadership from transformational leadership. Many versions of the prescriptive model of transformational leadership emphasize sharing power with followers, yet the charismatic leader, armed with special gifts, does not have to permit or encourage participation, and indeed the followers of charismatic leaders may not want to share power with the leader. By definition, charismatic leaders have an appeal to followers that makes the leaders unaccountable in the conventional sense.[87] Charismatic leaders may not achieve transformation, and may not wish to do so, whereas noncharismatic leaders may achieve transformation even if they do not enjoy the asset of charismatic appeal. The obvious problem here is that defining both transformational leadership and charismatic leadership as prescriptive models—with the same defining characteristics of leaders who are ethical, visionary, power sharing, articulate, inspirational, sensitive to followers' needs, and willing to make personal sacrifices—ignores the potential for problematic charismatic leadership. Although charisma is a *potential* asset for good leadership, the full range of implications of leadership by charismatic individuals can be explored only by leaving open the question of whether this quality leads to positive or negative outcomes in specific contexts. The useful way to explore charismatic leadership is to resist the temptation to present charismatic leadership as a prescriptive model, and instead to see it as a *transforming* process and keep open the question of whether charisma will have good or bad effects.

The complex reciprocity represented by the triple-appeal principle and the insistence on viewing leader–follower relationships as exchange are crucial to understanding why efforts to discover simple correlations between potential follower characteristics and the appeal of different leadership styles are consistently disappointing. Consider the 2001 study published in the prestigious *Leadership Quarterly* by Ehrhart and Klein, which carefully developed statements that hypothetical supervisors would write to reflect their commitment to styles of charismatic, relationship-oriented, and task-oriented leadership. Ehrhart and Klein examined 10 personality characteristics of their college-age subjects, and then correlated these traits with the subjects' preferences for the leaders associated with each statement. The predictions were based on similarity and "needs" (e.g., a measure of the preference for close interpersonal relations at work should correlate with preference for the relationship-oriented leader). The study was constructed with admirable care, yet the correlations are strikingly low and inconsistent because many correlations run counter to the predicted directions, and only 2 correlations of leadership style preference exceed 0.2 (one at .23 and another at .27) among the 30 correlations linking the 3 preferences with the 10 personality variables. This is all the more remarkable in light of the partial overlap between the questions measuring the followers' traits and the leadership statements. Consider, for example, that the preference for close interpersonal work relationships correlates with the relationship-oriented leadership preference at .17—the trait thus accounts for less than 3% of the variance in leadership-style preference (Ehrhart & Klein, 2001).

The predictions assumed that follower traits would correspond with preferences in leadership traits, rather than more complicated relationships of complementarity. Is it not also possible that some of the individuals who have a high personal need for structure would on occasion desire to be led by someone who could serve as a channel for vicarious gratification through identification with a leader of opposite temperament?

The hypothetical leader is the immediate supervisor. This is a fair question if one is interested in determining the appeals of immediate supervisors at the lower- or middle-management level, but is hardly relevant to understanding the appeals of more remote, higher-level political leaders. Moreover, in posing a hypothetical scenario, the Ehrhart–Klein research design minimized the degree to which the exercise can engage the anxieties of the respondents. Insofar as political leadership appeals resonate with the management of anxiety, the findings can give little insight into this function.

Most important, the Ehrhart–Klein study did not attempt to gauge the *content* of the appeal that the charismatic leader presents to the potential followers. It is one thing for an aspiring charismatic leader to say that he or she wishes to inspire followers; it is another for the charismatic leader to present an appealing principle with which to inspire. Lasswell's insistence on assessing the substantive and symbolic content of the appeal clarified why such weak findings would result from experiments that did not introduce this content. This was echoed in Jay Conger's (1989) insight that if "followers do not think that their leader's formulation of a strategic vision matches their own aspirations, they are less likely to perceive him or her as a charismatic leader" (pp. 23–24). Without any information on the content of the vision, the potential for charismatic appeal is largely unengaged.

LASSWELL'S THEORY
OF DEMOCRATIC LEADERSHIP

In 1929, the 27-year-old Harold D. Lasswell returned to the United States from a second extended European stay, bringing back two stunning insights. First, any observer of Europe's downward political spiral could not help but note that European leaders were displaying a far more authoritarian side than anything experienced in the United States. Second, Lasswell was thoroughly imbued with the in-depth methods pioneered by Freud and other psychoanalysts. Lasswell had devoted nearly 3 years of study to the work of analysts in Vienna, Berlin, Paris, Prague, and Budapest. Thereby, he grasped the applicability of their theories for understanding elite behavior.[88] In 1930, Lasswell published one of the earliest American political treatises within the psychoanalytic tradition, *Psychopathology and Politics*.[89] The book focused on the life histories of political leaders, in large part to demonstrate the intimate roots of public stances and behaviors.

Lasswell's most basic contribution to the study of leadership was his warning about the destructive characteristics of the *extreme* power-centered personality. Such personalities are intent on imposing their wills on others, sacrificing other values in the pursuit of their own power, and displaying highly rigid behaviors. The power-centered personality is not necessarily involved in "politics" in the conventional sense of political parties, elections, government, and public affairs. The preoccupation with power may be seen in certain individuals in all sorts of groups and organizations.

Nor do all, or even most, individuals holding considerable power and authority have power-centered personalities. Thus, Lasswell was not arguing the inevitability that power corrupts, but rather that certain personality types hold power to be an overwhelming priority, so that when leadership recruitment brings authority to such people, the objectives of the group or organization risk being sacrificed to the leader's pursuit of power. In this circumstance, conflicts with other members and leaders will be severe, and followers with complementary destructive predispositions may also be empowered as they are mobilized to follow the distorted vision of the power-centered leader.

Lasswell's values framework, in posing power as both a *scope value* (something desired in itself) and a *base value* (a resource for the pursuit of goals), immediately suggests two motivations for power. Lasswell proposed that individuals who receive deference[90] when assuming leadership roles at an early age will be motivated to become leaders in order to enjoy the power and the deference that such leadership brings. For those who find that leadership accomplishes other objectives, leadership roles will also be preferred. These theories of positive reinforcement allow for the healthy pursuit and exercise of power. Yet, Lasswell also proposed that when individuals are in great need of deference because of early deference deprivations, a leadership role that brings deference will create a consuming craving for power. Thus, in many cases the desire to have influence over shaping the future through leadership is not pathological, but some patterns of leadership are based on this last pattern of desperate power seeking.

Lasswell (1954) provided a succinct summary of the development of the power-centered personality:

- *Origins:* Political personalities come into being by the use of power as a defense against threatened or actual loss of values.

- *Expectations:* The value position of the self is regarded as low either on the assumption of actual or threatened loss. Nonpower values are appraised as likely to be unsuccessful means of defending and improving the position of the self. The use of power, on the contrary, is viewed as comparatively successful.

- *Demands:* Success fosters the demand to use power or to pursue power as a major goal.

- *Identifications:* The boundary of the self depends on the indulgences received from the environment during early years. Egocentricity is most pronounced when early support is weakest. In all cases, a basic minimum of support is essential to keep the individual alive and active.

- *Skills:* The person possesses the aptitudes for acquiring the skills by which at least a minimum degree of participation can be acquired in the decision making process. (p. 207)

Regarding the most potent losses or threats to the power-centered personality, Lasswell (1954) added:

It is adverse estimates of the "self by the self" that appear most likely to precipitate efforts at active defense. . . . Our hypothesis relates to *deprivations from the standpoint of one who regards himself as deprived.* In general the hypothesis affirms that *deprivations of deference values are of the greatest significance as occa ions of active defense.* More specifically, this applies to *rectitude, respect* and *affection.* (1954, p. 214; emphasis in original)

One other hypothesis is crucial for understanding Lasswell's developmental model of the power-centered personality. As power-centered personalities expand their interactions beyond the most intimate circle of a family to more "remote" individuals and issues, and have to account for orientations on these issues to others as well as to themselves, the need for cognitive consistency prompts a process of rationalization that construes their beliefs and actions in terms of the public good.[91] The "public" here may be limited—the members of the group or organization, or the beneficiaries of the group or organization's actions—or it may extend to the entire society. Yet, the same underlying impulse is involved: to justify actions truly motivated out of the hunger for power. Other leaders must be toppled not because they are rivals for power, but rather because their beliefs and actions are off mission; followers must be manipulated because more transparent approaches would subvert the organization or its mission. Of course, everyone engages in a degree of rationalization, but Lasswell's point was that leaders who engage in acts of power with great frequency have a greater need to work out coherent rationalizations. Reinforcing the need and thoroughness of their rationalizations, power-centered personalities have low tolerance for ambiguity. Because inconsistencies in private beliefs and expressed beliefs can exacerbate ambiguity, and such inconsistencies can arouse anxiety-producing guilt, the rationalizations are often genuinely held beliefs rather than cynical propaganda.

It is worth noting that some of the more contemporary studies of the origins of leadership motivation have picked up on or independently discovered Lasswell's insight on the role of earlier deprivation. Popper and Mayseless (2002) cited eight studies published since 1990 that emphasized "narcissistic deprivation" to account for "the persistent desire to acquire leadership position so as to win admiration" (p. 206).

Lasswell distinguished among three basic leadership styles to assess risks stemming from personality-driven behavioral pathologies. His categories of "agitator," "theorist," and "administrator" have certain parallels with the categories in contemporary use. Agitating, theorizing, and administering are neither intrinsically democratic nor basically undemocratic, but the personality types that gravitate to these leadership styles have predispositions that are relevant for democratic, responsible leadership.

The *agitator* places high value "on arousing emotional responses from the community at large" (Lasswell, 1930/1960, p. 125), rooted in narcissism and difficulties in relating to the closer individuals. Craving the gratifications of deference derived from the interactions with followers, agitators subordinate personal considerations for the sake of higher principles, and often display an emotional detachment from their own personal well-being and apparent emotional needs, thus creating the aura of being above it all. In some circumstances, this can be the basis for charismatic appeal (Lasswell, 1930/1960).

For Lasswell, the *theorist* path to leadership tends to attract individuals who are driven by their preoccupation with their ideologies and broad programs, as well as the acceptance of these broad principles.[92] The problem is that theorists may be displacing their personal psychological issues onto the public sphere, and may be raised to leadership positions because the theory resonates among followers who are also displacing their internal motives. The theory and its implications may therefore have a problematic connection with the needs for action that the external reality requires. Moreover, Lasswell's theorist tends to be aloof from followers. The theorist does not seek leadership positions for the sake of leading or power; he or she takes on a leadership position to gain support for and implement the theory, and to receive gratification from its increasing support. The specific tasks of the movement may be secondary; the human relations within the movement may be as well, leaving the leader weak in both task orientation and human relations orientation. Or perhaps the theorist becomes a leader not through any intrinsic motivation, but rather is lifted to a leadership position because the theory resonates with followers. Theorists are also susceptible to projecting personal psychological problems onto the content of their visions.

For Lasswell, the *administrator* was most likely to be attracted to transactional and task-oriented leadership roles. The typical administrators (as distinct from the agitators who happen to end up in administration):

> display an impersonal interest in the task of organization itself, and assert themselves with firmness, though not with overemphasis, in the professional and in intimate life. Their lack of interest in abstractions is due to the fact that they have never needed them as a means of dealing with their emotional problems. They can take or leave general ideas without using them to arouse widespread affective responses from the public. Tied neither to abstractions nor to particular people, they are able to deal with both in a context of human relations, impersonally conceived. Their affects flow freely; they are not affectless, but affectively adjusted. Very original and overdriving, administrators seem to show a fundamental pattern which coincides with that of the agitators; the differences in specific development are principally due to the cultural patterns available for identification at critical phases of growth. (1930/1960, pp. 151–52)

Thus, the "administrator" does not have the emotional need to transform the organization or the reality that the organization addresses, nor is there a strong motivation to personalize the professional interactions. Home life and friendship circles meet these needs. According to this model, the administrator is strong and task oriented.

Clarifying the Transactional-Transformational Distinction

Lasswell's value framework provides a straightforward way to conceptualize transactional, transforming, and transformational leadership. The same set of value categories (power, wealth, well-being, skill, enlightenment, affection, respect, and rectitude) represent demands (desired outcomes or "scope values") *and* resources ("base values") for trying to achieve objectives. The capacity to meet followers' demands increases the leader's support and the willingness of the followers to sacrifice for the cause. This capacity is thus a resource in itself. Leaders can gain additional commitments of followers to higher-level demands (on themselves and on others) by offering rewards from within the leader's base resources. Insofar as the leader commands respect, affection, and power, he or she can achieve objectives preferred by the followers: accord them respect that they appreciate by virtue of their deference for the leader, gratify followers' needs for rectitude by behaving in virtuous ways on behalf of the followers, and so on.

Therefore, Lasswell's framework calls into question the analytic wisdom of considering transaction and transformation as different types of relationships. They are concepts pertaining to different dimensions: transaction to the fact of exchange, transformation to the nature of the orientation that the leader provides to the follower. Exchange is always present in the leader–follower relationship; hence, every such relationship has elements of transaction. As Burns (1978) put it, the political leader–follower relationship entails "exchanging gratifications in a political marketplace" (p. 258). Yet, in some circumstances, leaders transform the nature of the transaction or exchange, even while they do so through exchange. The success of Mahatma Gandhi is a clear example. Gandhi was able to further the cause of those committed to Indian independence and greater respect for Indians through his own rectitude, the respect and affection that it engendered, and his skill as an organizer, orator, and legal expert. The success in meeting their aspirations for respect and power enhanced Gandhi's capacity to ask his followers for more sacrifice. In addition, however, Gandhi convinced many Indians to *become* committed to the struggle for independence and greater respect. He did this, in no small part, by expressing his respect and affection for those who embraced this higher-order set of objectives. Thus, the exchange of commitment on the part of followers for respect and affection on the part of the leader—in other words, a transaction—was key to the transformation of goals of potential followers. Therefore, a meaningful conceptualization of the transactional-transformational distinction contrasts the solely transactional leader–follower relationship with the relationship that entails both transaction and transformation of goals.

Risks of Leadership Styles

Armed with the distinctions among these leadership styles and their personality correlates, Lasswell addressed the question of what kinds of individuals would be attracted to situations that permit transformational leadership—situations in which the followers are susceptible to transformative value change, either because of the leader's dominance over followers' outlooks or because the followers are so ripe for change. Lasswell's answer was that of the three leadership types that he defined—administrators, agitators, and theorists—the agitators and theorists are more likely to be attracted to such opportunities. The agitator grasps a vision, but its content is less important than its value as a vehicle for mobilizing followers. The theorist formulates a vision, but the content of the theory may be of greater attraction to the leader than its impact following implementation.

The predispositions that Lasswell attributed to agitators and theorists raise grave concerns about the riskiness of transformational leadership. Lasswell argued that the impulse to change the motives of followers—the heart of the definition of transformational leadership—is frequently found in the extreme power-centered personality (Lasswell, 1930/1960). Insofar as the extreme power-centered personality is likely to pursue the agitator path, fundamentally motivated by the need for deference, the imposition of a vision onto the followers is driven by the appeal of exercising power rather than the intrinsic value of the vision.

Lasswell's displacement hypothesis reinforces these concerns over transformational leadership. If, as Lasswell emphasized in *Psychopathology and*

Politics (1930/1960), "political man displaces private motives onto public objects, rationalized in the public interest" (p. 75), the question is whether transformational visions arise to serve private motives when the actual tasks at hand do not really need transformation, or when the effort to transform poses unacceptable risks of disintegration. Some circumstances simply do not require transformation. For example, it is not at all clear that a well-functioning tax service or postal system would benefit from a transformational leader. Other circumstances may benefit from successful transformations, but the risks may outweigh the potential benefits. Yet, if the impetus for changing followers' objectives is derived from the leader's psychological needs rather than the logic of the situation, ill-advised efforts at transformation may be launched.

When power-centered leaders are involved in apparently transformational leadership, there is also a risk of "pseudo-transformational" manipulation that Bass and Avolio (2002) outlined.[93] The leader claims to be committed to a mission of transcendent objectives, but the apparent mission is a pretext for maintaining control. Extreme power-centered leaders are likely to find transformation a distraction and a risk to their capacity to maintain power. The use of power as a resource for other ends will often deplete power; those who seek power as an end in itself will be intolerant of depleting power in this way. Therefore, power-centered leaders who attempt to transform followers' values often do so in ways that only enhance the stature of the leader and the movement, rather than improving the reality that the movement ostensibly intends to address. This is the tragedy of such countries as Zimbabwe, where Robert Mugabe twisted the fervor for independence into a corrupt dictatorship.

Closely related to this concept of pseudo-transformational leadership is that of impostorship. According to Lasswell, impostorship has a double aspect. One is the tendency of some leaders to portray themselves in exaggerated ways: as more adept, more powerful, or more distinctive in ideology or temperament than they really are. Lasswell argued that power-centered leaders are particularly susceptible to this temptation, as a strategy for securing their power. In *Psychopathology and Politics*, Lasswell (1930/1960) emphasized the power-centered personality's "large capacity for playing the impostor upon himself and others" (p. 50). In particular, he addressed the agitator type as portrayed as narcissistic and highly prone to exaggeration:

> The hallmark of the agitator is the high public value which he places on the response of the public. As a class the agitators are strongly narcissistic types. Narcissism is encouraged by obstacles encountered in the early love relationships, or by overindulgence and admiration in the family circle. Libido is blocked in moving outward toward objects and settles back upon the self. Sexual objects which are like the self are preferred, and a strong homoerotic component is thus characteristic. Among the agitators yearning for emotional response of the homoerotic kind is displaced upon generalized objects, and high value is put on arousing emotional responses from the community at large. The oratorical agitator, in contradistinction to the

publicist, seems to show a long history of successful impostorship in dealing with his environment. (1930/1960, pp. 262–263)

In the case study of one former politician whom Lasswell categorized as an agitator, Lasswell described the following psychohistory:

> He had long practice in the art of the imposter. . . . He resolved never to do anything to cause his father to withdraw his affection, and when he was not entirely successful in living up to this ideal, he pretended to virtues which he did not possess. Never once was he found out, and his life was the life of a "model" boy and man. This reputation he owed in part to his abstinences, but likewise to his concealments. He learned to cultivate the mask of rectitude, and succeeded in carrying off the role so successfully that he was never found out during adolescence or adulthood. (1930/1960, pp. 96–97)

The other risk of impostorship is that leaders, believing themselves to be in power under more or less false pretenses, will lack the confidence and equanimity to lead responsibly. Some of the most spectacular crashes of prominent leaders occur when they are set off course by the irreality of the fact of their leadership, when at some level they doubt their own qualifications to lead. If, in the agitator mode, the leader has exaggerated his or her characteristics and accomplishments, there is all the more reason for the leader to experience the insecurity of impostorship.

Risks of Charismatic Leadership

Lasswell's studies of individual and policy appeals also clarify why the charismatic appeal is a double-edged sword. His insights on the peculiar dangers of charismatic leadership begin with the premise that leadership entails reciprocity between leaders and followers. The continued support by followers in turn hinges on what the leader does concretely to further the motives and interests of his or her followers. However, the attraction of and continued support for the charismatic leader is derived less from expectations of whether that leader can deliver with respect to the followers' interests (the heart of transactional leader–follower relationship) and more from the purely psychological gratification of affiliation with the charismatic leader. In this respect, the theory of charismatic leadership can be seen as a special case of the triple-appeal principle, with id and superego appeals accounting for the attribution of special gifts that do not coincide with instrumental considerations. In *Psychopathology and Politics* (1930/1960) Lasswell argued, "Ascendancy involves dependence, a reciprocal relationship. . . . But there are some who combine easy success with indifference. These are no doubt recruited from among those who have natural suggestive power to certain groups—they possess the *charisma* of Max Weber" (p. 52; emphasis in the original).

The two key insights here lie in *indifference* and *suggestive power*. The indifference comes from the fact that charismatic leaders can afford to be indifferent to the political and policy interests of their followers—whether the leader is in fact indifferent is another matter. This potential indifference is possible because the charismatic leader holds *suggestive power* in a sense that comes close to the notion of hypnosis: The appeal of charismatic leaders is so psychologically compelling that the followers are attracted without regard to the mere pursuit of their interests. The triple-appeal principle encompasses the psychodynamics of projecting the individual's impulses, both admirable and not, onto specific public figures and characteristics of such figures. The appeal of the saint reflects our aspirations to be saintly; the appeal of the ruthless leader is in the vicarious thrill of witnessing domination and ruthlessness. Whether the characteristics are positive or negative, the emotional component is stronger than leadership appeals based on considerations of material benefit, such as choosing a candidate who most faithfully will defend one's economic interests.

Lasswell's conception of the leader–follower relationship as *exchange* also implies that transactional leadership may be preferred by potential followers who have the maturity to demand predictability and instrumental responsiveness of their leaders. His work on the allure of emotionally domineering leaders highlights the problematic motivations of some followers who allow themselves to be swayed by the extremism of certain transformational leaders. Thus, one problem with the operation of charisma is keyed not to the failings of any particular leadership style, but that it diminishes the filters of reason and demand for accountability in the selection of leaders.

Some contemporary experts on charismatic leadership have echoed this concern over the potential lack of accountability of the charismatic leader. Jay Conger (1989) enumerated the consequences of the lack of leader's accountability in charismatic leadership situations. Whether or not intended by the leader, charisma may entail the voluntary surrender of followers' power, insofar as the leader's special gifts[94] compel a following regardless of whether the leader is acting according to the preferences or interests of the followers. Leaders with charisma will not necessarily behave—and are not necessarily emotionally capable of behaving—as positive leaders. Moreover, although a "good" charismatic leader may be sensitive to the needs of followers, charismatic leaders, according to Conger (1989), are often impatient and intolerant of followers, peers, and superiors.

Lasswell also pointed to the risk that the charismatic leader will come to believe in his or her special status, and therefore fail to adhere to ethical standards. Contemporary leadership studies have echoed this concern of how and why leaders regard themselves as exceptions to the ethical strictures that they acknowledge ought to govern the behavior of others (Price, 1998).

Charisma also increases the risks of impostorship outlined earlier. Charisma allows individuals to rise to leadership roles even if they lack the skills specific for that role. Therefore, charismatic leaders, more than other leaders, are prone to misunderstanding the basis of their own success, and this success is less likely to be well integrated into their self-images.

It is reasonable to hypothesize that those who succeed through charisma rather than accomplishment are more likely to harbor self-doubt and a sense of impostorship.

Is charismatic leadership associated with particular personality profiles? Are such profiles associated with democratic or undemocratic predispositions? Conger rejected the possibility of a personality profile of the charismatic leader, on the grounds that the same personality profile could not hold for individuals as different as Hitler and Gandhi. Lasswell's framework of exchange suggests a more ambitious strategy: to explore whether *several* personality types could elicit a charismatic following, predispose potential leaders to accept leadership roles, and use their charismatic power responsibly or irresponsibly.

Let us focus first on the individual who, in addition to having specific competence for the leadership role, also has charismatic appeal. Weber's 1925/1968 analysis of charismatic characteristics posited that the charismatic appeal typically lies in extreme talent, extreme motive, or a highly distinctive relationship with entities of special significance to potential followers. The Nobel Prize-winning physicist, the brilliant chess player, the amazing athlete, and so on may fit the first criterion. Robert McNamara's "steel trap mind" endowed him with charisma in the minds of some of the people who worked under him, even if others had a negative reaction. The display of extreme motive may endow charisma to the self-sacrificing nun devoted to assisting lepers, the man who runs across the entire country, the hardest-driving corporate executive, or the revolutionary. The characteristics of special relationship may come from accomplishment, such as serving as advisor to many presidents, or from nonempirically based belief, such as seeming favored by the gods. Some individuals are talented in many spheres, and may be highly skilled in the specific leadership capacities as well as possessing whatever characteristics are the basis for the followers' perception of special gifts. For such cases, the only analytical leverage would be to assess the whole range of personality types that would elicit charismatic attraction in potential followers across many types of situations and psychological needs. Obviously, no general answer can be found, but specific cases can be analyzed with the triple-appeal principle.

However, leaders who prefer the administrator style of leadership, with its typical reliance on businesslike, transactional exchange, may well be uncomfortable being cast in a charismatic role. Similarly, although theorists may yearn for the adulation of their ideas, their characteristic aloofness with respect to personal involvement may run counter to the followers' demands on the charismatic leader. Theorists are low on the human relations dimension. Thus, the self-selection to charismatic-based leadership may favor agitators over administrators and theorists.

Let us focus next on the individual who has a chance at charisma-based power even if the basis of that charisma is basically unrelated to the skills called for by the position. The actress who finds that her celebrity opens up a political career, and the extreme ideologue whose very extremism gains an ardent following, would fit this model. We should first ask, therefore, how the characteristics that may lead to an attribution of charisma by potential followers might interact with the characteristics associated with democratic or undemocratic predispositions. In Lasswellian terms, the appeal of the charismatic leader is likely reflect an id or superego impulse for the fulfillment of identification aspirations.

Will the potential leader accept and exploit the charismatic asset? Weber presumed that the charismatic leader accepts the leadership role as a natural and comfortable privilege. Lasswell, in contrast, never presumed that any particular role would be filled by well-adjusted individuals. As indicated in the discussion of impostorship, the followers' belief that charismatic leaders are special and worthy may not be shared by the leaders themselves. If so, why would the self-doubting charismatic leader not simply bow out? This would depend on the indulgences that the charismatic leader receives, as well as his or her sense of self respect or self-aggrandizement. One possibility is that the individual who accepts a leadership role without the specific competences may well be highly power centered; the attraction of wielding power may outweigh the risks of failure and the danger of being found out. Another possibility is that the leader values the possible accomplishments of leadership highly enough to take the risk.

POLICY IMPLICATIONS

Insofar as these risks of transformational or charismatic leadership merit concern, one might ask whether particular recruitment and selection structures can minimize these risks. Rather than take the line of many popular publications that transformational or charismatic leadership should be encouraged across the board, we should ask how to identify and discourage irresponsible charismatic leadership, and how to channel charismatic leaders toward tasks that are within their competence.

One antidote to irresponsible or undemocratic leadership is transparency, so that both potential followers and opponents can be aware of leaders' problematic behavior. A prime example is the news media's success in taking up Gary Hart's dare to find out whether he was involved in an affair during his 1988 bid for the presidential nomination. Hart's bizarre behavior, perhaps on some level intentionally bringing his emotional stability into question, may have passed unnoticed in an earlier era.

Of course, irresponsible or undemocratic leadership can be contained through process rules and institutions of enforcement that effectively check and punish illegal behavior of undemocratic political movements, without martyring the charismatic leaders and their movements. Western European nations have been much more successful in containing extremist movements with flamboyant leaders during the post-World War II period than in earlier decades.

If the public requires a vehicle for expressing its impulse for a charismatic leader, roles that do not challenge the skills limitations of the charismatic individual can be created. States such as Israel have separated the presidency from the prime minister's position. The presidency may be occupied by individuals distinguished for qualities removed from political and policy leadership, such as scientific accomplishment.

CONCLUSION

When disciplines forget the contributions of earlier generations, no matter how convenient this may be for asserting the originality of new work, it is certainly costly for progress in the field and the capacity to address real-world problems. Lasswell's work emphasized the risks of being swept away by the magnetic leader. Yet, the potential pathologies and antidemocratic predispositions of such leaders have largely escaped the enthusiasms of leadership studies.

This myopia may well be due to the neglect of Lasswell's most fundamental message that individuals arrive at leadership roles through psychodynamics that produce problematic leaders as well as sound ones. It is telling that Popper and Mayseless asserted in 2002 that:

> Although there is remarkable progress in understanding . . . leaders' impact, the internal world of these leaders remains to a great extent unstudied. . . . By borrowing from developmental and personality psychology research . . . the leadership domain may gain a better understanding of psychodynamic processes that have not been the focus of research so far. These angles might also add practical contribution relevant to the selection of leaders, placement in leadership roles, and the development of transformational leaders. (p. 223)

This is true, but the groundwork has been available for over half a century.

Lasswell's treatment of leadership styles still enlightens, because it goes beyond the characteristics of the leader–follower relationship to focus on the internal psychodynamics of the leader. This complements his triple-appeal analysis (discussed in chap. 3 of this text), which asks how various appeals, both constructive and destructive, serve followers' psychological needs. Instead of simply asking how to promote charismatic or transformational leadership—which in any event often begs the crucial question of whether these relationships are advisable—Lasswell's analysis of leadership styles focuses on the likely behavior of leaders attracted to particular roles because of their own psychological needs. Lasswell warned that the more heroic roles may attract the more psychologically problematic leaders.

Finally, Lasswell's coherent, functionalist analytic categories can help to clear away much of the confusion in contemporary leadership studies. The "manager" is not the dull foil to the exciting "leader," and Lasswell's depiction of the "administrator" demonstrates that the managerial temperament may well be associated with success in achieving major organizational and societal changes. Transactional and transformative leadership are not opposing roles or styles; understanding the breadth of the concept of exchange led Lasswell to recognize that transactions, whether tangible or symbolic, exist in all leader–follower relationships. Charisma is not fundamentally a characteristic of leaders, but rather of the appeal to followers, implying that the characteristics that thrust an individual into a charismatic leadership role depend fundamentally on the needs of the followers.

Chapter 6

Political Climate, Mood, and Crisis

The psychology of political character and political symbols goes a long way toward understanding the baseline behavior of political leaders and citizens under typical circumstances—the "political character" that typifies individuals or, perhaps, entire peoples. However, additional considerations must be invoked when circumstances give rise to collective moods that push public sentiment and action into different and often unpredictable directions. How can a political psychology based on political character account for political behavior that is out of character? How and why do extended periods remain in the grips of moods that define the political and policy discourse, highlighting particular preoccupations such as intergroup hostility, unbridled greed, religious fervor, or rigid conformity? How and why do such moods change?

Much of Lasswell's work explains why great variation exists among individual personalities and political predispositions. Yet, political moods represent both a departure from normally prevailing predispositions and a convergence of predispositions that are all the more baffling in light of this variation. Some earlier psychologists created entire theories of "crowd" or "mob" psychology with necessarily fuzzy transindividual constructs. Lasswell combined his framework of individual psychological traits and dynamics with his theory of symbols and communication to account parsimoniously and clearly for collective moods, and to demonstrate, as did Freud in *Group Psychology and the Analysis of the Ego* (1921/1959)[95] that there is no need to develop the concept of a separate "group mind." His framework can account for how diverse characters come to share predispositions that clash, in many cases, with their normal predispositions. His approach can explain how usually ethical and cautious people can participate in a destructive mobs, but also how the media, government, and interest groups precipitate and perpetuate more enduring moods.

Issues and Challenges

One of the most intriguing and difficult challenges for political psychology is to anticipate the directions and magnitudes of societal mood swings. For example, the euphoria from the fall of the Berlin Wall was followed quickly by pessimism and anxiety over the socioeconomic and political implications of absorbing impoverished East Germany into affluent West Germany. For many Russians and other peoples of the Soviet Union and Eastern Europe, the collapse of Communism and the subsequent vacuum led to similar mood swings. In Germany, the pessimism and anxiety apparently gave way to dogged resolve to get the job done; in Russia and many other transitional areas, pessimism and anxiety persisted, generating cynicism and the opportunism associated with it. Such mood swings often leave leaders and other policymakers unprepared to cope with the consequences of changed perspectives and intensities. Much of Lasswell's concerns over collective moods rested on his worries—obviously of great relevance prior to World War II and the Cold War period—that the self-discipline that distinguishes sensible, democratic political behavior would be swamped by the impulsivity of climates triggered by perceived crises.

Rapid and drastic shifts in mood and climate of opinion have long startled political observers. Consider the savagery of the interethnic conflict in Yugoslavia following the death of Josip Broz Tito, despite four decades of relative civility among Serbs, Croats, and Bosnian Muslims. Sometimes seemingly small changes in objective conditions seem to trigger reversals in mood, limiting the predictability of political mood and climate of opinion, even for leaders steeped in their own political culture. The inability to recognize and address mood swings was the root of dramatic political failure for the Shah of Iran, the Porfirio Diaz regime at the outbreak of the Mexican Revolution, Nicaragua's pre-Sandinista regime, and many other cases (Ascher & Overholt, 1983). Often, mood swings are triggered by obviously major crises. On the international level, wars, terrorism, huge influxes of unwanted immigrants, and so on can have enormous impacts on perspectives and predispositions to act in contradictory fashion. On the domestic level, outrages such as assassinations, school massacres, hate crimes, discoveries of major corruption, economic depression, or stock market collapses are among the innumerable negative events that can create political moods that challenge existing attitudes and practices. However, the mystery of mood swings is revealed in the major mood changes that result from events that do not represent major crises from an objective, material perspective. For example, the Argentine defeat at the hands of the British in the Falklands/Malvinas conflict did not entail significant political or economic losses for Argentina, but led to dramatic changes in Argentinians' perspectives across many dimensions of identifications, expectations, and demands.

Mood swings can also arise from unusually positive events or conditions, such as economic boom, military victory, oil discoveries, or vindicating events such as the fall of the Berlin Wall. Yet, even these events can create moods that threaten democratic practices and sensible policy. Political success can breed arrogance and overoptimism; boom mentalities characterized by "irrational exuberance" can squander ultimately scarce resources. The "abnormality" perceived by people when unusual conditions prevail can provoke the neglect of norms that otherwise would be observed. Even so, individuals with democratic norms also have selfish, aggressive, and antidemocratic impulses that might normally be kept in check; however, under greater stress, these too may break through the normal self-discipline of conscience and reason. Lasswell argued that the greatest danger over time is that anxiety or other swiftly rising psychological challenges would sap the psychic energy that holds back antisocial impulses. In his brilliant essay on "The Psychology of Hitlerism," Lasswell wrote that "[t]he stress of battle, under-nourishment, inflation, and unemployment during these eventful years [WWI and the following period] has exposed many men and women to temptations which they could not resist" (1933/1948, p. 240).

Crisis can override the restraints of reason and conscience, reducing anxiety by making antisocial behavior compelling at the expense of the usual moral and rational considerations. In his essay on "Democratic Character" (1951), Lasswell relied heavily on Harry Stack Sullivan's insight that

> any event which tends to bring about a basic change in an *established pattern* of dealing with others, sets up the tension of anxiety and calls out activities for its relief. This tension and the activities required for its reduction or relief—which we call *security operations* because they can be said to be addressed to maintaining a feeling of safety in the esteem reflected to one from the other person concerned—always interfere with whatever other tensions and energy transformations with which they happen to coincide. (Sullivan, 1948, cited in Lasswell, 1951, p. 510; emphasis in Sullivan's original)

On the other hand, mood swings—whether triggered by major crises, symbolic setbacks, or positive events—may also represent opportunities for constructive change, inasmuch as certain moods may predispose individuals to accept positive change when it is clear that the situation is not normal. Therefore, we are especially concerned with a particular class of moods that involve the subjectivity that the prior equilibrium has been disrupted and perhaps new goals and new rules are in order. Crisis situations are prominent triggers of such moods, although they are not the only triggers. Lasswell's premises concerning the political outcomes of unusual climates begin with three insights: first, an unusual climate typically entails an altered level of emotional intensity; second, appropriate political behavior requires a modicum of personal discipline that is often threatened by emotions that are out of the ordinary; and third, the uncertainty that comes with unusual situations brings preexisting perspectives into question.

These concerns raise a number of basic questions:

- How do collective political moods come to be established and durable?
- How, and to what degree, does an unusual mood pull people away from prevailing norms of appropriate behavior?
- What determines whether a mood is characterized by the sense of normalcy?
- Are there categories of mood for which similar psychological processes occur?
- What determines how extreme the swings in mood will be; can policy influence the swings?
- What aspects of political character make people more—or less—resilient to abandoning their discipline when unusual moods arise?

Intellectual Contributions

It is not difficult to show that Lasswell's framework and theoretical toolkit provide great insight into the questions just raised, without requiring a separate theoretical apparatus to account for the reactions to crisis and other conditions that trigger unusual moods. The triple-appeal principle, the displacement hypothesis, the impact of propaganda and other symbol manipulations, and the anatomy of political character account for much of the otherwise bewildering behavior of people in unusual political moods. It is, of course, an indication of a unified theory that the same propositions can be employed to understand phenomena as different as political "business as usual" and behavior under crisis circumstances.

Yet, even though Lasswell's writings on mood and climate were securely within the framework of his other works, they illustrate points concerning his epistemology not brought out in previous chapters: his orientation toward group versus individual political phenomena; the conditions that shape the relative importance of impulse, reason, and conscience; and the psychological impacts of crisis.

Definitions

Mood refers to a higher-than-typical level of one or a few affects attached to some aspect of perspectives (identifications, demands, or expectations) that influence a broad range of perspectives and intensity of predispositions. When a mood influences a large proportion of the population, it can be called a *climate*. There are moods and climates of insecurity with respect to personal safety, euphoria based on expectations of victory, self-absorption due to narrow self-identification, avarice due to unusually high preoccupation with wealth, interpersonal hostility over competition for jobs or respect, panic over an apparently imminent attack, moral outrage over the perceived violations of sexual strictures, somberness growing out of lower expectations of economic growth, impatience over the pace of political change, self-confidence regarding political competition, the sense of betrayal over perceived inconsistencies in government action, superiority vis-à-vis other nations, shame over one's own nation's failures to live up to moral standards, and so on. Insofar as a mood permeates the perspectives and the intensity of affects, it will color the perceptions of events, the attractiveness of alternative policies, the likelihood of unified action, and a host of other aspects of predispositions. Steven R. Brown (1982) pointed out, "[a]mong the most distinguishing features of moods, on the individual as well as the collective level, is the fact that they saturate all aspects of existence—behavioral and cognitive as well as affective—hence are more diffuse than emotions or attitudes, which tend to be object-specific" (p. 169).

Climate refers to some degree of convergence or commonality of perspectives at a point in time—it refers to a collective mood.[96] It must be conceived not as uniformity of opinion, but rather as the aggregate difference from baseline levels across relevant individuals. For example, a climate of heightened distrust toward business executives following financial scandals would entail higher-than-ordinary skepticism in a considerable segment of the population, but does not mean that everyone shares this skepticism.

Crisis can be defined as a circumstance that creates a high level of stress toward extreme action. Crises are clearly a major cause of the swings in mood and climate, even though obviously not all politically relevant climates emerge from crises. Crises have to be understood in terms of temporal sequences, because one type of crisis often evolves into another. An initial event or circumstance may trigger a crisis that evokes a response leading to different form of crisis. For example, a sudden, unexpected military attack may create a mood of anger and insecurity; the failure of the authorities of the attacked nation may trigger a crisis characterized by a mood of frustration and skepticism toward the authorities; if this mood provokes a foolhardy response, a third crisis of condemnation of this response may arise with other impacts on the political climate. One policy implication is that political leaders are often confronted with rapidly changing, intertwined climates and crises, greatly complicating political and policy management.

In this summary and extension of Harold Lasswell's approach to understanding the psychology of crises, collective moods, and mood swings, we consider the temporal range from the short-term moods that drive collective action in surprising eruptions of mobs to the enduring moods that characterize whole epochs. In many of the cases relevant for public policy choices, the basal mood establishes a fundamental orientation toward politics and policy, whereas the unpredictability arising from abrupt mood swings greatly complicates foresight and policy choices. For both extremes, Lasswell demonstrated that the interactions between individual psychological appeals and interpersonal communications lead to differences in the modes of communication.

CLASSIFICATIONS OF MOODS

Perhaps the most obvious dimension of moods and mood swings is *duration*. Very short-term "flash" moods triggered by immediate threats or highly provocative events (e.g., terrorist attacks or desecration of religious facilities) often leading to crowd or mob behavior, are likely to be subject to different dynamics than are the moods and climates marking longer time periods that can extend to entire epochs.

Beyond duration, Lasswell offered nine dimensions for classifying moods, each helping to generate insights and hypotheses about the origins and impacts of moods and mood swings. The utility of making these finer distinctions reflects the overall analytic value of Lasswell's general approach of breaking down broad phenomena into more specific dimensions.

Affect. Moods are characterized by affects such as sadness, apprehensiveness, relief, exhaustion, pride, excitement, and so on. The distinction between positive and negative affects is relevant for some of these, which relates to whether subsequent actions are intended to change or maintain the conditions believed to be responsible for the mood. Other aspects of affect, such as excitement or exhaustion, relate to the intensity dimension reviewed later in this chapter.

Identifications, Demands, and Expectations. Lasswell's distinction among identifications, demands, and expectations (which together constitute "perspectives") is a centerpiece of all of his work in political psychology. One can characterize some moods as *dominated* by a particular identification, demand, or expectation (e.g., the "significant fact" that characterizes the period may be the rejection of prior identifications, as in the rise of ecumenism; demands for a new government; or expectations of calamity; Lasswell, 1965a) but a fuller characterization flows from the nature and intensity of all three of these components of perspectives. Thus, the threefold distinction of identifications, demands, and expectations is also the basic organizing principle for defining other dimensions of moods.

Inclusiveness of Identifications. Moods can be characterized in terms of the degree of inclusiveness or narrowness of the defining identifications. The inclusiveness dimension is particularly important politically, insofar as it shapes the alignments of political conflict. When Americans are in an intensely "We are Americans" mood—with national loyalty and patriotism as dominant demands and affects—the unity vis-à-vis international rivals is likely to be heightened. By the same token, a climate of strong religious identification obviously affects the likelihood of sectarian conflict.

Change in Identifications. The rate and degree of change in identifications entailed by a mood swing are also of great importance, leading to changes in values and demands and the potential for clashes with existing institutions and practices. For example, the apparently dramatic rise of

Islamic fundamentalism in the Middle East, Southeast Asia, and South Asia presents severe challenges to the political institutions and formulae of many nations in these regions. Lasswell noted that revolutionary periods often coincide with or follow dramatic changes in mood principally defined in terms of changes in identifications; for example, from loyal workers to Bolsheviks, or from loyal colonialists to independence fighters (1965a).

Value Preoccupation. The demands component points first and foremost to whether the climate is dominated by one or a narrow set of values. In keeping with the value categories prominent in so many of his contributions, Lasswell noted that moods are often characterized by the preoccupation with one or a few of the values that he categorized broadly as power, wealth, well-being, affection, respect, rectitude, skill, and enlightenment. This categorization not only covers most of what people aspire to achieve, but also reflects the resources that people regard as means to other ends. Thus, a preoccupation with affection, for example, may reflect a desire to be loved, but it may also reflect a strategy to gain fame and fortune through popularity.

Preoccupations with particular values are especially relevant for characterizing rather long periods of moods. Whole eras have been denoted for religious fervor (rectitude), individualistic self-absorption (wealth and well-being), straightlaced conformity (respect), and so on. Much of Lasswell's work on the content analysis of communications was dedicated to tracing long-term trends in value preoccupations, based on the premise that the frequency of references to each value is a more or less valid indicator of the degree of preoccupation. This approach was extended to the contemporary era by Brunner and his collaborators (Brunner, 1987; Brunner & Morrow, 1984). Lasswell's treatment of value preoccupations has a prescriptive element, in that he warned against narrow value preoccupations. The preoccupation with just one of these categories often poses a risk to balanced politics and policy, and frequently endangers democratic practice. Much of Lasswell's work in political psychology assessed the dangers of the power-centered personality who restricts meaningful participation by others in a pursuit of power unrestrained by considerations of respect, affection, or rectitude (1930/1960). The unrestrained pursuit of either deference values or welfare values abandons the balance required for sharing respect for others' rights and interests. Even the all-out pursuit of rectitude bodes ill for democratic practice, insofar as a full and rigid commitment to morality is prone to intolerance for others' behavior.

Intensity of Demands. The intensity of the demands is an obvious complement to the dimension of value preoccupation. It has a straightforward role in determining the stress toward action. As Lasswell argued in his essay on "The Climate of International Action" (1965a), moods can range from lethargy to great urgency. Moods entailing high levels of emotional mobilization often provoke action even if no actions are likely to be constructive.[97] Later political psychologists have confirmed the utility of separating out a dimension of intensity or arousal from the evaluative dimension of like or dislike, approval or disapproval. Marcus, Neuman, and MacKuen (2000) argued that both brain physiology and survey results confirm that moods focusing on political objects cannot be defined as bipolar, but rather reflect a dimension of anxiety/arousal and a distinct dimension of enthusiasm.

Nature of Impulses.   Moods can also be categorized in terms of whether their appeals lie predominantly within the personality structures responsible for raw instinctual desires, reason, or conscience—in psychoanalytic terms, id, ego, or superego. Moods of aggressive hostility will obviously color political action differently than will moods of cautious calculation or moods embracing the moral high road. Sometimes long periods of time are dominated by a mood characterized by a prevalence of one of these personality components. These eras are often given popular labels that reflect this dominance, although the labels may exaggerate the uniformity of mood by implying the uniformity of mood. For example, the "Gay '90s", the "Roaring '20s", and the "Age of Aquarius" all denote periods in which greater impulse indulgence is presumed to have prevailed.

Degree of Optimism/Pessimism.   The expectations component suggests the dimension of optimism versus pessimism. In addition to the obvious connection between optimism and confidence—which shapes the predispositions toward assertive rather than defensive actions—optimism often has an extraordinarily strong impact on the favorability of attitudes toward the prevailing political institutions and leaders. In the realm of international relations, the expectation of violence is a particularly important form of pessimistic expectation that Lasswell emphasized in *World Politics and Personal Insecurity* (1935b/1965), his essay on "Climate of International Action" (1965a), and *World Politics Faces Economics* (1945). This last monograph is a brilliant, concise statement of the emerging conflict between the United States and the Soviet Union, emphasizing how economic expansion, if managed poorly, can exacerbate international tensions because the expectation of violence colors all other expectations.

Normative Abnormality.   Expectations, as well as demands, are affected by moods characterized by the subjective sense that changed circumstances bring into question the preexisting norms. Wars and revolutions, among other events, often create a climate of normative uncertainty. Does the individual expect that others will demand the same norms and commitments? Does the individual believe that the standards of behavior of others will and should prevail? At that critical time when it seems that all bets are off and the certainty about conventional demands declines, political behavior is susceptible to great heights and great depths. People may be inspired to develop more compelling ethics, freed from the constraints of old hypocrisy. However, they may also lose their moral bearings.

CLASSIFYING CRISES

Crises can be characterized by linkages between objective conditions and the moods they engender. Lasswell drew a distinction between "crises of abundance" and "crises of scarcity" (1935b/1965, p. 109). Abundance brings unequal distribution and thereby conflict and acrimony; material temptation undermines the morality of simple living, prompting contempt and guilt; individuals liberated from concern over survival begin to struggle over deference, leading to envy. Scarcity brings physical deprivation and desperation; disappointment breeds discontent. Another differentiation that Lasswell applied to war crises similarly focuses on the mood that arises from the threats or deprivations that the public perceives from others. In classifying war crises, Lasswell (1935b/1965) defined an *insecurity crisis* as one that occurs among rivals of roughly even strength over significant issues; thus, the insecurity stems from the concern of defeat and the deprivations that would follow. He defined an *exasperation crisis* as one in which a lesser power frustrates the objectives of the stronger power. An *indignation crisis* is triggered by perceived brutality by a weaker power. The logic behind this classification is the linkage between the circumstance (nature of the perceived offense, relative power of the actors) and the mood likely to emerge because of these circumstances.

UNDERSTANDING EPHEMERAL CLIMATES:
THE CROWD AND THE MOB

Although Lasswell's theorizing on mood and climate largely focused on durable moods, he also addressed the very short-term moods that drive actions in acute crises. In *Psychopathology and Politics* (1930/1960), Lasswell analyzed the political riots in Austria in the 1920s. In Lasswell and Kaplan's *Power and Society* (1950), the more generic case of mob or crowd action was addressed.

Here, we are concerned with moods triggered by immediate, flash collective events often do not provide the opportunity for elites to plan and execute control over the symbols that shape the underlying mood. Therefore, except for the impact of elite-controlled provocateurs, these events lead to an unmediated, reactive response by affected individuals.

The most intriguing puzzle of crowd or mob action is that impulsive and often illegal behavior emerges from individuals who would not engage in such behavior without the presence of the group. Political psychologists who could not account for such behavior by invoking individual behavior often resorted to questionable concepts of the "group mind." Lasswell, following Floyd Allport (1924/1967), found the answer in communication and individual adjustment.

In *Power and Society* (1950), Lasswell and Kaplan wrote that "in a crowd, there is *psychic contagion*, a maximum of sincere, unreflective, excited dissemination of symbols" (p. 40; emphasis in original). The key here is not the obvious point that crowds often experience a form of contagion, but rather that the contagion is spread through the dissemination of symbols; that is, through communication, even if it is so rapid and ephemeral that it does not leave an easily discernable record. Consider sectarian mob violence, organized against a perceived outrage such as an attack against a mosque, church, synagogue, or temple. An intense, sometimes nearly instantaneous set of words, gestures, deeds, and other symbols evokes predispositions toward action on the part of each member of the mob; the actions of each individual reinforce the judgment of each other that the initial attack warrants the outrage of the mob; the mob's counterattack signals to each participant that the normal rules do not apply. The validation of impulsive behavior by others allows for the expression of raw impulse by each member of the mob. As Lasswell wrote in *Psychopathology and Politics* (1930/1960):

> The study of personality genesis shows that the sublimation of primitive impulses is possible on the basis of a kind of primitive "social contract." The individual forgoes direct indulgences (which have the disadvantage of bringing him into conflict with authority), and substitutes more complex patterns of behavior on the tacit understanding that love and safety will thereby be insured. When another individual breaks over and gratifies his illicit impulses directly on a primitive level, the equilibrium of every personality is threatened. The conscious self perceives that it is possible to "get by," and this threatens the whole structure of sublimation. The superego tries to maintain order by directing energy against the possibility of illicit gratification, and seeks to turn the ego toward activities which reduce temptation. (p. 182)

In short, the social contract may be suspended when others signal that the circumstances obviate it, giving room for the expression of otherwise suppressed impulses.

However, another factor is at play in crowd behavior: Individuals are sometimes driven—or inspired—to heroic feats of self-sacrifice. The Russians who climbed onto tanks to precipitate the fall of the Soviet Union illustrate such behavior. Sometimes group interaction leads not to the suspension of norms, but to demands for even higher morality. This may result from a concern for respect from other participants, but it can also reflect the fact that individuals are engaged in a potentially continual process of learning about what norms ought to prevail. Rather then taking norms as givens, we must recognize that individuals experience uncertainty as to the appropriateness of particular norms and the specific situations in which they ought to be applied. Interpersonal communication, even in "microtransactions," are often extremely rich in cues about what constitutes appropriate behavior (Reisman, 1999). Finally, the intensity aroused by unusual circumstances, especially crisis situations, often distracts attention away from the multiple mundane considerations of self-interest.

UNDERSTANDING LONGER-TERM CLIMATES

In considering enduring rather than ephemeral political climates, our analytic challenge is to explain how distinctive moods come to be crystallized and consolidated despite both the variations in individual perspectives and the enormous variety of information in all but the most isolated contemporary contexts. Both the change and continuity in collective moods must be explained. Lasswell offered a four-pronged theory to explain enduring mood swings.

Objective Conditions

Lasswell acknowledged that objective conditions with similar impacts on broad populations will have some commonality of impact on perspectives: identifications, demands, and expectations. Clearly, the expectations of success are important to this choice. Understanding whether an individual or community will embrace a particular value is therefore closely connected to the mood component of optimism or pessimism. The mood swing from one preoccupation to another is shaped by the expectation that a value is at risk, or that rewards would result from action related to that value.

Such changes in objective conditions certainly have an impact. Lasswell argued that moods, even if reinforced by elite consensus, are most likely to change when "elite or non-elite experience . . . flagrantly contradicts the expectations that sustain the mood." Although "mood stability is a self-perpetuating and self-extending process to the extent that it screens perceptions to harmonize with it . . . [i]t is not probable that acquired expectations will be firmly enough embedded to exclude forever the recognition of incompatible events" (1965a, p. 346). Insofar as economic collapse, the outbreak of war, victories or defeats in war, and similar major crises have largely (but certainly not uniformly) common impacts on affected populations, these events provide a "first cut" approach to predicting the expectations component of collective mood changes in obviously straightforward ways: Disasters provoke pessimism; successes generate optimism.

The most important use of Lasswell's perspectives framework (i.e., identifications, demands, and expectations) for understanding responses to crisis or other climate-altering conditions is in connecting changes in expectations to changes in identifications and demands. Reality enters through the recognition of changing prospects, which often provoke shifts in identifications and demands through several mechanisms.

Frequently, circumstances bring into question the integrity and attractiveness of prevailing identifications, which are then open to change. For example, the collapse of the Soviet Union had enormous impacts on the identifications of its citizens. The sense of belonging to a dominant political and economic entity, realization of the growing irrelevance of communism, and the newly available identification with unabashed capitalism have changed the demands for geopolitical prominence and the internal economic demands. In turn, the demands dependent on preexisting identifications may change. For example, Russians' demands on their government have changed dramatically.

The circumstances bring into question the validity of prevailing expectations of trends and of the success of various strategies. Altered expectations change demands by changing what is seen as feasible and altering perceptions of risk. Originally low demands to protect particular aspects of life may come to have priority if those aspects are seen as threatened. For example, military defeat shifts the expectation from dominance to possible subjugation, in turn changing demands from conquest to coexistence. By the same token, the economic collapse in Thailand, similar to such collapses in many other developing countries, dramatically changed the expectations of future economic growth and the viability of existing economic institutions and policies. The mood of dread and disappointment led to severe scalebacks in investment and the unwillingness to purchase defaulted real estate, even when the prices were extremely low.

Both of these patterns clarify how changed expectations can undermine existing identifications and demands, but this level of theory is not as useful for anticipating the specifics of the new demands that will arise, because the impact of objective conditions on value preoccupations is not straightforward. A deprivation with respect to a particular value may, of course, lead to a preoccupation with that value. Economic recession or depression may give rise to a preoccupation with wealth. However, adverse economic conditions may also discourage such a preoccupation and refocus attention on values perceived to be more attainable. By the same token, economic boom may either satiate the desire for greater economic gain, or increase the preoccupation because of the perceived opportunities and a general climate that legitimizes this preoccupation. By this reasoning, all of the efforts to relate simple characterizations of the objective conditions to climates such as revolutionary fervor are doomed because of their lack of sensitivity to how details of the objective reality can alter subjective needs. Lasswell offered a detailed account of how individuals become preoccupied with a particular value.[98] However, the question for this analysis is: How does a preoccupation come to be shared across a large number of individuals with presumably different psychohistories and therefore different predispositions to seek particular values?

Predispositions

A second level of explanation provides greater explanatory power for understanding changes in value preoccupations. Lasswell defined two aspects of the predispositions to moods and climate, emphasizing that these predispositions are often deeply sociocultural phenomena. The first aspect is the *repertory* of past mood patterns, focusing largely on the range of values that have been strongest historically in mobilizing intense affect and action (Lasswell, 1965a). For example, Colombia has long been beset with extraordinary levels of violence and the preoccupation with personal security.

The second aspect of predispositions is the *mood agenda*, a more complicated notion covering the patterns by which moods are expressed in symbols and actions. These agendas are the more detailed patterns relating to the specific elements of the mood repertory. Agendas as such consist of the potentially wide range of symbols, prescriptions, anecdotes, foci of admiration ("miranda"), and dominant explanations that reinforce a mood or provide precedents for how emerging moods will be defined and supported (Lasswell, 1965a). The basic premise is that past or existing patterns will predispose individuals to define (or respond to) the imagery and beliefs about a mood. For example, in Argentina, where political instability and economic decline have long been popularly associated with the moral failings of top political leaders and the vivid accounts of their dealings, any economic downturn is likely to trigger a similar interpretation and therefore contribute to the climate of political cynicism that often has a self-fulfilling impact.

These constructs of mood repertory and agenda thus provide another connection between the individual psychodynamics generating preoccupations and the broader societal understandings that crystallize particular moods. Even without active propaganda efforts, many people will come to common understandings and orientations related to the power of different values and the threats or opportunities that these values face.

As an application of psychoanalytic theory, the hypothesis that particular groups or societies are predisposed to a repertory of moods presumes the generalization of the overall patterns: The place to start in asking what patterns are likely to occur is to identify the patterns that occurred before. Yet, it does not rule out the dynamics of displacement that we examined in chapter 2. In theory, a particular mood, if emotionally painful because of the threats to a specific value, may be supplanted by a different, less painful preoccupation. The lust for power may be transformed into greed or religious fervor; pacifism may supplant militarism as, say, in post-WWII Germany and Japan; frustrated greed may yield to asceticism. However, the strength of the repertory concept is that if there is a predisposition to displace one form of value preoccupation with another, it may have been manifested earlier. For example, certain countries, including the United States, seem to go through alternating periods of Puritanism and moral liberalism. Displacement dynamics may be at work in this alternation, and each phase may seem to contradict its predecessor, but the pattern as a whole and each of its elements can be regarded as part of the repertory.

The mood predisposition hypothesis can also be cast in terms of the cognitive theories of heuristics. As Kahneman et al. (1982) argued, complex new situations tax the capacity of individuals to understand, because of limited information, time, and analytic resources. Therefore, assessing the new situation from scratch is often not feasible, and thus people look to prior circumstances and understandings and presume, as analytical shortcuts, that they will hold for the emerging conditions. Although the basis for choosing the prior cases that will be taken as parallel to the new situation may vary,[99] the convergence is that the cognitive elements underlying particular collective moods are likely to be replicated as the new situation is interpreted as if it were a repeat of past situations.

The Triple Appeal

Lasswell applied the triple-appeal principle to account for collective moods as well as to the attraction of politicians and policy appeals. In the triple-appeal principle, he applied the Freudian notion of the clash among id, ego, and superego to explain why certain appeals of persons, actions, and symbols resonate better than do others, depending on the psychological needs of the individual. Of the three categories of interactions covered by the triple-appeal principle, that of person-to-occasion relationships is clearly relevant to the explanation of moods and mood swings that are triggered by crises or other events and conditions. Mood repertories and agendas appeal differentially to personality components, which correspond roughly to raw impulse, reason, and conscience. To examine this contribution in terms of *collective* moods requires combining this insight with an analysis of how individuals are influenced by others in terms of the importance that they attribute to impulse, reason, and conscience at any point in time.

To find a window on how the triple-appeal principle applies, we follow Lasswell's insight that internal psychodynamics are most clearly revealed by examining the seemingly contradictory cases rather than the typical, consistent cases in which impulse, reason, and conscience reinforce one another. Two such anomalous types of cases can be found.

First, as outlined earlier in the section on flash moods that culminate in mob behavior, a mood of impulsivity sometimes reigns among people who otherwise would be far more cautious and conscientious. The explanation already provided is that both the intensity of emotion and signaling from others permit id impulses to be expressed. Similarly, intensity and signaling may result in putting conscience before calculation. In either case, an obvious hypothesis is that heightened intensity of crisis makes people more susceptible to appeals that clash with preexisting perspectives. In *Psychopathology and Politics* (1930/1960), Lasswell argued:

> Political crises are complicated by the concurrent reactivation of specific primitive impulses. War is the classical situation in which the elementary psychological structures are no longer held in subordination to complex reactions. The acts of cruelty and lust which are inseparably connected with war have disclosed vividly to all who care to see the narrow margin which separates the social from the asocial nature of man. The excesses of heroism and abnegation are alike primitive in their manifestations, and show that all the primitive psychological structures are not antisocial, but asocial, and may often function on behalf of human solidarity. (p. 179)

We can hypothesize that id or superego appeals, individually or together, will have higher salience when emotions are more intense. Insofar as crisis raises anxiety, crises impel actions intended to dispel anxiety. In many instances, no rational, calculated options would satisfy the psychological needs. Simplistic actions and policies then occur—some destructive, some heroic.

A reinforcing pattern often occurs when extreme conditions increase the uncertainty as to what constitutes rational behavior. With greater uncertainty about appropriate demands and expectations, the rational becomes less compelling. This may increase anxiety for those still preoccupied with rational coping strategies, but it can be liberating for those predisposed to headlong action.

The second, and even more perplexing anomaly, is that crises causing or threatening severe deprivations sometimes create positive affects, whereas many crises that produce less actual damage instill only negative mood elements. For some individuals, the most fearful crises bring peace or even exhilaration. In *Psychopathology and Politics* (1930/1960), Lasswell wrote that the "individual who is sorely divided against himself may seek peace by unifying himself against an outsider. This is the well-known 'peacefulness of being at war'" (1930/1960, pp. 193–194).

We can contrast this counterintuitive outcome with the pattern that emerges when a threat exists but is not consummated to the point of acute crisis and an obvious deprivation with a clear perpetrator. Consider the Cold War mood vis-à-vis the Soviet Union, which was largely marked by grim vigilance, hyperattentiveness, and desire for avoidance rather than confrontation. The Cold War was a crisis, insofar as it entailed a serious threat to important values, but it was a prolonged crisis marked by threats that never culminated in the most feared outcomes. There was no support for direct confrontation, and little pressure for the U.S. government to go beyond the superficial battles with the Soviet Union on cultural and diplomatic affairs. The orientation toward the Soviet Union per se was bereft of bravado or open competitiveness, in contrast with the support for surrogate wars. The efforts by the Right to mobilize an anti-Communist crusade directly against the Soviet Union largely fell on deaf ears, in contrast to the domestic Red Scare. Unlike the arrogance that many Americans felt toward other nations, attitudes toward the Soviet Union were characterized by grudging respect. In dealing with other nations seen as potential allies of either the United States or the Soviet Union, the American public largely tolerated the *Realpolitik* approach of cultivating pro-U.S. forces and undermining pro-Soviet forces, regardless of the moral considerations of supporting dictators and destroying democrats. In short, the Cold War, even though an enormous victory for the United States, elicited virtually no peace of mind or exhilaration.

The first hypothesis to account for the difference between the mood of exhilaration or peace that sometimes comes with the out-and-out attack (Pearl Harbor, September 11) and the hypercaution of the Cold War is that in the former cases the inner conflict among impulse, reason, and conscience is temporarily resolved. Aggressive impulses, formerly regarded as id-indulgent, become respectable in terms of reason, conscience, and duty. Prior to the outbreak of all-out conflict, an antagonist such as the Soviet

Union may represent a threat, an affront, or perhaps a source of humiliation, but attacking the antagonist runs counter to morality, instrumental behavior, or both. A dramatic precipitating event, in contrast, makes the counterattack compelling when the emergency overrides the normal constraints. Some who abandon family responsibilities to enlist in the armed forces, engage in terrorism, or undertake other aggressive activities may reflect this dynamic—although others may do so primarily out of conscience.

Crisis can also alter the salient level of identifications, in two ways that can relieve emotionally draining anxieties. Danger to the whole community can create an identification of solidarity, lifting people beyond their own narrower anxieties. The petty but multiple anxieties of self-centered normal life are downgraded in importance. In other types of crises, self-interest may dominate over conscience, such that the "every man for himself" mentality can be indulged with fewer qualms.

Another angle to these patterns rests on the rough correlation between the id-ego-superego division and value preoccupations, although the correlations are complicated by the fact that values are both resources and ends in themselves. Superego demands are typically reflected in preoccupations with rectitude, and possibly with respect, enlightenment, and affection. Id impulses are most likely to be expressed as preoccupations with well-being (especially in its security aspects), power, and affection. Ego demands are often manifested as preoccupations with wealth, skill, respect, and power. For those personalities predisposed to preoccupation with a single value, for whom leading the "balanced life" is psychologically draining, refocusing from myriad small preoccupations to one large one because of a crisis or other abnormal circumstances can be emotionally liberating. Therefore, in addition to the straightforward reduction of anxiety through the reduction in ambiguity, a mood of crisis can combine the fundamental gratification of indulging raw impulse with the relief of anxiety arising from holding impulse in check.

The crucial insight from psychoanalytic theory accounts for the susceptibility of the public to different perspectives in times of major crisis. In addition to the direct effects of uncertainty mentioned earlier, a transformative crisis often creates a mood of lost bearings, "all bets are off," and consequent openness to radically different perspectives. The "uncanny feeling" that Harry Stack Sullivan attributed to anxiety, understood in the broader psychoanalytic sense of emotional mobilization rather than the narrower contemporary sense of unpleasurable nervousness, is relevant here (Sullivan, 1948). In many of his works, Lasswell made a distinction between equilibrium circumstances and developmental circumstances, a distinction that seems puzzling in light of the fact that every situation has elements of continuity and change. However, the important insight here is that conditions change when people *perceive* them as changing in significant ways. The perception of change opens up the possibility that the existing norms and constraints will no longer hold, that expectations pivotal to the individual's perspectives are in question. It is perhaps the heightened vigilance and arousal, akin to being in an unfamiliar city in a foreign country, that accounts for both exhilaration and openness to new perspectives. This line of explanation has been carried forward in Marcus et al.'s theory of dual affective subsystems, which posits that in addition to the disposition system that reflects habitual routines that are reinforced by both internal and external feedback, there is a surveillance system that "monitors the environment for novel and threatening stimuli" (Marcus et al., 2000, p. 53). Insofar as the surveillance system is activated, the individual assesses and reassesses the situation, loosening the bounds of habitual affects and cognitions.

Communications, Propaganda, and Sanctions

An additional element of the theory of enduring political climates elaborates on the influence that the actions of elites and the media, as well other members of the crowd or mob, have on the predispositions to adopt or maintain a particular mood.

Elite Communications. Lasswell argued that political climates are crystallized and sustained by the uniformity and consistency of messages originating from the relevant elites. Lasswell argued in "The Climate of International Action" (1965a) that elites often perceive advantages in maintaining a particular political climate, even if it has negative aspects, and will direct their communications to the public accordingly. The key premise is that stable climates enhance predictability. They reduce uncertainty regarding how the population will react to symbols. Even the leaders of international rivals such as the United States and the Soviet Union had common cause in being able to resort to the symbols of Cold War rivalry to reinforce loyalty, discredit critics, and mobilize resources. Stable climates reduce the volatility in expectations and standards of appropriate behavior, making it easier for elites to maintain respect and find political common ground. From an economic perspective, stable climates can even aid in predicting how markets will react to new products.

The question facing the world today is whether terrorism, which may be able to persist without state sponsorhip, will lead to a pattern of continued or even increased instability and insecurity. The incentives of the "haves" to maintain some degree of stability in political climate may be irrelevant to the "have nots" who resort to terrorism.

If a political climate is perceived to be in the interest of particular elites, their options for maintaining the climate include both fashioning reinforcing communications and punishing other elite members for sending out dissenting communications. Reinforcing communications are both results and causes of the prevailing climate. If policy appeals are conveyed with affect and symbols consistent with the prevailing mood, they are not only more likely to strike a responsive chord with nonelites, but also may reinforce the existing climate.

The capacity to punish dissenting communications is more obvious when the climate involves dire threats, as in the case of the Cold War (the major case addressed by Lasswell's "Climate of International Action"), than in cases of positive climates, because dissenters from mainstream interpretations of threat can be accused of insufficient vigilance or, in the extreme, even treason. Yet, even dissent from largely positive moods can be negatively sanctioned, as when those who communicate negative information are accused of undermining optimism and progress.

When the prevailing political climate challenges the objectives of government elites, their dilemma is whether to minimize the conditions and issues that underlie the mood, or to take strong action in order to signal that the underlying problems are being addressed. This calculus of managing the focus of attention is analyzed insightfully in Murray Edelman's *The Symbolic Uses of Politics*, which emphasizes the reassurance function of the sheer existence of government activity—hearings, commissions, planning, and so on—that signals that problems are being addressed (1964/1985).

Manipulating Intensity. In addition to reinforcing or diminishing the prevailing political climate, elites often engage in efforts to alter the intensity of collective moods, in order to make the public more receptive to the government's preferred policy strategies and to dampen public actions that may run counter to these strategies. If the leader determines that the emotional intensity must be reined in for sensible policies and actions to be pursued, then the appeal to reason, and the restoration of the dominance of ego over id and superego, may be the appropriate strategy. Occasionally an antagonistic climate threatens to emerge vis-à-vis an ally, prompting efforts to defuse the intensity, as in the case of spy scandals involving "friendly" powers. In contrast, when great sacrifice is desired—for example, in mobilization for war—governments obviously strive to maximize the intensity of the mood and narrow the value preoccupation to the focus of action.

However, in many cases the challenge is to *calibrate* the intensity level rather than maximize or minimize it. For example, the September 11 terrorist attacks posed a difficult challenge for the U.S. government: to mobilize public opinion in favor of a war in Afghanistan, but not to create such hatred and fear of Muslims as to trigger anti-Muslim riots or killings; to tolerate more stringent security measures, but not to abandon air travel; and to mobilize support for a war against Iraq, even though the connection between the terrorist attacks and Iraqi misdeeds was murky.

Climate intensity can be manipulated through at least three strategies: attribution, symbolic action, and labeling. The attribution of responsibility for events or conditions can focus the source of threat broadly or narrowly, from an individual such as Osama bin Laden to an entire religion. Attributing motives also influences intensity by shaping expectations as to the seriousness of threats: Are rivals just trying to survive, or do they seek world domination? Attribution often permits more discretion of interpretation than is recognized once an attribution comes to be accepted. In the case of the September 11 terrorist attacks, should blame have been attributed to "the Saudis" and Saudi Arabia, because the majority of the terrorists, as well as Osama bin Laden, were from that country, and (arguably, of course) the corruption of that society had driven the terrorists to their actions; or to Afghans and Afghanistan, because the Afghan government harbored Osama bin Laden and some of the terrorists? How broadly should blame be attributed? To the terrorists and those who planned the specific attacks? To those who aided them in various ways? Or to all Islamic fundamentalists?

Symbolic action entails signals as to the response to the conditions or events that created or sustained the climate. Both words and deeds influence public opinion in assessing how dire the situation is. Measured words and deeds imply that less intensity is warranted. Leaders sometimes strive to communicate a business-as-usual mood in the midst of crisis so that individuals will not abandon balance in their actions.

Finally, the very labeling of the precipitating events and the subsequent circumstance provides the opportunity to link the existing situation with other situations of known intensity. Calling an attack an act of war obviously impacts differently than calling it a provocation, a foolish mistake by lower-level individuals, or an act of terrorism. Commonality of labels encourages the assumption, conscious or not, of commonality of agenda and intensity. The use of labels that connect the new situation semantically to other situations increases the likelihood that the intensity and other affects associated with the old will bleed over to the new. This result is predicted from both the theory of heuristics reviewed earlier, and the generalization of affect that Sapir and other Lasswell collaborators attributed to "condensation symbols" that cover multiple phenomena.[100]

Thus far we have largely considered the role of government elites. But, of course, they are not the only interpreters and signalers of events and climates. William Kornhauser, in *The Politics of Mass Society* (1959), argued that the monopoly of mood setting by a small government elite leads to extremes, if the elite's preoccupations and particular interpretations are the only ones available to mass audiences.

The mass media, where they are permitted some independence, play a central role in determining the intensity of political climate and the labeling of both events and climates. A potentially important climate-triggering event or condition can fade if the media ignore it; alternatively, it can become prominent if the media emphasize it and then continue to do so because of how widely it has been recognized. The stability of collective moods is often reinforced by the very fact that the media assign a broad label to the climate. People come to accept these characterizations as valid even if the implied uniformity is greatly exaggerated. Consider how the media's interpretations of the emergence of young anti-Viet Nam War protestors and flower children in the late 1960s and early 1970s came to be accepted by the participants themselves as the defining climate of the times.

Reinforcement of Mood, Institution, and Practice.   Lasswell's frame-work emphasized institutions as well as predispositions. The durability of political climate is often strengthened by the mutual reinforcement of climate and the institutions that grow up around them. Lasswell's most explicit example of the institutional anchoring of mood was his chilling exposition on the possibility of the *garrison state:* a "developmental con-struct" (or provisional hypothesis) that the rising mood of physical inse-curity will give increasing power to the specialists of violence (military, policy, intelligence agencies, security-oriented ministries, etc.). Security concerns dominate other considerations. The dominance of these roles, and their preoccupations, perpetuate the mood of insecurity. The inter-actions with potential antagonists, whether domestic or foreign, escalate and exacerbate the climate of insecurity. Rivals are symbolized as enemies. Standard operating procedures, communications, training, and the out-looks of its chief functionaries all reinforce both the mood of insecurity and the dominance of the elites whose power rests on the prominence of the climate (Lasswell, 1941a; 1962). The prescience of the garrison state hypothesis in anticipating the rise of the "military-industrial complex" and the tensions between defending against terrorism and protecting civil liberties is reflected in the hundreds of publications on civil–military rela-tions that cite Lasswell's two primary works on the topic, and the repub-lication of these essays as late as 1997.[101]

POLICY IMPLICATIONS

Lasswell conceived of the policy problems arising from the changes in pub-lic climate in terms of both the intelligence function and the challenges of preempting and coping with the rise of destructive moods. Insofar as political leaders and policymakers are aware of emerging moods, the strat-egies for addressing them constructively correspond to the same insights that Lasswell brought to bear in dealing with negative affects, with the special consideration that rapid mood swings entail distinctive problems of uncertainty and abnormalcy.

The Intelligence Function

Lasswell's assessment of the challenges stemming from mood swings began with the insight that policymakers often remain dangerously unaware of the moods that have emerged. In "The Climate of Interna-tional Action" (1965a), he noted that officials in the cities are frequently ignorant of the mood in the small towns and the countryside, and that the mood differences of younger generations are often overlooked. He called for more careful, systematic monitoring, through interviews and content analysis. In this regard, Lasswell expressed confidence that quantitative content analysis can reveal moods that the policy elite would not perceive through their own informal assessments of the moods of other groups. He cited Karen Dovring's content analysis of 18th-Century Swedish hymnals, which reflected democratic and egalitarian aspirations that the elite only came to appreciate after the hymnal reform led to a dramatic increase in church attendance.[102]

However, Lasswell (1963) voiced reservations about the conventional opinion survey, because responses to the same question change meaning in different contexts and over time—a case of "index instability." His concern was that survey responses are easily taken out of the broad context of the respondents' perspectives and referents. Lasswell gave strong support to the more intensive, configurative approach of the Q technique, which employs factor analysis to identify perspectives defined by the overall configuration of responses rather than individual responses (Brown, 1980). Lasswell also applauded the typical reliance of the Q technique on the discourse of the respondents rather than having to impose the language (and therefore the perspectives) of the researcher.

Preempting and Discharging Disruptive Impulses

In "The Politics of Prevention," the most original chapter of Lasswell's extremely provocative *Psychopathology and Politics* (1930/1960), he wrote that:

> The problem of politics is less to solve conflicts than to prevent them; less to serve as a safety valve for social protest than to apply social energy to the abolition of recurrent sources of strain in society.
>
> This redefinition of the problem of politics may be called the idea of preventive politics. The politics of prevention draws attention squarely to the central problem of reducing the level of strain and maladaptation in society. In some measure it will proceed by encouraging discussion among all those who are affected by social policy, but this will be no iron-clad rule. In some measure it will proceed by improving the machinery of settling disputes, but this will be subordinated to a comprehensive program, and no longer treated as an especially desirable mode of handling the situation . . .
>
> The politics of prevention does not depend upon a series of changes in the organization of government. It depends upon a reorientation in the minds of those who think about society around the central problems: What are the principal factors which modify the tension level of the community? What is the specific relevance of a proposed line of action to the temporary and permanent modification of the tension level? (pp. 197–198)

The "politics of prevention" thus proceeds by identifying and addressing the underlying causes of irresponsible and undemocratic responses to adverse conditions. In addition to the standard processes of democratic governance, such as giving voice and vote to citizens and offering fair mechanisms of conflict resolution, resiliency in the face of crisis requires reducing the deep-seated insecurities and perverse reaction patterns (e.g., scapegoating and other displacement mechanisms reviewed in chap. 2). It is nothing less than an effort to change the components of fundamental political character that are manifested in times of crisis and deprivation, whether physical, psychological, or both. Using Lasswell's distinction of impulse, subjectivity, and expression, we can elaborate on the effort of the politics of prevention:

• Addressing impulse calls first for interventions to reduce sources of destructive impulses that arise under stress, such as feelings of inferiority, lack of respect, powerlessness, loss of meaningfulness, and alienation. Second, it entails finding cathartic alternatives for the discharge of impulses into nondestructive, or at least less destructive, ways. Within the past century, spectator sports have become a major outlet for the displacement of competitive, aggressive impulses. Both their potency—and limitations—for channeling aggression can be seen by the marauding soccer fans who occasionally erupt at European matches. Election campaigns also serve as channels for these impulses, allowing for some discharge in less destructive ways as long as electoral rules are observed. Unfortunately, political leaders sometimes resort to war to discharge impulses initially directed against domestic targets (Volkan, 1988).

• Addressing subjectivity calls for influences on how individuals perceive the conditions and their own impulses, especially in how and to whom they attribute responsibility or blame for their troubles. The management of symbols in framing issues is obviously crucial. Lasswell's diagnosis of Hitlerism and Nazi propaganda's attribution of blame for Germany's humiliation and economic deprivation revealed the pernicious potential of such framing; the politics of prevention requires turning around the subjectivity so that tensions can be discharged in less destructive ways.

Avoiding the symbols and activities that exacerbate mood swings:

• Civic education as well as shorter-term symbol management by government and civic institutions must also be engaged.
• Addressing expression by shaping habitual responses to adversity. Civic education is again relevant, but so too are the patterns of response by public figures who serve as role models. Is it taken for granted that a political leader besieged by criticism will counterattack by accusing the opposition of treason; will the military be prodded to intervene? Does a labor group respond to economic adversity by mounting a strike intended to paralyze the economy, or does it respond by first seeking redress by appealing for policy changes?

CONCLUSIONS

We return to the question of how individuals can be out of character. Lasswell had two answers to this puzzle. First, Lasswell's conception of political character entailed a range of predispositions depending on circumstances. The full description of political character addressed the wide variety of circumstances that an individual might face, not just the normal.

An individual of "democratic character" under normal circumstances does not necessarily behave democratically under more adverse circumstances. Democratic character is a matter of where the thresholds are—how much adversity can the individual endure without succumbing to the temptations to act undemocratically?

Second, Lasswell could attribute the out-of-character behavior that arises in group situations, such as mobs, to the communicative context that shapes demands and expectations. Consider an individual who believes that violence outside of legally constituted channels is inappropriate in general, except when morally outrageous acts are committed. Under usual circumstances, judgments as to whether a given act is so morally outrageous may come from newspaper or magazine articles, from the constituted legal system via government pronouncements, or from other channels that may moderate the judgments. In contrast, mobs forming immediately after learning of an outrage (e.g., the 1992 acquittal of the four Los Angeles police officers tried for brutalizing Rodney King) must decide whether immediate action is necessary. The communications bombarding any given individual within the mob may exaggerate the degree of outrageousness. In addition, political character usually entails some elements of conformity and desire to embrace the orientations of friends and neighbors, which may be greater in times of crisis. When friends, neighbors, coworkers, or coreligionists go to the barricades, the needs for conformity and solidarity that were previously latent may be expressed. This does not mean that political character has changed, but rather that new information has mobilized previously dormant aspects of political character.

Let us presume that a nation's citizens are normally predisposed to democratic norms and behavior. What are the conditions that would undermine these basic predispositions? A nonpsychodynamic view that might be asserted by the rational choice approach would be that democratic behavior would be jettisoned as soon as the costs of such behavior were perceived to outweigh the benefits. Lasswell rejected this position in arguing for the importance of the self-system, which encompasses norms—that is, demands on the self. Rather, Lasswell posited that stress and the resultant anxiety of crisis push individuals into behavior that they would otherwise not entertain. This led him to the "politics of prevention," which rests on all of the psychodynamics and normative stances of Lasswell's framework. Our concluding chapter 8 takes up the question of how the politics of prevention can be pursued without compromising democracy.

Chapter 7

Integrating Lasswell's Contributions: Brief Applications

In presenting the various elements of Harold Lasswell's framework, analytic categories, and theories, we have not yet shown how these elements can be fit together. However, Lasswell's insistence on a "configurative approach"[103] is as important a lesson as any in his repertoire. Therefore, in this chapter we present thumbnail applications, addressing single or multiple cases, to illustrate the applicability of Lasswell's psychodynamic functional theories and analytic categories to crucial public policy issues. Of course, these vignettes do not do full justice to any of the cases; each issue warrants full-length books. These applications do, however, demonstrate the relevance of a host of potential psychodynamic insights that conventional positivist, empirical approaches may neglect.

The first four applications concern diagnoses of intergroup conflict and violence, focusing on how understanding the psychodynamics of such conflicts can guide the search for strategies to reduce the predispositions to violence. The fifth application addresses the strategies for developing democratic character in Latin American military officers, with a special emphasis on the troubled case of Argentina. Together, these five applications hinge on the interplay of identifications, demands, and the triple-appeal principle in the socialization toward or away from democratic character.

Turning to domestic policy issues directly relevant to the United States, we address the peculiar symbol associations facing nuclear energy, and, lastly, the issues of labor union bargaining and leadership. The nuclear energy case highlights the importance of symbol associations as conveyors of affect from one policy issue to another. The labor union discussion emphasizes (a) the potentials and dangers of charismatic leadership in the interactions among leaders, rank-and-file members, and employers; and (b) how union members' interests can be pursued without excessive influence from symbolic associations that might stand in the way of constructive negotiations.

ATTITUDES SUPPORTING
INTERETHNIC VIOLENCE

The predisposition to engage in or support interethnic violence can some-times be found among populations that adhere, at least in principle, to general tenets that condemn violence except in the extraordinary circumstances of the "just war."[104] The just war doctrine legitimizes violence only when grave injustices exist, nonviolent approaches to redressing these conditions have been exhausted, the violence required is in proportion with the intended improvements, and the violence will bring about these improvements. Thus, retribution is not a legitimate motive, and violence is unjustified if its success in redressing egregious conditions is improbable, or if those targeted are blameless.

Therefore, when outside observers judge the achievement of the objectives of violence as improbable or the victims of violence as innocent, interethnic violence is typically interpreted as the unchecked expression of primal impulses of revenge and aggression. The premise is that these impulses overwhelm any moral tenets that otherwise would deter such predispositions.

If this diagnosis of support for interethnic violence is correct, then the remedies might include invoking moral arguments, reducing tension levels that weaken the discipline against the expression of raw impulses, or emphasizing the instrumental costs of indulging aggressive impulses. However, the Lasswellian framework invites more complex explanations that may lead to other strategies. The mid-1980s attitude structures of U.S. supporters of Irish Catholic violence against British officials and soldiers in Northern Ireland, and of those Armenian-Americans who supported attacks on Turkish officials and soldiers, revealed the power of the triple-appeal principle, and the interplay of identifications, demands, and expectations.

In 1986, the Q technique was used to explore the attitude structures of members of Northern Irish Aid ("Noraid"), a U.S.-based group supporting the Irish Republican Army, and members of the Armenian Assembly, an American-Armenian association (Ascher, 1986). The Q technique, which typically calls on respondents to sort statements according to the degree of agreement, was chosen because it affords greater capacity than do conventional survey techniques to capture the interrelatedness of belief structures.[105] For this analysis, the items—gathered from the respondents' own discourse from previous open-ended discussions—included identification, demand, and expectation statements.

At that time, many Noraid members supported the attacks against British targets in Northern Ireland, and a minority of Armenian Assembly members supported attacks on Turkish targets. Therefore, one might have expected these proviolence respondents to manifest straightforward revenge and an eye-for-an-eye mentality. Instead, the analysis revealed how superego and id impulses come into congruence in ways that can be understood through the combination of expectations and demands that reinforces moralistic aggression. Specifically, moralistic perspectives arise that adhere to the just war doctrine, but also serve the id impulses of revenge and dominance.

In both of these cases, outside observers would doubt that the criteria of the just war would pertain. Then—and now—the prospects for Armenian independence from Turkey would be highly implausible. Given that the 1915 Armenian Genocide occurred under a regime that collapsed after World War I, and that the vast majority of the perpetrators were long dead by the mid-1980s, the blameworthiness of the targeted Turkish officials and soldiers would appear to be highly questionable. Similarly, the fact that the majority of the Northern Irish citizenry is Protestant has made the reunification of all of Ireland improbable if not unthinkable, and the civilian-targeted bombings committed by the Irish Republican Army raise comparable questions of the appropriateness of violence against the innocent. The premise that nonviolent means had been exhausted was also questionable in the case of Northern Ireland, in light of the ongoing negotiations with British and Northern Irish Protestants.

And yet, the belief structures of the violence-supporting respondents were indeed congruent with the just war tenets. The first key to this congruence comes in holding the very expectations that outside observers would consider to be far-fetched. The most significant expectation among Noraid members and those members of the Armenian Assembly who expressed support for violence was that violence could achieve independence. Where outside observers would see futility, those who support violence would see a different scenario: that the violence would ultimately convince the British or the Turks to capitulate to demands for independence. The fact that the violence-prone respondents were joined by others striving for independence undoubtedly reinforced the plausibility of this expectation in the respondents' minds.

The related expectation was that nonviolent means would fail, an expectation necessary for concluding that violence is necessary. This is certainly reasonable with respect to Armenian independence—which outside observers would consider to be highly unlikely under any circumstances. Yet, even in the Northern Irish case, the supporters of violence viewed the British as unyielding in peaceful negotiations, and the rest of the world unsupportive of the Irish Catholic cause (Ascher, 1986). The fact that efforts at a political solution have been ongoing for decades could be interpreted as hopeful for nonviolent approaches, but the supporters of violence could also interpret it as indicating the futility of peaceful negotiations.

The most important demand was that current conditions be treated as egregious and unjust, or even as tantamount to violence. For the Armenians, this demand was supported by the view that the refusal to acknowledge the Armenian Genocide was itself an egregious affront to Armenians, especially to the survivors still alive at the time that the analysis was undertaken. This moral indignation (which Strawson termed "resentment on behalf of another")[106] appears to be a powerful motivator because it simultaneously combines selflessness—it is to vindicate the elderly survivors, not oneself—with a demand for immediate action before the survivors die without recognition for their suffering.

For the Noraid case, the supporters of the Irish Republican Army frequently referred to the employment and wage discrimination against Irish Catholics in Northern Ireland as "economic violence," blurring the concept of violence but reinforcing the premise that prevailing conditions were intolerable. Equating economic discrimination with violence bolstered the argument that the IRA's violence is no different from the treatment of Irish Catholics by Protestants and the British, nor disproportionate to the injustices suffered by the Catholics. It is a perspective that a state of war existed at the time of the survey—and indeed still exists, even if the British and the Ulster Protestants pretend that it does not.

The significantly missing demand was for personal material gain. Despite the fact that the common concern over the independence issue provided social and possibly economic linkages for members of these groups, respondents were adamant that they would not benefit from independence or reunification, and emphasized the material sacrifices they had made or were prepared to make for the cause. Therefore, these cases provided an important insight about the triple-appeal principle (see especially chap. 3). Under many circumstances, an appeal is strongest when it serves id, ego, and superego at the same time. However, when moral indignation helps to reconcile id impulses that otherwise might violate moral precepts, the motive of personal gain would pose the risk of diminishing the moralism of violence.

What advice would emerge from such an analysis? There is nothing in this assessment that would fault the strategy adopted by the British government in negotiating an autonomy arrangement that would permit neither the Ulster Protestants nor the Catholics to take on a greater identity as victims. The official Turkish approach—of attributing the Armenian deaths to the chaos of World War I, questioning the numbers of casualties, emphasizing the innocence of the current Turkish officials, or otherwise minimizing the responsibility of the Turkish government and people—is based on a misdiagnosis of the emotional basis of the Armenians' indignation. The Turkish position keeps the Genocide and the independence movement linked as "current issues"; symbolically, the Genocide is not simply an historical event, but rather a pattern of atrocity and continued affront. It may be that an official Turkish acknowledgment that the Genocide occurred, along with an expression of regret, would diminish the emotional charge of the Armenian cause.

PROVOKING THE SENSE OF VICTIMIZATION THROUGH SYMBOL MANIPULATION

To extend the analysis of the sense of victimization, we present a brief vignette of a case of interethnic violence that entailed explicit manipulation of symbols in order to revive a sense of victimization and moral indignation that had been largely extinguished through the passage of time. The capacity to identify and monitor this form of symbol manipulation may be crucial for anticipating the outbreak of interethnic violence and human rights violations.

The shocking retrogression in Serb behavior in the post-Tito era—after decades of relatively peaceful coexistence with Croats, Bosnian Muslims, and Kosovar Muslims—has been a tormenting puzzle. The Serbs had dominated the Yugoslav Republic politically and economically. The separation of the Republic into nations roughly corresponding to the significant ethnic groups would certainly have undermined the aspiration of "Greater Serbia," but hardly constituted the victimization of the Serbs. The Ottoman Empire, of course long in the past, would not normally serve as the focus for either moral indignation or aggressive impulses. The predisposition of Serbs to disregard the human rights of other ethnic groups seems to lack the requisite emotional basis.

Yet, Vamik Volkan (1997, 2002) related that in 1989, the year before the 600th anniversary of the Battle of Kosovo, Slobodan Milošević ordered the disinterment of Serbian hero Prince Lazar, who, along with many of the Serbian nobility, had been killed in that battle against the invading Ottomans. Prince Lazar's status as the tragic hero of the Serbs is enshrined in religious icons, folk songs, and art. Prince Lazar's remains were taken from town to town over the course of the year, and then reburied in the battlefield on the anniversary of the Battle. As Volkan (2002) wrote:

> Lazar was, in effect, "reincarnated" and "reburied." A "time collapse" occurred as well, meaning that feelings and perceptions associated with the mental representation of this historical event were compounded with feeling or perceptions found in the existing "enemy." Thus, an emotional atmosphere was created to enhance Serbian national identity, and a task of revenge was added to the Serbian identity at that time. This atmosphere was necessary in order for individuals to carry out atrocities against the Muslims, this time Bosnian and Kosovo Albanian Muslims, rather than the citizens of the Ottoman Empire, the original nemesis that no longer existed. (p. 12)

In this case, the full triple-appeal principle pertained, as the impulses for revenge, the defense of Serbian integrity, and the desire to regain or preserve territory reinforced one another. The propaganda coup involving Prince Lazar was to create the basis for Serbian self-pity and sense of victimization that could rationalize extreme measures against the separatist movements.

IRAQI IDENTIFICATIONS

In emerging democracies beset with histories of intergroup conflict, governance arrangements must take into account the relative salience of existing and potential identifications. The composition of the Iraqi Governing Council set up by the U.S. government after the fall of Saddam Hussein was based on two premises: that the country was divided between pro-Saddam Hussein Baathists and the anti-Baathist opposition, and that this division essentially overlapped with the Shiite–Sunni religious difference as the most important dimension of Iraqis' identifications. Basing the political formula on religious division as the most salient dimension of identification has serious consequences. It shapes political cleavages and coalition possibilities, creates expectations that the religious division will continue to be the defining aspect of politics, and may reinforce its importance in the long run. The quotas applied to balance the Shiite–Sunni representation may have the effect of signaling to the Iraqis that this dimension will continue to be the defining difference in the U.S. strategy toward Iraq.

Therefore, it is crucial to determine whether the religious division is, and will inevitably be, the most salient identification for Iraqis. Yet, there is controversy over which dimensions of identification are currently and potentially most important. Toby Dodge (2003) argued that the Shiite–Sunni distinction is seriously overemphasized by non-Iraqi analysts. Similarly, the very aggressive treatment of the city of Falluja by U.S.-led forces, strongly shaped by the characterization of the city as a Baathist stronghold, has been criticized as ignoring the more important identification of the people of that city as conservative Sunnis. Dodge also argued that U.S. policy is flawed because of U.S. policymakers' underestimation of the importance of the identification of Iraqis who remained during the Saddam Hussein period as those who were victimized, in distinction with those who went into exile. He also asserted that Iraqis identify themselves more as Iraqis than as members of a religious following, and therefore have much greater resentment toward the occupying forces than U.S. strategists assume. And this does not limit the dimensions of identification: There are clan loyalties, regional loyalties, and divisions between secularists and fundamentalists as well as along the conventional right-left ideological dimension. These dimensions intersect to create an even more complex set of identifications. For example, although fundamentalist Shias might identify strongly with Iran, secular Shias may not, despite what Saddam Hussein presumed about them.

How can the potential salience of alternative identifications be assessed from the outside? A Lasswellian perspective would begin by asking which identifications serve the personalities of particular Iraqis in light of their upbringing, personal experiences, and current situations. The salience of identifications is partly rooted in life history, but is also partly plastic in response to evolving conditions. Vamik Volkan (2002) argued that the key to understanding large-group identity "is the psychodynamic process of linking the child's core identity to the large-group identity that is historically primary at the time of the child's development. . . . [T]he most compelling identifications are formed in childhood, reinforced by distinctive practices" (p. 4). He also maintained, "as a large-group organizing principle, ideology is less durable than religion, ethnicity, or nationality because it is less basic and more intellectual" (2002, p. 4).

A Lasswellian perspective would question the reductionism of this view, and point to a host of dynamics affecting the relative strengths of identifications. One possibility is that the identifications that are most congruent with the triple-appeal principle when individuals come of age will prevail. For example, Kurdish adolescents who were attracted to (or pressured into) Abdullah Ocalan's Marxist-oriented, Turkey-based Kurdish Workers Party (PKK) may have been heavily influenced by the fact that the PKK is associated with particular Kurdish clans. Yet, once the commitment to the PKK was established, the leftist revolutionary ideology may have become as central as ethnicity. The importance of Kurdish identity notwithstanding, the bloody clashes with other Kurdish groups led by Massoud Barzani or Jalal Talabani reinforced the ideological differences that have distinguished one group from another.[107] Ideological commitment can also help to counter the challenges to the superego that engaging in violence—especially against other Kurds. Is this fundamentally a matter of ideology or subethnicity? Lasswell would say that the more appropriate questions are how these identifications are linked to one another, and how unfolding events and conditions can influence the salience of multiple identifications.

In Iraq, then, the analytic challenge is to determine how the U.S.-led occupation, the governance options, and the diagnostic statements themselves would influence the salience of identifications. It is important to consider that specifying a dimension of identification as primary can have a self-fulfilling result. On a practical political level, people who are defined by the rules as constituting a particular group may act that way; on a psychological level, the official endorsement of a distinction may reinforce it as well (but note that the official denial of a particular identification can trigger a strong counterreaction, as in the case of Kurdish identity in Turkey).

What hypotheses are worth exploring to assess the likely strength of identifications, and what might influence their salience? One underlying psychological principle for assessing the salience of identifications is that particular identifications are rewarding in terms of id, ego, and superego. Another, more specific developmental principle is that the identifications that yielded deference and self-esteem at formative stages are likely to retain their strength in the long run. This latter principle suggests that an intensive analysis of Iraqi attitudes might reveal that different age cohorts have quite different profiles of identification salience. We would, of course, be interested in the identifications of politically pivotal cohorts: those of an age to be politically prominent now, those who are of the age to be active as insurgents, and so on.

This developmental principle notwithstanding, it would also be worthwhile to assess whether, as the climate of insecurity changes, the salience of different identifications would change as well. We can hypothesize that greater levels of stress and anxiety may induce the reversion to earlier identifications. Narrow ethnicity may prevail over broader identifications.

Assuming that elections will be held in Iraq, the identifications that women possess must also be assessed. It is possible that the new opportunities for women will attract them to identifications that are consistent with a democratic Iraq, but it is also possible that their possibly closer identifications with family and clan will prompt women to hold narrower ethnic identifications. Finally, recalling that *identification* refers to how individuals symbolize themselves (Lasswell & Kaplan, 1950), we can determine the salience of identifications by examining the narratives that are emerging from the experiences of Saddam Hussein's rule and the U.S.-led occupation.[108] However, this is a complicated task that requires anticipating the emergence of narratives in a situation in which various forces are likely to be trying to shape narratives in order to promote particular identifications. The strategic propaganda question is whether democratic forces can shape credible narratives that will reinforce democratic predispositions.

TRUTH COMMISSIONS

"Truth commissions"[109] are the most high-profile form of psychodrama in the contemporary era.[110] They have been established in a host of countries with recent histories of human and civil rights violations, and have been proposed in many more. Their proponents have had multiple goals: to address and heal the psychological scars of past human rights and civil rights violations; to publicize past offenses; to resocialize the population to regard human rights violations, dictatorship, and violence as unacceptable; and to promote political reconciliation.[111] These commissions have been prevalent in Latin America (Argentina, Bolivia, Chile, Ecuador, El Salvador, Guatemala, Haiti, Honduras, Panama, Peru, and Uruguay), Africa (Burundi, Chad, Nigeria, Uganda, South Africa, Sierra Leone, and Zimbabwe), and Asia (East Timor, Nepal, the Philippines, South Korea, and Sri Lanka). In Europe, Germany had one in the early 1990s following reunification, and Serbia and Montenegro launched a commission in 2002. There have been recent calls for truth commissions in Afghanistan, Bosnia-Herzegovina, Cambodia, Indonesia, Kenya, Malawi, Mexico, Pakistan, Rwanda, the Solomon Islands, and Venezuela.

Truth commissions are usually compromise strategies, situated between war crimes tribunals and blanket amnesties. Although in certain circumstances the most prominent perpetrators have been prosecuted through conventional criminal prosecutions, and some investigations and hearings conducted by truth commissions can lead to conventional criminal procedures (Hayner, 2002), truth commissions typically entail partial or full amnesty for many human-rights abusers and government officials involved in dictatorial practices. They sometimes entail limitations in the access to information about the activities of individuals receiving amnesties. Their essential narrative is that success means confession, forgiveness, and reconciliation. Indeed, the most prominent truth commission, at least in terms of analysis by international experts, has been the South African "Truth and Reconciliation Commission," which by its very title conveys that reconciliation is desirable and achievable.

The questions facing a government and society considering a truth commission include whether to launch the commission, how the commission is to be symbolized and framed, how to articulate its objectives, how to calibrate the expectations of retribution versus leniency, who should serve on the commission, when to launch the commission's work, what timetable to impose, and many other strategic and tactical issues. The Truth Commission Project—a joint venture of the Harvard Law School's Program in Negotiation and the international nongovernmental organizations Search for Common Ground and the European Centre for Common Ground—outlined nearly 50 policy-design dimensions for truth commission structures and procedures.[112] Another strategic dimension is the politics of gaining agreement on launching the truth commission and subsequent cooperation. How can the adherents of a particular truth commission initiative understand and respond to potential opposition or reluctance to participate?

A Lasswellian perspective would help to frame many of these issues. Lasswell's assessment of the politics of prevention raises the question of whether a particular design for a truth commission would channel emotions into constructive or destructive directions. Insofar as truth commissions are established after crises, one challenge is how to avoid the "reactivation of specific primitive impulses" (Lasswell, 1930/1960, p. 179). Will the activities of the truth commission revive and intensify the hatreds created by the original crimes?

Through the lens of the triple-appeal principle, the question is whether the proceedings of the truth commission will provoke aggressive impulses of retribution more than it will reinforce the superego demands for treating others with dignity, while also having the instrumental benefit of promoting attitudes favorable to intergroup cooperation. In favor of the truth commission logic, a psychodynamic perspective would point to the possibility that insofar as truth commissions can legitimately publicize offenses by actors on all sides of the conflict, they can minimize the tendencies of groups to demonize one another and reinforce narrow identifications rather than more inclusive ones. The victimization narratives, and particularly the "chosen trauma" (to use Vamik Volkan's term—see Volkan, 1997) can be modified with convincing information that offenses were not committed exclusively by "the enemy." In addition, documenting and publicizing past offenses can lessen the id impulses of revenge by minimizing the perception of a "double crime"—the original offenses and the denial that they occurred. As the Armenian–Turkish conflict assessed earlier in this chapter attests, removing the current cause of victimization and humiliation may reduce the moralistic underpinnings of further violence.

Although the focus on truth commission impacts has largely been on the perpetrators and the victims, a Lasswellian democratic character perspective would also focus on the impacts on the population in general, particularly those young enough to be susceptible to significant changes in predispositions (Lasswell, 1951). However, Lasswell's emphasis on broad identifications and optimism about societal improvement as elements of democratic character sounds the alarm that the truth commission could politically traumatize the impressionable if graphic testimony provokes cynicism rather than optimism.

The Politics of Truth Commissions

In light of this compromise nature, it is not surprising that truth commissions have been criticized from both sides. Although the avowed intentions of truth commissions include healing the traumas of the victims, the victims and their sympathizers often condemn the commissions for leniency toward alleged perpetrators, or for trying to diminish the importance of the violations. Alleged perpetrators and their sympathizers frequently condemn the commissions for failing to take into account the difficult situations that provoked their actions, or for dredging up issues that increase the desire for revenge.[113] In ethnic conflicts, the nondominant ethnic groups may fear that the truth commission will be used as a vehicle for legitimizing retribution. Both sides may object to the possibility that the truth commissions might undermine existing judicial institutions.

Disagreements on whether to proceed with truth commissions can easily be misunderstood if one does not employ all of the aspects of perspectives. Much of the discourse on truth commissions pits those most concerned with the implications of leniency and amnesty against those focusing on reconciliation and psychological healing. Differences in expectations explain much of the support for or opposition to truth commissions. Those who expect that truth commissions will reduce intergroup conflict and reinforce the superego demand that human rights violations are horrific will be strong adherents; the pessimists are more likely to see the dangers of the halfway status of the commissions.

Some critics, often associated with the international human rights movement, believe that the lesson drawn from truth commissions is that individuals guilty of heinous crimes not only avoid full criminal prosecution, but also entitled to forgiveness. Rather than instilling the strongest possible shame for the commission of human rights violations, the perpetrators—and potential future perpetrators—are or will be eligible for forgiveness and respect. Insofar as truth commissions situate human rights violations in the specifics of difficult conditions for all, they convey that these conditions, rather than the moral failures of the perpetrators, account for the violations. These critics assert that truth commissions promote "impunity," using this term in place of "amnesty." For example, Richard Mosier, in "Truth Commissions: Peddling Impunity" (2002) wrote, "The reasons for questioning amnesty grants, whether issued by a truth commission or by the fiat of a ruling regime, are manifold . . . granting amnesty (read impunity) to a human rights perpetrator is the victim's ultimate injury" (p. 1). Contrast this with the view espoused by Brandon Hamber (1995):

> The [South African Truth and Reconciliation Commission], by creating an accurate picture of the past, could liberate individuals and broader society from this skewed view of humanity constructed solely around the inhuman legacy of South African society. Furthermore, by creating a realistic perspective of past human rights abuses, individual and collective cognitive recovery could be aided by allowing survivors to accept what happened to them and deal with their resultant emotional responses. Importantly, through acknowledgement and uncovering the roots of the traumatic incident it could also serve to absolve the feelings of guilt and personal causal responsibility . . . that survivors often experience after traumatic events. (p. 3)

Some actors clearly have stronger demands for retribution, whereas others, identifying more strongly with living victims, are concerned with whatever psychological healing they believe the psychodrama will effect. Some demand that the aftermath of human rights violations must instill enough shame for these violations that future generations will not relapse; for these individuals, "truth and reconciliation" may very well fall short.

With valid objectives and concerns on both sides, how should policymakers proceed? Lasswell's consistent insistence on the importance of context is crucial for assessing the decision to launch a truth commission as well as decisions on design. Consider the issue of timing. Priscilla Hayner, the author of the most definitive assessment to date of truth commissions, wrote that "although the circumstances of each country differ, as a general rule a truth commission should begin as soon as possible after a political transition, should carry on for at least nine months and no longer than two or two and one-half years, and should always be given a deadline for completion, even if extendible" (2002, pp. 220–221). Yet, in a climate of insecurity and pessimism—perhaps occasioned by economic decline, political instability, or international conflicts—levels of stress and anxiety may amplify the antagonisms aroused by publicizing human rights violations (Lasswell, 1965a; also chap. 6 of this book). Vamik Volkan (1998) invoked an additional psychodynamic rationale for concern about an immediate truth commission:

> The idea of a group or its leader asking for forgiveness from another group or its leader may be a potentially powerful gesture if the groundwork has truly been laid. Forgiveness is possible only when the group that suffered has done a significant amount of mourning. The focus should be on helping with the work of mourning and not on the single (seemingly magical) act of asking forgiveness. Stubborn large-group conflicts cannot be solved by an instant-coffee approach. (p. 226)

More generally, each dimension of truth commission design ought to be assessed in terms of the psychodynamics of relevant groups and age cohorts, taking into account the prevailing general climate of crisis and levels of intergroup hostility. One would have to expect that the dynamics will be different in different countries, and that the effects—positive and negative—will be different for different groups.

INCULCATING DEMOCRATIC VALUES
IN LATIN AMERICAN MILITARIES

Many efforts have been undertaken to try to inculcate democratic values among military officers of nations struggling to consolidate democracy. Lasswell's very broad definition of democratic character—as the set of predispositions for sharing, give and take, and respect for human dignity—suggests a broader problem definition than simply whether the military will desist from intervening in the civilian sphere of governing the country. It extends to whether the military cooperates with civilian authorities, how the military interacts with civilians in areas contested by guerrillas or narcotraffickers, whether the officer corps will be open to entrée by individuals from outside of the military "caste," and whether the military will be willing to reduce its social isolation.

The predominant strategic thrust of efforts at the democratic socialization of the military has been on the content of their education. This is a cognitive orientation of the most basic sort—focusing not on cognitive processing of information, but on the information per se that is conveyed in the training in military academies and higher command schools.[114] To a certain degree, the curricula on democratic governance and human rights have been adopted by the military academies and command schools in many Latin American countries. In support of these efforts, as well as to cement relations between the armed forces of the host and guest countries, the militaries of established democracies (especially the U.S. military) have provided slots in their military schools for officers of countries with histories of military authoritarianism.

There are strong indications that this approach is of limited utility. Despite the addition of prodemocratic modules to varying degrees in Latin American military curricula, Frederick Nunn (1998) reported that "professional military thought and self-perception were comparable and evinced consistency across national borders and decades" (p. 350).

The Lasswellian framework suggests that the efforts to instill and reinforce democratic norms within the military officer corps should give greater emphasis on life experiences within their own organizations and countries, and on the personality formations that stem from these experiences. Consider this passage from Herbert Huser's 2002 book on Argentine civil–military relations:

> Argentina represents the refinement of this military socialization process through successive educational endeavors. Many observers credit the country's system of military schools with instilling the Argentine military officer with such a sense of professional perfection that he presumes himself suited for national decisionmaking at the highest levels. The system

includes military high schools, *liceos militares*, a principal source of reserve officers; the *Colegio Militar de la Nación*, the only source for army regular officers (with counterpart academies in the other services); and an array of branch, service, technical, and command and staff schools for each service. Moreover, the intensity and isolation of these experiences and their emphasis on the traditional military values of honor, discipline, and duty have until recently left little room for support of democracy (and the free expression and consensus that accompany it) in the military education process. In the words of an Argentine general of the Peronist era, antidemocratic feelings have been inculcated in the military. He expressed that the fundamentals of Argentine military doctrine on this issue are a phobia against the essential forms characterizing political cooperation in the great Western democracies; a lack of confidence and a deprecation for every citizen who feels a vocation for problems of a public nature (so-called professional politicians); and a lack of faith in the citizenry. (p. 16)

Few familiar with Argentina and its struggles would question the validity of most of Huser's interpretation, at least prior to the Argentine military's humiliating defeat over the Falkland (Malvinas) Islands at the hands of the British in 1982. The criticism of the content of military education for conveying the superiority of the military over civilians in public affairs is standard. Certainly the multiple failures of democratic experiments in Argentina make it unsurprising that the Argentine armed forces would have a jaundiced view of politicians and citizens.

Yet, Huser's interpretation is problematic in depicting the military as confident in the capabilities of the armed forces and the professionalism of fellow officers. In fact, the Argentine military has been riven by internal conflicts and recriminations, as evidenced by severe interservice rivalries, the clash between pro- and anti-Peronist officers, the succession of military coups against military presidents in the late 1960s and early 1970s, and the abortive revolts in 1986 and 1987. Thus, the military officer corps has displayed a high level of *general* distrust and pessimism characteristic of the antidemocratic, power-centered character that Lasswell sketched out in his essay on "Democratic Character" (1951; see also chap. 4 of this volume). Lasswell (1951) emphasized the importance of optimism as a basis for democratic character, especially with respect to the willingness to engage in give and take and the willingness to delay rewards while others share in power. Some elements of the military also displayed shocking callousness in the treatment of suspected subversives during the "Dirty War" of the mid-1970s. The Argentine officer corps has also held perspectives (e.g., that Peronism was a form of Communism; that in order to save democracy, the military had to ban democratically elected leaders; and that Argentina could prevail in a territorial confrontation with Great Britain) that have been so unrealistic or bizarre to outside observers that it is compelling to seek deeper explanations.

Could it be that the patterns of rewards and advancement within the premilitary and military training of the Argentine officer corps, reinforced by social isolation, instilled these jaundiced perspectives? The Lasswellian theory of political character would emphasize that insofar as the driving motivations for cadets and young officers are power, respect, and affection in relation to fellow officers and the rise within the military, these reward structures will shape the repertoire of actions that the individual will adopt to strive for deference and advancement. Could it be that officers were elevated not for their professional competence in general, but rather for their capacity to prevail in the infighting that marked the internal politics of the military in the post-World War II period? Could it be that capricious reward patterns, deliberate denial of respect, and rewarding dominance contributed to the development of the power-centered personalities, as Lasswell (1951) theorized?

None of these questions can be answered without in-depth analysis of individuals. Yet, insofar as these factors may have relevance in the Argentine case and in other armed forces with similar structures and conditions, we would look more deeply at the interpersonal interactions in premilitary and early military training in shaping character formation. Because the contact with the mechanisms of military socialization begins, in many instances, in the midadolescence of high school (if not before for those of military families), the potential for shaping democratic or antidemocratic character is stronger than for virtually any other institution.

A Lasswellian perspective would ask how id, ego, and superego demands can be reconciled in military actions and the articulation of doctrines that would shape the thinking of the future generations of military leaders. The impulses to assert superiority over civilians have found their channel in cultural criticism that paints civilian society as decadent and in continuing decline. Silvio Waisbord's interviews with midlevel officers in 1988 (following three abortive military revolts in 1987 and 1988) revealed that the greatest affront to military self-esteem was the prosecution of military officers accused of human rights violations during the "Dirty War" against leftist and Peronist activists (Waisbord, 1991). By magnifying the Communist threat, the officers rationalized the military's integrity, and painted the civilian sector as hypocritical as well as ungrateful. One might expect that the Argentine military would have been chastened or even humiliated by the human rights violations, yet it is in contrast with civilian decadence that the officers affirmed their moral superiority.

The plasticity of identifications also serves to protect the younger cohorts of officers from humiliation. Waisbord's interviews revealed that the middle-ranking officers (captains and majors) he interviewed in 1988 identified most strongly with their "generation" as distinct from those of more senior officers, and attributed the failure to convince the civilian sector of the necessity of all-out war against subversion, and folly of the Falklands War, to the generations of the generals in the mid-1970s and 1982.

Cultural criticism, published in military journals, aims at keeping cadets and junior officers from succumbing to decadence and other challenges to national values, but it also signifies the moral high ground that the officer corps asserts as part of its self-image. The centrality of articulating an ideology that upholds the military's righteousness may be a key to understanding the rise of extreme military leaders and eccentric positions. Despite the apparent equation between military leadership and the control over force and violence, some of the men who have risen to the highest prominence within the Argentine military have been the military intellectuals, such as General Ramón Díaz Bessone, whose "Guerra Revolucionaria en la Argentina 1959–1978" presented extreme premises concerning the thorough infiltration of Communism and the moral failure of civilian politicians. With the declining plausibility of a significant Communist threat in the Southern Cone countries, the criticism of civilian politics and society leveled by the militaries has come to focus on the general decadence of the civilian society—sex, crime, and the decline of religion (Nunn, 1998).

If we then return to the question of the efficacy of various models of democracy training for Latin American militaries, we would highlight the importance of embedding the content of military education in the interactions that make this content relevant—in the home context. Frederick Nunn (1998), who has used articles appearing in the journals of the Argentine, Brazilian, Chilean, and Peruvian armed forces as a window on their thought, noted that the predisposition for the military to intervene is more closely connected to the doctrines inculcated by the domestic military educational institutions than to those taught at the U.S.-based School of the Americas or other U.S. military training programs in which officers from these countries participate. Indeed, if we were to ask how discussions of democracy in a U.S. military school are likely to be interpreted by Latin American participants, we would have to consider the possibility that the contrast between the entrenched nature of democracy in the United States and the fragility and superficiality of democracy in many Latin American countries would reinforce the pessimism that underlies antidemocratic predispositions.

What, then, can be done by a democratic government that wishes to influence military attitudes? Gaining some control over the reward structures of young military officers would be an important step, as long as the interactions with civilians provide reliable, predictable rewards for good performance. This can be done in terms of controlling education, promotions, or both. Civilian involvement in cadet or officer instruction is important not only in terms of the content of education, but also because it would require junior officers to interact with civilian instructors. David Pion-Berlin (1992) noted that the Argentine military had the least overall autonomy of the five armed forces he assessed,[115] and yet military education was still the province of military officers, with no requirement for officers to be exposed to civilian instructors. Civilian instructors would also place civilians in positions of authority over officers, rewarding or punishing them in terms of evaluations that presumably would have some influence over career advancement. Other means of civilian control over junior officer advancement do not appear to be feasible for filtering out antidemocratic personalities. Pion-Berlin judged that all of the militaries he assessed had high levels of autonomy over junior officer personnel decisions.

However, civilian authorities play significant roles in senior officer advancement in all but Brazil among the countries assessed by Pion-Berlin, and particularly in Argentina and Peru (Pion-Berlin, 1992). Insofar as character is established early, senior-level advancement is a matter of screening rather than character formation. Insofar as power-centered, pessimistic, or narcissistic personalities can be recognized, these insights can (and probably often do) influence promotion decisions. Yet, optimism about the possibilities of detecting unusually problematic individuals among military officers should be tempered by the realization that antidemocratic orientations are often widespread within Latin American militaries. Moreover, authoritarian personalities are less likely to manifest themselves in neuroticism in military settings (Davids, 1957; Redl, 1971), reducing the chances that a particularly problematic individual could be recognized as such.

If the military high command is committed to instilling democratic character, what can it do? Even with more civilian interaction, the bulk of the interactions shaping cadets and junior officers will be with the military—both more senior officers and peers. Therefore, it is important to assess how young cadets or officers are rewarded, and for what attributes. Are excessive boldness, bravery, disregard for one's own well-being (which may be signs of narcissism), and the other pathologies of the agitator (Lasswell, 1930/1960) applauded or censured?

The political character profile of the officer corps can also be reshaped by changing recruitment patterns, bringing in young officers who had not been exposed to the earlier socialization of military families. This has been a common theme in the United States, Canada, and Western Europe, where diversity of the officer corps has been pursued through recruitment targeted at minorities, college-level reserve officer training programs, and reforms in aptitude testing. It has occurred in some Latin American countries, most notably in Brazil (McCann, 1989).

Another approach suggested by the Lasswellian framework is to redefine the military's identity by redefining its role. Nunn (1998) also pointed out that, following the Falklands disaster, the Argentine armed forces embraced the role of UN peacekeepers. He wrote, "Although the Argentine defense budget has shrunk and obligatory service (for decades a mainstay of the South American military ethos) has been eliminated, Argentines see their prestige restored by participating in peacekeeping" (p. 356). This new identification appears to be a tidy integration of practical and psychological needs.

NUCLEAR ENERGY AND SYMBOL ASSOCIATIONS

The various symbol associations related to nuclear energy add great complexity to the discourse on energy policy. The term *nuclear* (like the older symbol *atomic*) spans a broad range of phenomena, raising the possibility that affect from one flows to another beyond the actual connections that link the phenomena to one another. The fact that the public perceives nuclear technologies as the province of "big science," and as controlled by central governments, adds to this complexity.

The proponents of the nuclear power industry claim that public attitudes toward nuclear energy are irrational, because they are strongly colored by the associations between nuclear weapons and nuclear power. Perhaps the most explicit statement of this claim is the following:[116]

> The vastly different perception of a serious reactor accident by members of the public stems, in the first place, from a simple and subconscious word associations: atomic bombs and atomic energy in the early days, and nuclear weapons and nuclear energy now. Many people are still unaware that nuclear reactors simply cannot explode like nuclear weapons. These associations are reinforced by the media which, either deliberately or out of ignorance of the science involved, illustrate features on nuclear energy with images of mushroom clouds . . . and are shamelessly exploited by critics of nuclear energy. For instance, they compare the amount of radioactive material in a reactor with the amounts produced at Hiroshima and Nagasaki, concealing the fact that the vast majority of the bomb deaths were due to blast and fire, not radiation, and that the number of deaths were comparable to those in conventional fire-bomb raids on Tokyo. Some technologies are common to weapons and the peaceful applications but several are unique to the weapons. (Robertson, 2000/2003, p. 1)

More neutral observers harbor the same speculation. In its 1984 report on nuclear power, the U.S. Office of Technology Assessment noted, "[G]iven the level of national concern over the arms race, public acceptance of nuclear power cannot be expected to increase substantially until the two nuclear technologies are separated in people's minds" (p.). In 2002, a report of the Nuclear Energy Agency of the Organisation for Economic Co-Operation and Development asserted:

> Although the corresponding infrastructures are fairly separated, the applications of nuclear energy outside the electricity sector, i.e. nuclear weapons and use of isotopes mainly in medicine, remain interconnected in the minds of most members of the public. The perceived association of military uses and the risk of weapon proliferation with peaceful applications of nuclear energy is a key issue for assessing social risks and benefits of nuclear technologies. (p. 28)

Spencer Weart, author of the most extensive history of the antinuclear movement, concluded that the embrace of anti-nuclear-energy positions by anti-nuclear-weapons advocates "was partly due to a merging of images. Polls found a third of the world public still convinced that a reactor could blow up exactly like an atomic bomb, while many more thought that reactors offered at least a vague danger of 'nuclear explosion'" (1988, p. 321). Weart (1988) also asserted a displacement mechanism, referring to one antireactor activist as follows: "As a youth in Australia she had been deeply impressed by *On the Beach*, and when she grew up she helped lead a campaign against French bomb tests in the Pacific. When she moved to the United States and found nobody there interested in bombs any longer, she began to fight reactors" (p. 320).

It *may* be that symbol associations go beyond the actual relationships between nuclear energy and a host of other phenomena, ranging from nuclear war and irradiated food to big government and skepticism toward science. From a theoretical perspective, the connection would certainly not be surprising. "Dread," aroused by possibilities that have high uncertainty and whose negative consequences are difficult to grasp, has been shown to be most strongly evoked by unfamiliar risks that are outside of the individual's control and are associated with vivid images and large numbers of deaths (Slovic, 2000). Hiroshima and Nagasaki, and the image of the mushroom cloud, provide the otherwise missing attributes to heighten the dread of nuclear power plant meltdowns, which by themselves lack vivid imagery and large casualties. Attitudes toward "things nuclear" were formed in the context of atomic bomb drills, the Cuban Missile Crisis, and the Cold War confrontation in general.

However, the empirical evidence that the dread associated with nuclear energy exceeds the level appropriate for the very real risks of nuclear power plant accidents and other impacts of developing nuclear power is thin. It is not enough to demonstrate that those who oppose nuclear weapons also oppose nuclear energy, nor even that public assessments of nuclear energy risks are higher than are those assigned by experts. Nuclear weaponry and nuclear energy are not completely separate spheres. The technologies have some overlap, as do the fuels, and the development of nuclear energy industries has been a vehicle for the development of nuclear weapons systems (even if the proponents of nuclear energy can always counter that napalm is made from petroleum, and other weapons of mass destruction can emerge from the development of biotechnology). And although the public perception of nuclear power accidents is far greater than that assigned by risk experts,[117] various explanations have been offered, such as the argument that the public's concern with long-term consequences goes beyond the experts' preoccupation with historically based statistics.

The very limited empirical evidence, such as it is, comes from survey trends. Roper survey data show that the Reagan administration's heavily publicized 1982 deployment of missiles in Western Europe was followed by a very large increase in opposition to nuclear energy—from 41% to 56% (Rosa, 2001). Yet, here again it may be that the greater salience of nuclear weapons increased the proportion of the U.S. public convinced that no aspects of nuclear development should be pursued in those circumstances. It is, however, incontestable that the discourse on nuclear energy, and the structure of the organizations involved in the debate, explicitly link weapons, energy, big government, big science, and the environment.

Although the relative environmental merits of nuclear energy compared to other fuels are debated, it is certainly not clear that nuclear energy is more environmentally damaging than, say, oil and coal burning. Nuclear energy does not contribute to carbon dioxide emission, and therefore is benign in terms of global warming. However, antinuclear groups often embrace environmentalism, as well as "small is beautiful" and antigovernment orientations.[118]

Thus, energy policy analysts and policymakers have to decide how to interpret the public's reactions—are they colored by the symbol associations to a degree that compromises the pursuit of the common interest? The first effort should be to design explorations of belief systems to examine the flow of affects, such as focus groups, Q technique studies, and experiments that determine whether invoking nuclear weapons imagery alters the emotions toward nuclear energy.

If these analyses demonstrate that the symbol associations are creating an excessive level of negativity, strategies for decoupling the symbols should be explored. Yet, a number of challenges emerge even if we assume only that mention of nuclear energy evokes thoughts of nuclear weapons and war. Can the public assess the probabilities of nuclear accidents on their own terms? Can the discourse differentiate adequately between the phenomena, without denying that they do have some connection? Can constructive alternatives be presented and considered without being rejected out of hand? Does the debate have to be posed in crude "pronuke" versus "antinuke" terms?

It is important to inventory the characteristics that individuals attribute to nuclear energy to determine whether some of these characteristics are inaccurate. For example, it is likely that the vast majority of the public presumes that all nuclear reactors are potentially subject to core meltdown, whereas in fact new nuclear reactor designs, such as the pebble-bed modular reactor system, have zero risk of meltdown. What are the worst-case scenarios if a nuclear power plant accident occurred?

The analysis could also examine the history of how nuclear phenomena were linked, in order to determine whether greater differentiation could be accomplished. In the United States, nuclear energy development was defined in relation to nuclear weapons since the early 1950s.[119] Eisenhower's "Atoms for Peace" program was explicitly dedicated to transforming the horrors of the atomic bomb into the marvel of bountiful, cheap, and clean atomic energy. Thus, even for those who accepted the exaggerated claims of costs and safety, the connection between nuclear energy and nuclear weapons was apparent. Although the debate about the military's role in the development of nuclear technologies culminated in a civilian Atomic Energy Commission, the nuclear plant designs were scaled-up versions of the reactors designed for nuclear submarines, creating a further association with the military.

Nuclear energy, nuclear weapons, and other phenomena involving radiation are also connected in their associations with centralized government and big science. Just as nuclear arms are under federal control, the federal government's Atomic Energy Commission (later the Nuclear Regulatory Commission) was the dominant voice in public discourse, and for decades was unabashedly in favor of nuclear energy. The antinuclear movement's distrust of big government resonates with the long-standing undercurrent of anticentralization, no doubt exacerbated by revelations of coverups of nuclear incidents and reports pointing to the risks of nuclear energy. Government scientists, in turn, were implicated in the coverups of nuclear-energy risk studies, some of which were later disclosed under the Freedom of Information Act. Yet, the vast majority of U.S. nuclear power reactors are built, owned, and operated by the private sector—the Atomic Energy Commission yielded these responsibilities a half century ago. The symbol cluster of nuclear energy, nuclear weapons, and dominance by big government may be historical as much as it is intrinsic.

The ambiguous symbolism of science is also complex. The Roper survey revealed that the majority of the American public opposes new nuclear reactors, but believes that nuclear energy ought to be an important part of *future* energy supply (Rosa, 2001). This may reflect a bifurcation involving skepticism toward the combination of government and scientists to implement safe technology, but faith in scientific advancement to create technologies beyond the possibility of failure. Thus, the invocation of "nuclear (or atomic) science" is likely to arouse multiple and entangled associations and affects.

In one of the very few intensive analyses of public attitudes toward U.S. energy issues, Brunner and Vivian (1980) used the Q technique to explore a cross-section of American attitudes in mid-1979, reflecting the painful energy decade of the 1970s:

> The predominant themes are resistance to energy price increases and concern for public health, safety, and the environment, particularly in connection with nuclear power plants. There is also widespread distrust of the oil and gas industry, local utilities, the President, and energy experts, coupled with disbelief, disorientation, disaffection, and undertones of moral outrage. (p. 148)

Another related effort would be to examine why nuclear energy appears to have been debated with greater dispassion in other countries. France would be an obvious focus of inquiry: Although France does have an antinuclear movement, the acceptance of nuclear energy in France has been among the most extensive in the world.[120] It would appear that the French concerns with energy vulnerability following the 1973 oil embargo were able to overcome the fears that paralyzed nuclear development in many other countries. Or perhaps the stronger tradition and acceptance of centralized government in France renders the association between nuclear energy and "big government" less salient than in the United States. Yet, beyond the fixed circumstances of energy supply, part of the French nuclear energy strategy has been to involve the public in a "concertation" process in the planning of nuclear facilities.[121] By bringing the public into closer contact with the details of nuclear energy issues, or at least providing the public the opportunity for closer involvement, any excessive associative connection between nuclear weapons and nuclear energy may diminish.

LABOR UNION BARGAINING AND LEADERSHIP

Establishing and maintaining constructive labor–management relations raises four challenges for political psychology. Let us examine these challenges strictly from the perspective of labor union members interested in optimizing their economic standing and working conditions. Of course, parallel analyses could be conducted from the perspectives of management or the government.

The first challenge is to determine whether particular charismatic union leaders are beneficial or detrimental to the interests of the union members. In many circumstances, strong leaders who can mobilize union members in order to mount credible strike threats can be a tremendous advantage. However, charismatic union leaders may derive their popularity from characteristics unrelated to whether they are being responsive to union membership. For union members who are less well educated or financially compensated than are the executives and officials involved in labor negotiations, the charismatic appeal of labor leaders may be based on the sense of deprivation of respect and power vis-à-vis employers and government officials. The articulate, dynamic, labor leader who conveys an image of combativeness and rejection of the socioeconomic pecking order can often capitalize on these deprivations. The capacity to arouse emotional responses through articulate expression, the demand for deference, and the appearance of disdain for personal consequences are often admired (Lasswell, 1930/1960), even if in reality the narcissistic leader is obsessed with personal consequences.

In some cases, especially in the United States, another basis for charisma is literal inheritance from father to son—Strauss (2000) noted the prevalence of national union leadership passing in this fashion at the national level of some of the most important U.S. unions. The literature on such succession emphasizes the entrenched leadership's dominance of the union's communication and decision-making mechanisms, but a political psychology perspective would also raise the possibility of the displacement of affection and loyalty from the father to the son.

The risk is that the charismatic union leader, taking advantage of the lack of accountability that charisma entails, will pursue narcissistic objectives. The problem is that it is very difficult to determine whether brinksmanship—sometimes necessary to obtain the best negotiating outcome—is actually self-indulgence. As Conger and Kanungo (1998) noted, "[C]harismatic leaders can be prone to extreme narcissism that leads them to promote highly self-serving and grandiose aims. As a result, the leader's behaviors can become exaggerated, lose touch with reality, or become vehicles for pure personal gain" (p. 211).

Determining whether a union leader is inappropriately power oriented is not an easy task. Political confrontation can be a legitimate strategy for the achievement of economic gain, and frequently labor's right to fight for economic gain becomes a political issue requiring confrontation, often beyond what is needed for the specific economic issue at hand, and sometimes involving confrontation with government as well as private employers. Even so, the potential for conflict (the principal–agent problem) arises, especially when union members would benefit from quick resolution of labor conflicts, but the leader prolongs the conflict in order to engage in and win the power struggle against employers or, in some instances, the government. However, in addition to judging whether the leader's relationship with actors outside of the union is ultimately counterproductive—a judgment that is inevitably arguable—the analyst can also look for clues in the behavior of the leader within the politics of the union, where the nature of tactics and confrontation ought to be different. We would begin by examining the life history of the leader as he or she rose to prominence within the union. Has the leader been rewarded by agitational activities more than by actions that provide economic benefits for followers? Has the leader ever sacrificed an opportunity for personal advancement for the interests of the union? Was the charismatic resource used to stifle the careers of other competent union leaders? Has the leader been faced with past opportunities to make major economic gains for the union, but instead chose confrontation? Union members may be able to examine how the leader privately diagnoses the utility of political confrontation, to determine whether the emphasis on power is a strategy or a compulsion.

The second challenge is to determine whether—and if so, how—charismatic appeals can be minimized in leadership choice. Union members who accept a leader as being above questioning lose their capacity to judge whether their interests are being served. One could explore the mechanisms for ensuring power sharing (broadly speaking, checks and balances in union decision making; specifically, union council approval of decisions on strikes, greater voice of the rank and file, secret ballots for elections and strike votes, etc.).[122] Narcissistic leaders are more likely to reveal their maladaptation in such contexts.

The third challenge is to determine whether the union's demands are taking on symbolic significance that interferes with the constructive pursuit of union members' interests. For example, demands for health care benefits may become symbolically important because of the associations with caring for one's family, even if their monetary value could be recouped through higher wage levels or other benefits. In many countries, governments and political parties are perceived as pro- or anti-union, giving the strike additional political and symbolic significance, which may or may not in the interests of union members. On some occasions union leaders must learn to capitalize on symbolism to mobilize union members, yet on other occasions they must learn how to deflate the intensity of particular symbolic associations.

The fourth challenge is to determine whether displacements are distorting the stance that union members and leaders take toward employers and the government. The typically lower education and income levels of union members can create deprivations of respect that may be difficult to address if the hostility is displaced onto economic issues such that the union membership becomes recalcitrant even when objectively attractive offers are made. Union leaders often recognize the promotional advantages of playing the respect card. Indeed, it is hard to find a union–management confrontation in which union leaders do not claim that management, the government, or both are treating unionists disrespectfully.

Chapter 8

Conclusion: The Role of the Political Psychiatrist

Lasswell presented positive models for leaders, citizens, and political discourse, but in focusing on the potential pitfalls of these models, most of his analysis centers on the pathologies that can undermine these models. Ultimate goals are neither rational nor irrational, but the concrete objectives that individuals set for themselves—and the strategies they choose to pursue them—may be irrational in terms of achieving the individual's interests, whether selfish or altruistic. Healthy political and policy discourse requires minimizing the irrational. If individuals act contrary to their own interests, the societal impact will often be destructive.

In light of Lasswell's pervasive emphasis on these pitfalls of psychopathology, human destructiveness, and the character deformations caused by deprivation and anxiety, one might be tempted to think of Lasswell as a Jeremiah. Yet, Harvard psychiatrist Miles Shore (2001) called Lasswell "one of the most hopeful and influential political scientists exploring ways in which [political science and psychiatry] might benefit one another" (p. 192).

What accounts for this positive, optimistic assessment of Lasswell as "hopeful"? Shore recognized that in identifying the deepest sources of unproductive, irresponsible, or undemocratic behavior, Lasswell held out the promise of being able to address and rectify these behaviors. He promised that the application of scientific approaches to political psychology would provide freedom from destructive compulsiveness and thereby from destructive behaviors (1951). However, the crucial questions are: How should these behaviors be addressed, and by whose authority? The answer hinges on the concept of self-insight, which is also a key to addressing the controversy over the use of the concept of the unconscious.

In this concluding chapter, we link Lasswell's fundamental diagnosis of political psychopathologies with his prescriptions for minimizing undemocratic and irresponsible political behavior. In so doing, we try to correct the most serious distortion of Lasswell's position, which comes from misreading his position on the role of the "political psychiatrist." Particularly in the "Politics of Prevention" chapter of *Psychopathology and Politics* (1930/1960, chap. 10), but also in two articles written in the dark years of the late 1930s (1938b; 1939), Lasswell called for intervention to address the gap between what individuals seek and what would truly serve their overall interest. He wrote that the:

> findings of personality research show that the individual is a poor judge of his own interest. The individual who chooses a political policy as a symbol of his wants is usually trying to relieve his own disorders by irrelevant palliatives. An examination of the total state of the person will frequently show that his theory of his own interests is far removed from the course of procedure which will give him a happy and well-adjusted life. (1930/1960, p. 194)

Lasswell (1930/1960) noted that, scaled up to the society or polity, "the politics of prevention draws attention squarely to the central problem of reducing the level of strain and maladaptation in society" (p. 197). As reviewed in chapter 6, Lasswell urged political leaders to address the fundamental causes of stress and personality deformation, lying largely in the deprivation of respect and human dignity. Yet, short of such societal transformations, he also recommended strategies that arise from applying psychiatric principles to politics.

This might seem to call for the conclusion that the political psychiatrist ought to play the role of philosopher king or queen, deciding what is best for the public whether or not the public acknowledges or accepts it. However, this conclusion is completely at odds with Lasswell's position, which is strictly in keeping with the treatment philosophy of psychoanalysis that psychopathologies are resolved only through the insight of the afflicted. In his 1951 essay on "Democratic Character," Lasswell wrote:

> It is insufficiently acknowledged that the role of scientific work in human relations is *freedom* rather than prediction. By freedom is meant the bringing into the focus of awareness of some feature of the personality which has hitherto operated as a determining factor upon the choices made by the individual, but which has been operating unconsciously. Once elevated to the full focus of waking consciousness, the factor which has been operating "automatically and compulsively" is no longer in this privileged position. The individual is now free to take the factor into consideration in the making of future choices. (p. 524; emphasis in original)

The philosopher king/queen who is tempted to enact what citizens "really want" without their knowing it would have to suppress the opposition of the very citizens whose welfare is being pursued, or would have to delude them into thinking that their demands are being addressed even when they are not. Lasswell (1930/1960) was explicit in rejecting these options as undemocratic:

The recognition that people are poor judges of their own interest is often supposed to lead to the conclusion that a dictator is essential. But no student of individual psychology can fail to share the conviction of Kempf that "Society is not safe . . . when it is forced to follow the dictations of one individual, of one autonomic apparatus, no matter how splendidly and altruistically it may be conditioned." (1930/1960, p. 197)

In fact, Lasswell's position, consistent with the therapeutic model of psychoanalysis, is that progress in treatment requires insight. Techniques for bringing the client, leader, or citizen to insight are the tools of the political psychiatrist. These range, as Arnold Rogow (1969b) pointed out, from education to "situational therapy" (p. 138).

The concept of insight is also crucial for finessing the disagreement over the unconscious. The issue of whether unconscious mechanisms need to be invoked has been engaged in most of the chapters of this book, particularly with respect to the mechanisms of displacement, the impact of id and superego impulses, and the spillover of affect among objects of overlapping symbol association. We have argued that some of the mechanisms that Lasswell offered to understand political behavior do not require reliance on notions of the unconscious. For example, chapter 2 outlined several mechanisms of displacement that involve social interactions and interpersonal communications rather than literal psychological repression. However, we must retain some notion of the lack of insight, or the heart of Lasswell's contributions would be lost.

For most practical purposes, lack of insight can be equated with lack of conscious awareness of the origins or implications of identifications, demands, and expectations, whether or not we wish to debate the usefulness of theorizing about the nature and mechanisms of unconscious dynamics. We retain the crucial point that individuals will not behave responsibly and democratically without insight into the forces that lead them into destructive actions. The political psychiatrist has the difficult, and sometimes risky, task of bringing leaders and citizens to these insights. At the same time, the debate over the nature of the underlying psychodynamics cannot be swept under the rug entirely, because the diagnosis on this point will shape the political psychiatrist's, and the leader's, assessment of the brittleness of the existing perspectives and how to address these perspectives if they persist (see the discussion on the management of unconscious and conscious displacements in chap. 2).

The concept of the political psychiatrist is, of course, not to be taken literally as someone who hangs up a shingle in an office opposite the White House or 10 Downing Street. Lasswell, as usual, was referring to a functional rather than a conventional role. Therefore, the question remains: Who would serve this function? The answer is that it can be performed by individuals in a number of different roles. Media commentators writing for newspaper editorial pages and serious opinion magazines have often pointed out inconsistencies of leaders' and the public's attitudes and behaviors. Courageous political advisors can inform leaders when their behaviors seem to reveal internal conflicts and inconsistencies. Civic groups sometimes launch campaigns to disabuse the public of prejudices that clash with norms and aspirations for a more just society. Government-sponsored efforts to confront the population about its prior or current destructive behavior can also play a role if they force the public to reexamine basic beliefs. South Africa's Truth and Reconciliation Commission has combined revelations of past crimes with a psychodrama on race relations, forgiveness, and accountability. The writings of political psychologists—at universities or think tanks—can also make a significant contribution if they are written broadly enough.

Political leaders themselves also have a responsibility to guide citizens to greater understanding of how to secure the common interest and maintain democratic practice and ethical behavior. This was epitomized by George Washington's efforts to discourage the charismatic impulse to make him king. These lessons sometimes require painful confrontations that risk the leaders' popularity. For example, President Jimmy Carter tried to convince the American people that the energy crisis of the late 1970s reflected the inconsistency of the public's desires for material indulgence and security. On July 15, 1979, Carter's "Crisis of Confidence" speech warned: "In a nation that was proud of hard work, strong families, close-knit communities and our faith in God, too many of us now tend to worship self-indulgence and consumption. Human identity is no longer defined by what one does but by what one owns." The reaction was decidedly negative, eroding Carter's already declining support. These dangers aside, the politician who aspires to healthy transformational leadership often has to enlighten followers about the id impulses that block their capacity to transcend their selfish or destructive impulses.

FINAL THOUGHTS

We have seen that Harold Lasswell pioneered in the careful analysis of psychological mechanisms such as displacement, the management of anxiety in periods of crisis and deprivation, and the nonrational id and superego appeals of leaders and policies. His analysis of the psychodynamics of the impact of political symbols was a great advance beyond the analysis of symbols that preceded him. His framework for linking political demands to identifications (also subject to symbol manipulations), connected communications, individual perspectives, and political action. His application of personality theory and learning theory to the development of democratic and antidemocratic character revolutionized the analysis of both political leadership and the behavior of the body politic. Through these constructs, Lasswell introduced American political science to the wide range of psychological mechanisms that can shape political behavior, and demonstrated that these mechanisms and their consequences can be analyzed with contextually sensitive sophistication.

Lasswell's project in political psychology should be seen as the broadest assessment of how psychodynamics can affect political behavior, without making psychopathology the reductionist explanation of politics. Many of these dynamics involve unconscious mechanisms, which present distinctive issues because of the importance of insight to address inappropriate behaviors. When emotions toward public figures or policies reflect displaced emotions, or when id and superego impulses dominate over reason, these mechanisms can be definitive, even though conscious mechanisms are in principle no less important. This synthesis provides the richest framework for political psychologists to recapture the full range of influences on political behavior.

Endnotes

[1] The UCLA group comprised of David Sears, James Sidanius, and their students exemplifies this commitment. See, for example, Sears, Sidanius, and Bobo (1999), and Sidanius, Feshbach, Levin, and Pratto (1997).

[2] An exception was Moore (1989).

[3] Excluding, of course, the political analysis still conducted in the psychoanalytic tradition. See, for example, the articles published in the *Journal for the Psychoanalysis of Culture & Society.*

[4] This term is chosen to denote the dual ideas that political predispositions serve needs; that is, they are "functional" in the sense conveyed by Daniel Katz (1960) in his classic categorization of attitudes (knowledge, instrumentality, ego defense, and value expression), and because some of these arise from internal psychological needs. However, we do not presume that these psychological needs are necessarily ego-defense functions. Therefore, the definition is very close to what Smith, Bruner, and White (1956) termed *externalization.* They wrote:

> *Externalization.* It would be all too easy to equate externalization of inner requirements with the classical conceptions of projection and displacement. These two mechanisms are two *examples* of what we mean by externalization. Externalization occurs when an individual, often responding unconsciously, senses an analogy between a perceived environmental event and some unresolved inner problem. He adopts an attitude toward the event in question which is a transformed version of his way of dealing with his inner difficulty. By doing so, he may succeed in reducing some of the anxiety which his own difficulty has been producing. (p. 43)

[5] Such patterns are parallel to the neurosis, which reflects an accommodation to anxiety or some other painful emotional state, but in so doing is maladaptive in a broader sense and may well bring on unhappy repercussions.

[6] We do not want to claim exhaustiveness, because the point here is to identify what is largely absent from contemporary political psychology, rather than to beg the question of the appropriate scope of useful psychodynamic functional theory within the definition per se.

[7] Harold Lasswell elaborated on this point in "The Psychology of Hitlerism" (1933/1948), which is reviewed more fully later in this book.

[8] Here we refer to the scientific positivism of Ernst Mach. See Mach (1897/1959). See also Thayer (1968).

[9] Cosin, Freeman, and Freeman (1982) described the scientific conception of Frank Cioffi, a prominent anti-Freudian, as follows: "A scientific theory consists essentially of related hypotheses each of which is empirically refutable, and there is an injunction upon scientists to expose their working hypotheses to (potentially falsifying) severe tests. Analysis of the generation of hypotheses is considered methodologically less important than their refutability" (p. 33).

[10] Consider the model (elaborated later in this book) of individuals who suffer from severe deprivations in respect, but find that strong assertions of power gain them defer-

ence; this reinforcement shapes a power-centered personality that contributes to extreme political beliefs in circumstances that may trigger radical action if the individual's political standing is threatened.

[11] Erwin (1996) provided a lengthy argument against the possibility of definitively demonstrating the existence of unconscious material, despite the many efforts to do so. McKeown (1984) offered a clever paradigm for detecting the effects of material beyond the subject's awareness via the Q-sort method. Yet the skeptics adopting Erwin's position would still find the demonstration unconvincing.

[12] This is not to deny that there are significant communities of psychoanalysts who work on social and political issues. However, these communities have little impact on the mainstream academic training of political scientists and social psychologists.

[13] We can point to the development of the Q technique as a remarkable innovation. See Brown (1980).

[14] It is telling that Freud himself warned of the dangers of extrapolating from the individual to the society. In *Civilization and Its Discontents* (1929/1961), Freud wrote:

I would not say that an attempt . . . to carry psycho-analysis over to the cultural community was absurd or doomed to be fruitless. But we should have to be very cautious and not forget that, after all, we are only dealing with analogies and that it is dangerous, not only with men but also with concepts, to tear them from the sphere in which they have originated and been evolved. Moreover, the diagnosis of communal neuroses is faced with a special difficulty. In an individual neurosis we take as our starting point the contrast that distinguishes the patient from his environment, which is assumed to be 'normal'. For a group all of whose members are affected by one and the same disorder no such background could exist; it would have to be found elsewhere. And as regards the therapeutic application of our knowledge, what would be the use of the most correct analysis of social neuroses, since no one possesses authority to impose such a therapy upon the group? (p. 110)

[15] Useful summaries of Lasswell's biography and intellectual history can be found in McDougall (1984), Muth, Finley, and Muth (1990), and Rogow (1969a, in particular the essay by Smith, 1969).

[16] For an account of pragmatism at the University of Chicago, where Lasswell received both his undergraduate and graduate training and taught until WWII, see Karl (1974).

[17] Lasswell and Kaplan (1950).

[18] In his 1939 essay, "The Prolonged Insight Interview of Freud," Lasswell (1939a/1948) wrote:

The propositions which have been stated by psychoanalysis have been tremendously stimulating, even to those who were without the special training necessary to understand them fully. Among social anthropologists of standing who have been explicitly affected by psychoanalytical hypotheses, Bronislaw Malinowski and Margaret Mead have been particularly prominent. Among sociologists, Erich Fromm and John Dollard are conspicuous examples. In the field of political sociology and psychology, the study of the genesis of attitudes toward authority has been given new impetus. The theory of law has not been unaffected, notably by way of Hans Kelsen. (Lasswell, 1939a/1948, p. 286)

[19] To Lasswell, conventional labels—what people call particular institutions or practices—were analytically treacherous because the same label may be placed on different things, and the same things from a functional perspective would be given different labels. Even mid-level generalizations are far more difficult when unlike things are treated as if they are the same, or the opportunity to aggregate like things is neglected because they receive different labels. Thus, all those things labeled as "government" are presumed to govern, but other institutions outside of "government" often wield authoritative power as well, and certain governments or subgovernmental institutions do not govern at all. See Lasswell and McDougal (1992, pp. 389–391).

[20] Lasswell and McDougal (1992) referred to Malinowski's interviewing approach as being "in typically brilliant fashion" (p. 903).

[21] See, for example, the chapter on "The Prolonged Interview and Its Objectification" in Lasswell (1930/1960).

[22] For example, Baas and Brown (1973), and McKeown (1984).

[23] In *The Ego and the Id* (1923/1960), Freud praised Otto Rank's "good examples of the way in which neurotic acts of revenge can be directed toward the wrong people" (p. 44).

[24] Two cases recounted by Lasswell demonstrate these patterns:

Although A never frankly faced his own animosity toward this brother, he was plagued by a sense of guilt for his unfraternal attitude. This conflict was partially resolved by a reactive formation and by displacement. The reactive formation was the reverse of the anti-brother drive, but it was only supportable by displacing his affection upon remote social objects. (1930/1960, p. 93)

O displaced much of his animosity on to remote, abstract symbols of authority, like kings and capitalists, and devoted himself to destroying them. Much of his affection was likewise displaced upon abstract ideals of a fatherless fraternal society, living together without coercion. (1930/1960, p. 159)

[25] Lasswell's use of the term *political man* is not the generic term for the political side of all individuals, in the fashion of saying that "man is a political/social/economic animal." Lasswell (1930/1960) referred to *non-political man* as one who is simply not involved in politics and public affairs in a significant way.

[26] Rogow (1969b) also noted that Lasswell's analysis of Hitlerism emphasized how anti-Semitism fended off feelings of guilt pertaining to declining piety, sexual propriety, and diligence.

[27] Freud (1940/1969, p. 17): "We have found that instincts can change their aim (by displacement) and also that they can replace one another—the energy of one instinct passing over to another."

[28] This is often termed the *Stockholm Syndrome*, after the episode of four Swedes who were held captive for 6 days in 1973 by bank robbers who treated them with a mix of threats and kindness. The captives resisted rescue efforts, strongly defended the robbers, and two subsequently became engaged to the robbers.

[29] Examining the intensity of our views of contemporary political leaders can be used as an introspective device for appreciating the nonrational aspects of the intensity of political attitudes. Consider the remarkable tendency of Americans to believe that we really know enough about George W. Bush and Albert Gore to have strong opinions of admiration or contempt toward them, despite the fact that many of us also know that their public images have been very deliberately manipulated; such figures are really fundamentally artificial, manufactured images. See, for example, Bill Turque's *Inventing Al Gore* (2000). Jay Martin (2001) argued that the politicians who can shift their apparent identities can take advantage of the public's tendency to accept superficial attributions of political figures as being more fundamental than they really are.

[30] The key difficulty of definitively demonstrating the operation of unconscious dynamics holds for any approach to inferring unconscious phenomena. When experimenters try to create unconscious material—for example, through subliminal messages designed to trigger particular behaviors—the skeptics ask how the experimenter definitively knows that the stimuli were not consciously perceived prior to or at the time that the behavior occurred. Thus, Silverman's experiments with provocative subliminal pictures do find measurable outcomes, such as increased stuttering or levels of depression, but critics question whether the subliminal messages are truly subliminal throughout the experiment (Erwin, 1996; Holender, 1986; Silverman & Weinberger, 1985). The approach of creating material through hypnotic suggestion (McKeown, 1984) such that the material is not consciously accessible until triggered by some cue, does not necessarily reflect the operation of repression. The approach of identifying inconsistencies between preexisting unconscious material and conscious material—for example, by showing that perspectives revealed through Q-technique analysis are surprising to the conscious awareness of the subject (Baas & Brown, 1973)—can be challenged on the grounds that these perspectives are complex, poorly understood implications of consciously accessible beliefs, rather than manifestations of unconscious material. Finally, it should be obvious that theories positing behavior resulting from totally inaccessible unconscious material have no chance of verification.

[31] This etiology of "intensification of emotion" was mentioned by Freud (1921/1959, p. 10) in his review of LeBon.

[32] This points to the essential connection between psychoanalysis as therapeutic technique and psychoanalytic theory. Psychoanalysis, with its methods of lengthy observation and free association, began as a treatment method to bring repressed material to the conscious level where it could be reassessed. As long as one is committed to the necessity of such intensive and lengthy procedures for bringing thoughts into consciousness, the distinction between materials requiring such efforts (i.e., unconscious materials) and materials that are merely outside of awareness at a particular moment must loom very large.

[33] This is most straightforwardly illustrated in his *Pre-View of the Policy Sciences* (Lasswell, 1971).

[34] In the afterthoughts of the 1960 edition of *Psychopathology and Politics*, Lasswell wrote that

the most comprehensive proposition [linking developmentally significant experiences to political roles and types] is that *power-centered personalities are developed by individuals who come to rely upon power practices (rôles) as the preferred means of maximizing their value position. This comes about in response to deprivations received from persons who are also regarded as sources of greatest indulgence. Strong rage and persistence responses find outlets that are successful in mitigating deprivations though not in reinstating full indulgence.* (p. 300; italics in the original)

[35] See Ellenberger (1970), especially chapter 4, for the history of this lineage.

[36] Lasswell's most directly applicable writings on symbolization and propaganda can be found in Lasswell (1927a, 1927b/1971, 1930/1960, 1932, 1933/1948, 1935a, 1935b/1965, 1950). A three-volume edited collection was published posthumously. (Lasswell, Lerner, & Speier, 1979–1980). An excellent analysis of Lasswell's contributions to the study of propaganda can be found in Horwitz (1962).

[37] James (1890/1950) wrote:

Why a single portion of the passing thought should break out from its concert with the rest and act, as we say, on its own hook, and other parts should become inert, are mysteries which we can ascertain but not explain. Possibly a minuter insight into the laws of neural action will someday clear the matter up; possibly neural laws will not suffice, and we shall need to invoke a dynamic reaction of the form of the consciousness upon its content. (pp. 1580–1581)

[38] *Politics: Who Gets What, When, How* (1936b/1958) is perhaps Lasswell's most widely cited book, and this distributional conception of politics is frequently taken as Lasswell's definitive definition of politics. A more refined definition, however, is "the shaping and sharing of values."

[39] The full statement is: "From the point of view of morality, the control and restriction of instinct, it may be said of the id that it is totally non-moral, of the ego that it strives to be moral, and of the super-ego that it can be hyper-moral and then becomes as ruthless as only the id can be."

[40] See the first case presented in chapter 7 of this volume.

[41] It is important to note that "ego" in this sense is not the personality component of id, ego, and superego, but simply refers to the individual, "minded" organism (Lasswell & Kaplan, 1950).

[42] According to Lasswell (1935b/1965), negative identifications arise when the other is identified "with some aspect of our own personality which we deplore as weak or disreputable. In this case we reject the profferred pattern and release profoundly destructive impulses" (p. 28).

[43] This corresponds to the "social adjustment function" of attitudes, as defined by Smith, Bruner, and White (1956, pp. 41–42).

[44] "Now people who act together get emotionally bound together. . . . Freud said that he was made clearly aware of the emotional factor in human relations by observing that those who work together extend their contact to dining and relaxing together" (Lasswell, 1930/1960, p. 185).

[45] In *Power and Society* (1950), Lasswell and Kaplan expressed the caveat in introducing these values that "it is not assumed that these are the only values which may be objects of scientific inquiry or practical action" (p. 55).

[46] Lasswell's position was consistent with Karen Horney's (1939) insight on neuroses:

When character trends are no longer explained as the ultimate outcome of instinctual drives, modified only by the environment, the entire emphasis falls on the life conditions molding the character and we have to search anew for the environmental factors responsible for creating neurotic conflicts; thus disturbances in human relationships become the crucial factor in the genesis of neuroses. A prevailingly sociological orientation then takes the place of a prevailingly anatomical-physiological one. (p. 9)

[47] Karen Horney (1939), a teacher and friend of Lasswell in the early 1930s, disputed the prevalence of the superego by arguing that

[t]he whole concept of the "super-ego" is fundamentally changed if we regard the individual's efforts as directed toward a "pretense" of perfection and infallibility, which for some reason it is necessary to maintain. The "super-ego" is then no longer a special agency within the "ego" but it is a special need of the individual. It is not the advocate of moral perfection, but expresses the neurotic's *need to keep up appearances of perfection.* (p. 216, emphasis added)

[48] "Rational choice theories" typically rest on three premises: Actors have "objective functions" (i.e., goals, and priorities among those goals) that are known to the analyst; these actors choose optimal ("rational") actions to achieve these objectives; and the analyst also knows which actions are optimal (and therefore can predict what the actors will do). For ease of analysis, rational choice theorists often presume that objective functions are stable, simple, and uniform across broad classes of roles. See Becker (1976) and Elster (1986).

[49] Doob was clearly targeting Lasswell, because *World Politics and Personal Insecurity* was the only publication that Doob (1935) cited in his discussion of symbols.

[50] In his 1933 essay on "The Psychology of Hitlerism," Lasswell wrote

There is a profound sense in which Hitler himself plays a maternal role for certain classes in German society. His incessant moralizing is that of the anxious mother who is totally preoccupied with the physical, intellectual and ethical development of her children. He discourses in public, as he has written in his autobiography, on all manner of pedagogical problems, from the best form of history teaching to the ways of reducing the ravages of social disease. His constant preoccupation with "purity" is consistent with these interests; he alludes constantly to the "purity of the racial stock" and often to the code of personal abstinence or moderation. (1933/1948, p. 240)

[51] The most sophisticated treatment of the Watergate and related symbols is found in the work of Ronald D. Brunner (especially 1987).

[52] The lack of receptivity to the term *character* is reflected in the fact that the journal *Character and Personality*, a collaboration between British and American psychologists, was retitled the *Journal of Personality* when it came under American dominance. (We are grateful to Steven R. Brown for bringing this to our attention via a personal communication, March 27, 2003.)

[53] This assessment of Lasswell's contributions to the study of democratic character has been enriched by earlier analyses from Brown (2000), Bryder (1998), Durning (2001), Greenstein (1968), Post (2001), and the essays found in Rogow (1969a).

[54] This is very much in keeping with the ego psychology approach of Hartmann (1939/1958), in the emphasis on defining healthy outcomes in terms of the degree to which the ego can gain autonomy from id impulses to establish constructive interactions with the external world.

[55] Segal (1973, p. 61).

[56] Opposition to the subjective, imaginative, and tender minded.

[57] "The disposition to believe that wild and dangerous things are going on in the world; the projection outwards of unconscious emotional impulses" (Adorno et al., 1950, p. 228).

[58] Aside from personality characteristics that overlap *by definition* with political attitudes or predispositions, personality traits per se rarely have significant correlations with either political affiliations or tendencies toward extreme political attitudes. Thus, *authoritarianism* is often found to be correlated with extremism—right or left (Lichter & Rothman, 1982)—but the definition and measurements of authoritarianism partially overlap with adherence to these extreme orientations; by the same token, social dominance is often found to be correlated with prejudice (Pratto, Stallworth, & Malle, 1994), but the social

dominance orientation entails belief in the legitimacy of prejudice. McFarland and Adelson (1997) and Altemeyer (1998) (based on U.S. and Canadian studies, respectively) found that out of 19 personality measures, only authoritarianism and social dominance correlate significantly with prejudice (cited in Lippa & Arad, 1999, p. 463). The recent efforts to bundle traits into broader constructs, most prominently the "Big Five" personality trait clusters (neuroticism, extraversion, openness, agreeableness, and conscientiousness) generally show low or inconsistent correlations with political orientations, with the exception of the cluster labeled "openness," which is frequently found to correlate negatively with "conservative political attitudes" (e.g., the longitudinal Harvard male student study with a 1939–1945 cohort; see Soldz & Vaillant, 1999). Other studies tend to confirm this result and the general lack of significance relationships of the other Big Five trait clusters. See Butler (2000) and Stone, Lederer, and Christie (1993). The openness cluster is indeed very close to Lasswell's organizing principle of the open ego capable of sharing and give and take.

[59] Shils (1954).

[60] Lasswell argued that

the democratic attitude toward other human beings is warm rather than frigid, inclusive and expanding rather than exclusive and constricting. We are speaking of an underlying personality structure which is capable of "friendship," as Aristotle put it, and which is unalienated from humanity. Such a person transcends most of the cultural categories that divide human beings from one another, and sense the common humanity across class and even caste lines within the culture, and in the world beyond the local culture. (1951, pp. 495–496)

[61] This analysis was drawn from the emerging literature on early childhood development, especially the notion of reinforcement by the "good mother." Compare this to Winnicott (1987), who employed the concept of the "good enough mother." Even so, Lasswell acknowledged the importance of recognizing potential benevolence had been emphasized by a host of political scientists (Lasswell, 1951). In a sense, Lasswell was reconciling the observation-based wisdom of such political scientists as Charles E. Merriam, James Bryce, and Hans Kelsen with the newly systematized insights of ego psychology.

[62] Lasswell and McDougal (1992) noted, "We assume that in a large scale modern society anxiety free personalities are almost nonexistent among adults" (p. 691).

[63] Anna Freud (1945/1998) wrote that ego strength "refers to the relative efficiency of the ego with regard to the contents of the id (instinctual drives) and to the forces of the environment with which the ego has to deal" (p. 218).

[64] See Duncan (2002) for an analysis of the problem of children with no apparent superego control, and the dilemmas this poses to the criminal justice system.

[65] See our discussion in chapter 2 of this volume.

[66] In his essay "Democratic Character" (1951), Lasswell noted that "from the point of view of modern personality research, the characters which are achieved by a complex process of balanced defense are viewed as constituting less enduring formations than those which evolve more directly" (p. 507).

[67] The synopsis can be found in Muth, Finley, and Muth (1990).

[68] Lasswell did recognize the work of radical psychoanalysts, such as Wilhelm Reich and Otto Fenichel, who gave much more credit to psychological dimensions in trying to develop a synthesis of Freud and Marx. See Fenichel (1967) and Reich (1930/1980, 1933/1980).

[69] This notion was explicated in greatest depth in his essay on "Democratic Character" (1951), but also in "Political Constitution and Character" (1959), which ended with a provocative list of hypotheses linking institutions with particular personality and character types.

[70] Edward Shils (1954, pp. 24–49), Dahl (1961, chaps. 27–28; cited by Greenstein, 1968, p. 707).

[71] Freud wrote earlier that "anxiety is based upon an increase of excitation which on the one hand produces the character of unpleasure and on the other finds relief through the acts of discharge" (1926/1977, p. 61).

[72] Rank (1923/1994) gave the greatest emphasis to how personality is shaped by the birth trauma. Sigmund Freud offered several, quite different interpretations of anxiety (see Freud, 1895/1962, 1917/1935, 1926/1977, 1933: Lecture 32).

[73] This problem existed from the very outset, owing to the fact that *Angst* in German has the broad meaning of "fear," even though Freud used the concept in a more specific way. See Laplanche and Pontalis (1967/1973).

[74] Lasswell and Sullivan were among the founders of the influential Washington School of Psychiatry. They shared in the development of several key constructs, such as the "self-system" (addressed earlier in this volume) and views on the importance of the impact of respect from others on the individual's level of self-esteem. See Perry (1982) for a biography of Harry Stack Sullivan.

[75] Freud (1925/1953) introduced this concept in his 1925 essay on the aesthetics of literature that evokes fear and fascination with the unfamiliar and uncertain.

[76] Lasswell confronted the debate concerning the possibility that anxiety arises solely from interpersonal interactions, a position advocated by Sullivan (1948). Lasswell realized that to link various anxiety states to political phenomena—as opposed to developing clinical treatments for anxiety—he did not have to engage in the theoretical and definitional debates over the scope of anxiety. In *Power and Personality* and in his essay on "Democratic Character," Lasswell avoided this predicament by limiting his attention to social anxiety while acknowledging the possibility that the fears of "relatively impersonal stimuli" such as the danger of falling could produce similar symptoms and reactions (1951, p. 509). The breadth of the term *social anxiety* as employed by Lasswell was, however, far greater than the contemporary label of *social anxiety*, which refers to anxiety that is basically limited to the panic attacks and phobic reactions of certain individuals in particular social situations. Whether or not anxiety due to interactions with the noninterpersonal environment add to social anxiety is hardly relevant if one simply wants to concentrate on the social origins of anxiety. Lasswell and those who wish to build on his legacy could afford to by-pass the theoretical issue of whether anxiety is strictly of interpersonal origins. Lasswell was content to limit his analysis to the anxiety that arises from interpersonal interactions without having to theorize as to whether the mental and physical manifestations with anxiety symptoms have exclusively interpersonal origins.

[77] Lasswell and McDougal noted that earlier treatments of the impact of anxiety focused on the effects of singular traumas and the repressions that they trigger, but that later so-called "ego psychology" came to emphasize the more gradual "mechanisms stressed in building defenses against anxiety." Nevertheless, they concluded that "[t]he conception of anxiety, however, continues to occupy a keystone position in the theory of personality growth and deviation. Specific patterns of character are related to the mechanisms stressed in building defenses against anxiety" (1992, p. 623).

[78] Lasswell and McDougal (1992, p. 691) argued that "anxiety is a function of two contrasting shifts in equilibrium: first, when id (impulse) patterns gain; second, when superego (conscience) factors gain. Anxiety is the motor that must reach a certain intensity before the personality system begins to resume its characteristic equilibrium relationship."

[79] Critics of the concept, both within and outside of psychoanalysis, have long questioned the utility of the analogy to physical energy and the theoretical implications of the premise of the principle of the conservation of psychic energy. Freud himself took varying positions on parallelisms between physical energy and psychic energy (Appelgarth, 1971; Freud, 1895, 1923/1960, 1926/1977; Germine, 1998; Swanson, 1977; Wallerstein, 1977). On the one hand, he saw it as was simply a metaphor to capture the idea that different aspects of mental life are more "charged," or have greater impetus for action than others. Pincus Noy (cited in Wallerstein, 1977, p. 531) noted that because Freud "sensed that many of the mental contents are charged by something like an impetus and peremptoriness, and their hold on mental life has something of power and strength, he tried to express it with the aid of concepts borrowed from the area of energy physics." Wallerstein (1977) maintained that to "Freud it was clear, or at least most people think it was clear, that the concept of psychic energy was always just that, a mental construct used metaphorically" (p. 532). On the other hand, Freud's early ambition was to unite the physiological with the psychological, and he employed the principle of the conservation of psychic energy as an important premise driving the models of repression, displacement, projection, the evolution of more mature drives, and the shifting of symptoms. In contemporary psychoanalytic literature, one prominent position is that psychic energy has some physiological basis

that is still difficult to identify and impossible to demonstrate definitively, until studies of brain physiology advance. Therefore, the more important task is to clarify the relationships among different psychological manifestations of intensity and stress toward action (libidinal energy, aggressive energy, ego energy, etc.) and with the psychoanalytic agencies such as id, ego, and superego (Applegarth, 1971).

[80] Several of the essays compiled in the section of *The Analysis of Political Behaviour: An Empirical Approach* (1948a) entitled "How to Observe and Record Politics" are illustrative. See also Lasswell's efforts to systematize the records of psychiatric interviews (1929, 1936a, 1938a).

[81] Almond and Verba's *Civic Culture* (1963) was the most prominent of these studies.

[82] Cook noted that after a proliferation of articles on political socialization in U.S. political science journals in the late 1960s, by the late 1970s and early 1980s the number of such articles had dropped dramatically (Cook, 1985, 1989). The general political science journals and even *Political Psychology*, the most prominent U.S. journal devoted to that field, have seen very few articles on political socialization in recent years, although there has been a resurgence of books on political socialization, especially in the field of education (Torney-Purta, 2000).

[83] See Brown (1980) for the most comprehensive and intelligent exposition of this approach to understanding attitude structures, and the journal for the Q-methodology, *Operant Subjectivity*. See also Durning (1999) for a highly relevant discussion of the role of the Q-technique in policy analysis.

[84] Bass & Stodgill (1990) noted over 3,800 works, and this is obviously only a partial list of the leadership literature; however, the literature on "elites" is largely absent from Bass' reference list.

[85] Burns (1978) used the terms *transforming* as well as *transformational*.

[86] Avolio and Yammarino (2002) asserted that "transformational and charismatic leadership are used interchangeably or as synonyms. The 'new genre' scholars argue that they are the same; the 'transformational' scholars argue that they are different; the 'charisma' scholars argue that they are addressing the important and unique component; and the 'leadership' scholars are just confused!" (p. xxiii).

[87] See Schiffer (1973).

[88] A very helpful and concise summary of Lasswell's European years can be found in Muth (1990).

[89] In the preface to *Psychopathology and Politics*, Lasswell noted that "[t]he procedures and findings of psychopathology are relied upon for the purpose in hand, since they are the most elaborate and stimulating contributions to the study of the person which have yet been made" (p. 217). Lasswell did not limit his views to psychopathology, nor to pure Freudianism, but used the set of well-elaborated and well-known theoretical constructs on which to build. Lasswell was well versed in the work of Harry Stack Sullivan, Abraham, Ferenczi, Reich, Deutsh, Horney, and countless others, as well as that of Freud.

[90] Lasswell's framework identified power, respect, rectitude, and affection as deference values. Power is influence: the ability to get someone to do something that he or she would not otherwise do. Respect includes both self-respect and the regard of others. Rectitude describes one's relationship with one's own superego as well as the moralistic expectations preached to others. Affection includes love and friendship (Lasswell & Kaplan, 1950). Deference may be accorded to an individual because he or she is perceived to be highly skilled, to possess power, to be respected by the community, to hold a prestigious position or role, to model rectitude, or to elicit affection. The possession of these different scope values by an individual leader may predict the direction of his or her efforts. For example, if a leader values power above the other base values, the leadership role is likely to be in the political arena. If the individual values respect, he or she may try to function in the role of patriarch or matriarch. One who prizes rectitude might lead in the realm of religion, whereas one who prizes affection may try always to be the people's favorite.

[91] This connection was made explicit in Lasswell (1954).

[92] The theorist is the least elaborated leadership type in Lasswell's works. In *Psychopathology and Politics* (1930/1960), the chapters on the characteristics of agitators and administrators are followed by a chapter on the psychodynamic origins of extreme beliefs,

rather than an analysis of the behavior and personality characteristics of the theorist. Lasswell did propose Karl Marx as the archetypical theorist, pointing out that "Marx wanted unreserved admiration for the products of his mind. He toiled through years of isolation and poverty to make his assertions impregnable" (p. 53). As Lasswell understood him, Marx did not want adoration toward his person, as an agitator might, but rather desired that his ideas be applauded.

[93] Popper and Mayseless (2002) referred to this as "personalized charismatic leadership" (p. 206).

[94] Weber's classic formulation of charisma is "a certain quality of an individual personality by virtue of which he is considered extraordinary and treated as endowed with supernatural, superhuman, or at least specifically exceptional powers or qualities" (1925/1968, p. 241).

[95] Freud wrote:

From our point of view we need not attribute so much importance to the appearance of new characteristics [of group psychology]. For us it would be enough to say that in a group the individual is brought under conditions which allow him to throw off the repressions of his unconscious instincts. The apparently new characteristics which he then displays are in fact the manifestations of this unconscious, in which all that is evil in the human mind is contained as a predisposition. We can find no difficulty in understanding the disappearance of conscience or of a sense of responsibility in these circumstances. It has long been our contention that "dread of society" [soziale Angst] is the essence of what is called conscience. (1921/1959, pp. 9–10)

[96] Like any terms in the behavioral and social sciences, *mood* and *climate* can have varying meanings. Although neither of these terms is defined in Lasswell and Kaplan's definitional exposition in *Power and Society* (1950), Lasswell's 1965 chapter on "The Climate of International Action" defined a mood as a broad subjective orientation (in contrast to images regarding specific references) marked by particular affects and preoccupations (p. 341). *Climate* is a collective mood. Elaborating on this concept, Brown (1982) defined *climate of opinion* as "a collective expression of relatively stable preferences for particular perceptions, outcomes, or courses of action" (p. 153).

[97] A population's political character, encompassing the major psychological aspects that account for political behavior, is comprised of two parts. The *self-system* consists of salient perspectives; the *intensity system* covers all drives and psychological dynamics that give intensity to various impulses toward action. This intensity system has its own baseline for any given individual under normal circumstances, reflecting his or her psychological development, but it is also affected by the events and conditions prevailing at any point in time. The intensity system is affected by crisis or other conditions that alter the intensity of emotions. In some instances, intensity is lower. For example, following a high-intensity episode, such as a war scare, a mood of relief or lethargy may follow.

[98] The individual will maximize satisfaction, reduce feelings of deprivation and anxiety, or some combination of these, as these factors are assessed through the individual's own perspectives and are shaped by the intensity toward each value. For some individuals, a preoccupation will emerge if the prospect of greater rewards and relief of anxiety by pursuing the value will be a net subjective gain; other individuals will flee from the painful preoccupation if the expectations are negative. As Lasswell (1965a) put it succinctly, the "maximization postulate suggests the fundamental point that mood events depend upon net value expectations. What gains or losses sustain stable or unstable moods?" (p. 344).

[99] Kahneman et al. (1982) suggested that the prior cases may be selected on the basis of representativeness or vividness. Other heuristics are possible.

[100] Edward Sapir (1934) noted that such a symbol "diffuses its emotional quality to types of behavior or situations apparently far removed from the original meaning of the symbol" (pp. 493–494). This phenomenon is examined in greater depth in chapter 3 of this text.

[101] These essays—along with Lasswell's 1937 essay, "Sino–Japanese Crisis: The Garrison State versus the Civilian State"—were published in the 1997 volume along with commentaries by Irving Louis Horowitz, Jay Stanley, and David R. Segal (Lasswell, 1997).

[102] Dovring (1959; cited in Lasswell, 1965a, pp. 344–345).

[103] The most explicit treatment of the "configurative approach" can be found in chapter 1 of *World Politics and Personal Insecurity* (Lasswell, 1935b/1965).

[104] The most prominent formulation of the just war doctrine is attributed to Thomas Aquinas. Contemporary expositions include Dugard (1982), Norman (1995), and Walzer (1977/2000).

[105] The most definitive exposition on the Q technique is found in Brown (1980).

[106] Cited in Strawson (1974, p. 15).

[107] See McDowall (2001) for a thorough exposition on the Kurds in Iraq and Turkey.

[108] See Ross (2002).

[109] Priscilla Hayner (1994) defined truth commissions as "bodies set up to investigate a past history of violations of human rights in a particular country—which can include violations by the military or other government forces or armed oppositions forces" (p. 558).

[110] See Bloom (1998) for an analysis of truth commissions as psychodrama.

[111] See the discussions in Minow (1998), Hayner (2002), and Rotberg and Thompson (2000).

[112] See the Truth Commissions Project website, www.truthcommission.org. The design dimensions range from the time and geographic horizons of the investigation to the severity of the penalties.

[113] Minow (1998) noted that former South African defense minister General Magnus Malan termed the Truth and Reconciliation Commission a "witch hunt."

[114] See, for example, the essays on the history of military training in both developed and developing countries collected in Converse (1998).

[115] The other nations were Brazil, Chile, Peru, and Uruguay.

[116] The quote is from J. A. L. Robertson, who was with Atomic Energy of Canada Limited from 1957 to 1985.

[117] Risk assessment experts typically place the risk of nuclear power fairly low down in the list of risky behaviors and technologies (e.g., ranked 20th out of 30 in the 1980 Slovic, Fischoff, and Lichtenstein survey), whereas the public typically ranks nuclear power accidents as the highest risk (Slovic et al., 1980). Experts recognize the greater historical lethality of pollution from conventional power plants (ranked 9th in the aforementioned survey), whereas the public ranks this risk as 18th (Slovic et al., 1980).

[118] According to the Agence France Presse (2001), antinuclear activists in Germany carried placards with the slogan "Atomic state equals police state."

[119] See Clarfield and Wiecek (1984) for the early history of U.S. nuclear energy policy. Freudenberg and Rosa (1984) provided a history of public attitudes.

[120] Roughly three fourths of France's electricity, and half of its total energy, are produced by nuclear power plants.

[121] See Touraine (1983) for the history of the French nuclear debate.

[122] See, for example, Estreicher, Katz, and Kaufman (2001), Fosh and Heery (1990), and Parker (1999).

References

Abelson, R. P. (1981). Psychological status of the script concept. *American Psychologist*, *36*(7), 715–729.

Adorno, T. W., Levinson, D. J., Sanford, R. N., & Frenkel-Brunswik, E. (Eds.). (1950). *The authoritarian personality* (1st ed.). New York: Harper.

Agence France Presse. (2001, March 30). Germany's Greens disappoint the anti-nuclear movement. Retrieved January 1, 2004 from http://www.commondreams.org/headlines01/0330–03.htm.

Allport, F. (1924/1967). *Social psychology.* Boston: Houghton-Mifflin.

Almond, G., & Verba, S. (1963). *The civic culture: Political attitudes and democracy in five nations.* Princeton, NJ: Princeton University Press.

Alsolabehere, S., & Iyengar, S. (1993). Information and electoral attitudes: A case of judgment under uncertainty. In S. Iyengar & W. McGuire (Eds.), *Explorations in political psychology* (pp. 321–337). Durham, NC: Duke University Press.

Altemeyer, B. (1998). The other "authoritarian personality." *Advances in Experimental Social Psychology*, *30*, 47–92.

American Psychiatric Association. (2000). *Diagnostic and statistical manual of mental disorders.* Arlington, VA: Author.

Applegarth, A. (1971). Comments on aspects of the theory of psychic energy. *Journal of the American Psychoanalytic Association*, *19*(3), 379–416.

Ascher, W. (1986). The moralism of attitudes supporting intergroup violence. *Political Psychology*, *7*(3), 403–425.

Ascher, W., & Overholt, W. H. (1983). *Strategic planning and forecasting: Political risk and economic opportunity.* New York: Wiley.

Atkins, W. E., & Lasswell, H. D. (1924). *Labor attitudes and problems.* New York: Prentice-Hall.

Avolio, B., & Yammarino, F. (2002). Introduction to, and overview of, transformational and charismatic leadership. In B. Avolio & F. Yammarino (Eds.), *Transformational and charismatic leadership: The road ahead* (pp. xvii–xxiii). Amsterdam: JAI.

Baas, L. R., & Brown, S. R. (1973). Generating rules for intensive analysis: The study of transformations. *Psychiatry: Journal for the Study of Interpersonal Processes*, *36*(2), 172–183.

Bandura, A. (1986). *Social foundations of thought and action: A social cognitive theory.* Englewood Cliffs, NJ: Prentice-Hall.

Barber, J. D. (1972). *The presidential character: Predicting performance in the White House* (2d ed.). Englewood Cliffs, NJ: Prentice-Hall.

Bass, B. M., & Avolio, B. (2002). Introduction. In B. M. Bass & B. Avolio (Eds.), *Developing potential across a full range of leadership: Cases in transactional and transformational leadership* (pp. 1–9). Mahwah, NJ: Lawrence Erlbaum Associates.

Bass, B. M., & Stogdill, R. M. (1990). *Bass & Stogdill's handbook of leadership: Theory, research, and managerial applications* (3rd ed.). New York: Free Press.

Becker, G. (1976). *The economic approach to human behavior.* Chicago: University of Chicago Press.

Bloom, S. L. (1998). By the crowd they have been broken, by the crowd they shall be healed: The social transformation of trauma. In R. Tedeschi, C. Park, & L. Calhoun (Eds.), *Post-traumatic growth: Theory and research on change in the aftermath of crises* (pp. 179–214). Mahwah, NJ: Lawrence Erlbaum Associates.

Brown, S. R. (1980). *Political subjectivity: Applications of Q methodology in political science.* New Haven, CT: Yale University Press.

Brown, S. R. (1982). Imagery, mood and the public expression of opinion. *Micropolitics, 2*(2), 153–173.

Brown, S. R. (2000). Harold D. Lasswell and the policy sciences. *Policy Evaluation, 6*(4), 4–8.

Brunner, R. D. (1987). Key political symbols—the dissociation process. *Policy Sciences, 20*(1), 53–76.

Brunner, R. D., & Morrow, K. M. (1984). The president's annual message. *Congress and the Presidency, 11,* 37–58.

Brunner, R. D., & Vivian, W. (1980). Citizen viewpoints on energy policy. *Policy Sciences, 12*(2), 147–174.

Bryan, W. J. (1896). Official proceedings of Democratic National Convention held in Chicago, Illinois, July 7–11. Logansport, IN: 1896.

Bryder, T. (1998). *The human face of politics: Essays on political psychology and politicised culture in the twentieth century.* Copenhagen: Copenhagen Political Studies Press.

Burns, J. M. (1978). *Leadership* (1st ed.). New York: Harper & Row.

Butler, J. C. (2000). Personality and emotional correlates of right-wing authoritarianism. *Social Behavior and Personality, 28*(1), 1–14.

Clarfield, G., & Wiecek, W. (1984). *Nuclear America: Military and civilian nuclear power in the United States, 1940–1980.* New York: Harper & Row.

Clarke, J. W., & Donovan, M. M. (1980) Personal needs and political incentives: Some observations on self-esteem. *American Journal of Political Science, 24*(3), 536–552.

Conger, J. A. (1988). Theoretical foundations of charismatic leadership. In J. A. Conger & R. N. Kanungo (Eds.), *Charismatic leadership: The elusive factor in organizational effectiveness* (pp. 12–39). San Francisco: Jossey-Bass.

Conger, J. A. (1989). *The charismatic leader: Behind the mystique of exceptional leadership* (1st ed.). San Francisco: Jossey-Bass

Conger, J., & Kanungo, R. (1998). *Charismatic leadership in organizations.* Thousand Oaks, CA: Sage.

Constable, P., & Valenzuela, A. (1989/1990). Chile's return to democracy. *Foreign Affairs,* 169–186.

Converse, E. V. III. (Ed.). (1998). *Forging the sword: Selecting, educating and training cadets and junior officers in the modern world.* Chicago: Imprint.

Cook, T. E. (1985). The bear market in political socialization and the costs of misunderstood psychological theories. *American Political Science Review, 79*(4), 1079–1093.

Cook, T. E. (1989). The psychological theory of political socialization and the political theory of child development: The dangers of normal science. *Human Development, 32*(1), 24–34.

Cosin, B. R., Freeman, C. F., & Freeman, N. H. (1982). Critical empiricism criticized: The case of Freud. In R. Wollheim & J. Hopkins (Eds.), *Philosophical essays on Freud* (pp. 32–59). Cambridge, UK: Cambridge University Press.

Dahl, R. A. (1961). *Who governs? Democracy and power in an American city.* New Haven, CT: Yale University Press.

Davids, A. (1957). Some social and cultural factors determining relations between authoritarianism and measures of neuroticism. *Journal of Consulting Psychology, 21,* 155–159.

Dodge, T. (2003). *Inventing Iraq: The failure of nation-building and a history denied.* New York: Columbia University Press.

Doob, L. W. (1935). *Propaganda: Its psychology and technique.* New York: H. Holt.

Dovring, K. (1959). *Road to propaganda: The semantics of communication.* New York: Philosophical Library.

Dugard, J. (1982). International terrorism and the just war. In D. Rapoport & Y. Alexander (Eds.), *The morality of terrorism* (pp. 77–98). New York: Pergamon.

Duncan, M. (2002). So young and so untender: Remorseless children and the expectations of the law. *Columbia Law Review, 102,* 1469–1526.

Durkheim, E. (1897). *Le Suicide.* Paris: Presses Universitaires.

Durning, D. (1999). The transition from traditional to postpositivist policy analysis: A role for Q-methodology. *Journal of Policy Analysis and Management, 18*(3), 389–410.

Durning, D. (2001). *Lasswell's unseasonable gift: Symbols, psychologically complex human beings, and policy analysis.* Unpublished manuscript.

Edelman, M. J. (1964/1985). *The symbolic uses of politics.* Urbana: University of Illinois Press.

Ehrhart, M. G., & Klein, K. J. (2001). Predicting followers' preferences for "charismatic leadership": The influence of follower values and personality. *The Leadership Quarterly, 12,* 153–179.

Ellenberger, H. (1970). *The discovery of the unconscious: The history and evolution of dynamic psychiatry.* New York: Basic Books.

Elster, J. (Ed.). (1986). *Rational choice.* Oxford, UK: Basil Blackwell.

Erdelyi, M. (1992). Psychodynamics and the unconscious. *American Psychologist, 47*(6), 784–787.

Erwin, E. (1996). *A final accounting: Philosophical and empirical issues in Freudian psychology.* Cambridge, MA: MIT Press.

Estreicher, S., Katz, H., & Kaufman, B. (Eds.). (2001). *The internal governance and organizational effectiveness of labor unions: Essays in honor of George Brooks.* Dordrecht: Kluwer Law International.

Eulau, H., & Zlomke, S. (1999). Harold D. Lasswell's legacy to mainstream political science: A neglected agenda. *Annual Review of Political Science, 2,* 75–89.

Farr, J. (1999). John Dewey and American political science. *American Journal of Political Science, 43*(2), 520–541.

Farrell, J. (1996). *Freud's paranoid quest: Psychoanalysis and modern suspicion.* New York: New York University Press.

Fenichel, O. (1967). Psychoanalysis as the nucleus of a future dialectical-materialistic psychology. *American Imago, 24,* 290–311.

Ferejohn, J., & Kuklinski, J. (1990). *Information and the democratic process.* Urbana: University of Illinois Press.

Ferster, C. B., & Skinner, B. F. (1957). *Schedules of reinforcement.* New York: Appleton-Century-Crofts.

Fiedler, F. E. (1967). *A theory of leadership effectiveness.* New York: McGraw-Hill.

Finlay, D. J., Holsti, O. R., & Fagen, R. R. (1967). *Enemies in politics.* Chicago: Rand McNally.

Fosh, P., & Heery, E. (Eds.). (1990). *Trade unions and their members: Studies in union democracy and organisation.* Basingstoke, UK: Macmillan.

Frame, M. (1995). Manager or leader: Which are you? *Business and Economic Review, 41*(3), 13–15.

Freud, A. (1936/1966). *Ego and the mechanisms of defense.* Madison, CT: International Universities Press.

Freud, A. (1945/1998). Indications for child analysis. In A. Freud, *Selected writings by Anna Freud* (pp. 201–228). London: Penguin.

Freud, S. (1895/1962). On the grounds for detaching a particular syndrome from neurasthenia under the description "anxiety neurosis." In S. Freud, *Early psychoanalytic publications* (Vol. III, pp. 87–122). London: Hogarth.

Freud, S. (1900/1965). *The interpretation of dreams.* New York: Avon.

Freud, S. (1913/1950). *Totem and taboo.* London: Routledge & Kegan Paul.

Freud, S. (1917/1935). *A general introduction to psychoanalysis.* New York: Norton.

Freud, S. (1920/1950). *Beyond the pleasure principle.* New York: Norton.

Freud, S. (1921/1959). *Group psychology and the analysis of the ego.* New York: Norton.

Freud, S. (1923/1960). *The ego and the id.* New York: Norton.

Freud, S. (1924/1961). *The economic problem of masochism.* London: Hogarth.

Freud, S. (1925/1953). The uncanny. In S. Freud, *The standard edition of the complete psychological works of Sigmund Freud* (Vol. XVII, pp. 219–252). London: Hogarth.

Freud, S. (1926/1977). *Inhibitions, symptoms and anxiety.* New York: Norton.

Freud, S. (1929/1961). *Civilization and its discontents.* London: Hogarth.

Freud, S. (1933). *New introductory lectures on psycho-analysis.* New York: Norton.

Freud, S. (1939). *Moses and monotheism.* New York: Knopf.

Freud, S. (1940/1969). *An outline of psychoanalysis.* New York: Norton.

Freudenberg, W., & Rosa, E. (1984). *Public reaction to nuclear power: Are there critical masses?* Washington, DC: Westview.

Germine, M. (1998). The concept in energy in Freud's Project for a Scientific Psychology. In R. M. Bilder & F. LeFever (Eds.), *Neuroscience of the mind on the centennial of Freud's Project for a Scientific Psychology* (Vol. 843, pp. 80–90). New York: Annals of the New York Academy of Sciences.

Gibson, J., Hannon, J., & Blackwell, C. (1998). Charismatic leadership: The hidden controversy. *Journal of Leadership Studies, 5*(4), 3–10.

Gordon, R. (2002). Conceptualizing leadership with respect to its historical-contextual antecedents to power. *The Leadership Quarterly, 13,* 151–167.

Greenstein, F. I. (1968). Harold D. Lasswell's concept of democratic character. *The Journal of Politics, 30,* 696–709.

Greenstein, F. I. (1977). Introduction. In H. D. Lasswell (Ed.), *Psychopathology and politics* (pp. vii–xxii). New York: Viking.

Grünbaum, A. (1984). *The foundations of psychoanalysis: A philosophical critique.* Berkeley: University of California Press.

Hall, C. S., & Lindzey, G. (1957). *Theories of personality.* New York: Wiley.

Hamber, B. (1995). Do sleeping dogs lie? *The psychological implications of the Truth and Reconciliation Commission in South Africa.* Centre for the Study of Violence and Reconciliation, Seminar No. 5, Johannesburg. Retrieved December 10, 2003, from www.csvr.org.za.papers/papsldog.htm

Hart, W. D. (1982). Models of depression. In R. Wollheim & J. Hopkins (Eds.), *Philosophical essays on Freud* (pp. 180–202). Cambridge, UK: Cambridge University Press.

Hartmann, H. (1939/1958). *Ego psychology and the problem of adaptation.* New York: International Universities Press.

Hayner, P. (1994). Fifteen truth commissions—1974 to 1994: A comparative study. *Human Rights Quarterly, 16,* 597–655.

Hayner, P. (2002). *Unspeakable truths: Facing the challenge of truth commissions.* New York: Routledge.

Hite, K. (2000). *When the romance ended: Leaders of the Chilean left, 1968–1998.* New York: Columbia University Press.

Holender, D. (1986). Semantic activation without conscious identification in dichotic listening, parafoveal vision, and visual masking: A survey and appraisal. *Behavioral & Brain Sciences, 9*(1), 1–66.

Horney, K. (1939). *New ways in psychoanalysis.* New York: Norton.

Horwitz, R. (1962). Scientific propaganda: Harold D. Lasswell. In H. J. Storing (Ed.), *Essays on the scientific study of politics* (pp. 225–305). New York: Holt, Rienhart, & Winston.

Huser, H. C. (2002). *Argentine civil–military relations.* Washington, DC: U.S. Government Printing Office.

James, W. (1890/1950). *The principles of psychology.* New York: Dover.

Janowitz, M. (1968). Harold D. Lasswell's contribution to content analysis. *Public Opinion Quarterly, 32*(4), 646–653.

Janowitz, M. (1969). Content analysis and "symbolic environment." In A. A. Rogow (Ed.), *Politics, personality and social sciences in the Twentieth Century: Essays in honor of Harold D. Lasswell* (pp. 155–170). Chicago: University of Chicago Press.

Kahneman, D., Slovic, P., & Tversky, A. (Eds.). (1982). *Judgment under uncertainty.* New York: Cambridge University Press.

Kardiner, A., & Preble, E. (1961). *They studied man.* Cleveland: World.

Karl, B. (1974). *Charles E. Merriam and the study of politics.* Chicago: University of Chicago Press.

Katz, D. (1960). The functional approach to the study of attitudes. *Public Opinion Quarterly, 24,* 163–176.

Kets de Vries, M. F. (1979). Managers can drive their subordinates mad. *Harvard Business Review* (July/August), 125–134.

Kohut, H. (1971). *The analysis of the self.* New York: International Universities Press.

Kornhauser, W. (1959). *The politics of mass society.* Glencoe, IL: Free Press.

Lane, R. E. (1959). *Political life: Why people get involved in politics.* Glencoe, IL: Free Press.

Laplanche, J., & Pontalis, J.-B. (1967/1973). *The language of psycho-analysis.* New York: Norton.

Lasswell, H. D. (1923). Chicago's old First Ward. *National Municipal Review, 12,* 127–131.

Lasswell, H. D. (1927a). The theory of propaganda, *American Political Science Review, 21,* 627–631.

Lasswell, H. D. (1927b/1971). *Propaganda technique in the World War.* London: Kegan Paul, Trench, and Trubner.

Lasswell, H. D. (1929). The problem of adequate personality records: A proposal. *American Journal of Psychiatry, 8*(1), 1057–1066.

Lasswell, H. D. (1930/1960). *Psychotherapy and Politics.* New York: Viking.

Lasswell, H. D. (1931). Review of "Civilization and Its Discontents." *American Journal of Sociology, 37*(2), 328–331.

Lasswell, H. D. (1932). The triple-appeal principle: A contribution of psychoanalysis to political and social science. *American Journal of Sociology, 37,* 523–538.

Lasswell, H. D. (1933/1948). The psychology of Hitlerism. *Political Quarterly, 4,* 373–384.

Lasswell, H. D. (1935a). The study and practice of propaganda. In H. D. Lasswell, R. D. Casey, & B. L. Smith (Eds.), *Propaganda and promotional activities: An annotated bibliography* (pp. 3–27). Minneapolis: University of Minnesota Press.

Lasswell, H. D. (1935b/1965). *World politics and personal insecurity.* New York: Free Press.

Lasswell, H. D. (1936a). Certain prognostic changes during trial (psychoanalytic) interviews. *Psychoanalytic Review, 23,* 241–247.

Lasswell, H. D. (1936b/1958). *Politics: Who gets what, when, how.* New York: Meridian.

Lasswell, H. D. (1937). Sino-Japanese crisis: The garrison state versus the civilian state. *China Quarterly, 2,* 643–649.

Lasswell, H. D. (1938a). A provisional classification of symbol data. *Psychiatry: Journal for the Study of Interpersonal Processes, 2,* 197–204.

Lasswell, H. D. (1938b). What psychiatrists and political scientists can learn from one another. *Psychiatry: Journal for the Study of Interpersonal Processes, 1,* 33–39.

Lasswell, H. D. (1939). Political psychiatry: The study and practice of integrative politics. In F. Moulton & P. Komora (Eds.), *Mental health* (pp. 269–275). Lancaster, PA: Science Press.

Lasswell, H. D. (1941a/1948). Radio as an instrument of reducing personal insecurity. *Studies in Philosophy & Social Science, 9,* 49–64.

Lasswell, H. D. (1941b). The world attention survey. *Public Opinion Quarterly, 5,* 456–462.

Lasswell, H. D. (1941c). The garrison state. *American Journal of Sociology, 46,* 455–468.

Lasswell, H. D. (1945). *World politics faces economics: With special reference to the future relations of the United States and Russia.* New York: McGraw-Hill.

Lasswell, H. D. (1948a). *The analysis of political behaviour: An empirical approach.* London: Routledge & Kegan Paul.

Lasswell, H. D. (1948b). *Power and personality.* New York: Norton.

Lasswell, H. D. (1950). Propaganda and mass insecurity. *Psychiatry: Journal for the Study of Interpersonal Processes, 13,* 283–299.

Lasswell, H. D. (1951). Democratic character. In *The political writings of Harold D. Lasswell* (pp. 465–525). Glencoe, IL: Free Press.

Lasswell, H. D. (1954). The selective effect of personality on political participation. In R. Christie & M. Jahoda (Eds.), *Studies in the scope of method of "The Authoritarian Personality"* (pp. 197–225). Glencoe, IL: Free Press.

Lasswell, H. D. (1959). Political constitution and character. *Psychoanalysis & the Psychoanalytic Review, 46*(4), 4–18.

Lasswell, H. D. (1962). The garrison state hypothesis today. In S. Huntington (Ed.), *Changing patterns of military politics* (pp. 51–70). New York: Free Press of Glencoe.

Lasswell, H. D. (1963). *The future of political science.* New York: Atherton.

Lasswell, H. D. (1965a). The climate of international action. In H. C. Kelman (Ed.), *International behavior* (pp. 339–353). New York: Holt, Rinehart & Winston.

Lasswell, H. D. (1966). Conflict and leadership: The process of decision and the nature of authority. In A. de Rueck & J. Knight (Eds.), *Conflict in society* (pp. 210–28). Boston: Little, Brown.

Lasswell, H. D. (1967). Political systems, styles and personalities. In L. J. Edinger (Ed.), *Political leadership in industrialized societies: Studies in comparative analysis* (pp. 316–347). New York: Wiley.

Lasswell, H. D. (1968). The impact of crowd psychology upon international law. *William and Mary Law Review, 9*(3), 664–681.

Lasswell, H. D. (1971). *A pre-view of policy sciences.* New York: Elsevier.

Lasswell, H. D. (1997). *Essays on the garrison state* (J. Stanley, Ed.). New Brunswick, NJ: Transaction.

Lasswell, H. D., & Blumenstock, D. (1939). *World revolutionary propaganda: A Chicago study.* New York: Knopf.

Lasswell, H. D., Casey, R. D., & Smith, B. L. (1935). *Propaganda and promotional activities.* Minneapolis: University of Minnesota Press.

Lasswell, H. D., & Kaplan, A. (1950). *Power and society: A framework for political inquiry.* New Haven, CT: Yale University Press.

Lasswell, H. D., Leites, N., & Associates (Eds.). (1949). *Language of politics: Studies in quantitative semantics.* Cambridge, MA: MIT Press.

Lasswell, H. D., Lerner, D., & Speier, H. (Eds.). (1979). *The symbolic instrument in early times.* Honolulu: Published for the East-West Center by the University Press of Hawaii.

Lasswell, H. D., Lerner, D., & Speier, H. (1980a). *The emergence of public opinion in the West.* Honolulu: Published for the East-West Center by the University Press of Hawaii.

Lasswell, H. D., Lerner, D., & Speir, H. (Eds.). (1980b). *A pluralizing world in transition.* Honolulu: Published for the East-West Center by the University Press of Hawaii.

Lasswell, H. D., & McDougal, M. S. (1992). *Jurisprudence for a free society: Studies in law, science, and policy.* Dordrecht, Netherlands: Kluwer Academic Publishers.

Lasswell, H. D., & Stanley, J. (1997). *Essays on the garrison state.* New Brunswick, NJ: Transaction Publishers.

Lau, R. R., & Sears, D. O. (1986). *Political cognition.* Hillsdale, NJ: Lawrence Erlbaum Associates.

LeBon, G. (1896/1986). *The crowd: The study of the popular mind.* London: Unwin.

Lichter, S. R., & Rothman, S. (1982). The radical personality: Social psychological correlates of New Left ideology. *Political Behavior, 4*(3), 207–235.

Lippa, R., & Arad, S. (1999). Gender, personality and prejudice: The display of authoritarianism and social dominance in interviews with college men and women. *Journal of Research in Personality, 33,* 463–493.

Lumley, F. E. (1933). *The propaganda menace.* New York: Century.

Lykken, D. (1995). *The antisocial personalities.* Hillsdale, NJ: Lawrence Erlbaum Associates.

Mach, E. (1897/1959). *The analysis of sensations.* New York: Dover.

Marcus, G. E. (2003). *The sentimental citizen: Emotion in democratic politics.* College Station: Pennsylvania State University Press.

Marcus, G. E., Neuman, W. R., & MacKuen, M. (2000). *Affective intelligence and political judgment.* Chicago: University of Chicago Press.

Martin, J. (1988). *Who am I this time? Uncovering the fictive personality.* New York: Norton.

Martin, J. (2001). Biographers and blue guitars. *Partisan Review, 68*(1), 91–104.

McCann, F. (1989). The military. In M. Conniff & F. McCann (Eds.), *Modern Brazil: Elites and masses in historical perspective* (pp. 47–80). Lincoln: University of Nebraska Press.

McDougall, D. (1984). *Harold Lasswell and the study of international relations.* New York: University Press of America.

McDowell, D. (2001). *A modern history of the Kurds.* London: IB Tauris.

McFarland, S. G., & Adelson, S. (1997). *An omnibus study of individual differences and prejudice.* Unpublished manuscript, Western Kentucky University.

McGuire, W. J. (1993). The poly-psy relationship: Three phases of a long affair. In S. Iyengar & W. J. McGuire (Eds.), *Explorations in political psychology* (pp. 9–35). Durham, NC: Duke University Press.

McKeown, B. (1984). Q methodology in political psychology: Theory and technique in psychoanalytic applications. *Political Psychology, 5,* 415–436.

Mead, G. H. (1934). *Mind, self, and society.* Chicago: University of Chicago Press.

Merelman, R. (1981). Harold Lasswell's political world—weak tea for hard times. *British Journal of Political Science, 11,* 471–497.

Merelman, R. (1989). Commentary. *Human Development, 32*(1), 35–44.

Minow, M. (1998). *Between vengeance and forgiveness: Facing history after genocide and mass violence.* Boston: Beacon.

Moore, S. W. (1989). The need for a unified theory of political learning: Lessons from a longitudinal project. *Human Development, 32*(1), 35–44.

Mosier, R. (2003). Truth commissions: Peddling impunity. *Human Rights Features, 6*(5). Retrieved December 25, 2003, from www.hrdc.net/sahrdc/hrfchr59/issue5/impunity .htm

Muth, R. (1990). A biographical profile. In R. Muth, M. M. Finley, & M. F. Muth (Eds.), *Harold D. Lasswell: An annotated bibliography* (pp. 1–48). New Haven/Dordrecht: New Haven Press/Kluwer Academic Publishers.

Muth, R., Finley, M. M., & Muth, M. F. (1990). *Harold D. Lasswell: An annotated bibliography.* New Haven, CT/Dordrecht: New Haven Press/Kluwer Academic Publishers.

Norman, R. (1995). *Ethics, killing, and war.* Cambridge, UK: Cambridge University Press.

Nuclear Energy Agency. (2002). *Society and nuclear energy: Towards a better understanding.* Paris: Organisation for Economic Co-Operation and Development.

Nunn, F. (1998). Beyond classrooms and parade grounds. In E. V. Converse III (Ed.), *Forging the sword: Selecting, educating and training cadets and junior officers in the modern world* (pp. 347–359). Chicago: Imprint Publications.

Ottati, V. C. (2002). *The social psychology of politics.* New York: Kluwer Academic/Plenum.

Ottati, V. C., & Wyer, R. S., Jr. (1993). Affect and political judgment. In S. Iyengar & W. McGuire (Eds.), *Explorations in political psychology* (pp. 296–315). Durham, NC: Duke University Press.

Parker, M. (1999). *Democracy is power: Rebuilding unions from the bottom up.* Detroit, MI: Labor Notes.

Perry, H. S. (1982). *Psychiatrist of America: The life of Harry Stack Sullivan.* Cambridge, MA: Belknap.

Pion-Berlin, D. (1992). Military autonomy and emerging democracies in South America. *Comparative Politics, 25*(1), 83–102.

Popper, M., & Mayseless, O. (2002). The internal world of transformational leaders. In B. Avolio & F. Yammarino (Eds.), *Transformational and charismatic leadership* (pp. 203–229). Amsterdam: JAI.

Post, J. (2001). Harold Lasswell: An appreciation. *Psychiatry, 64*(3), 197–210.

Pratto, F., Sidanius, J., Stallworth, L., & Malle, B. (1994). Social dominance orientation: A personality variable predicting social and political attitudes. *Journal of Personality and Social Psychology, 67,* 741–763.

Price, T. L. (1998). *Mistake and moral blameworthiness: An account of the excusing force of faultless mistakes of fact and faultless mistakes of morality.* Unpublished doctoral dissertation, University of Arizona, Tucson.

Rangell, L. (1980). *The mind of Watergate: A study of the compromise of integrity.* New York: Norton.

Rank, O. (1923/1994). *The trauma of birth.* New York: Dover.

Redl, F. (1971). The superego in uniform. In N. Sanford & C. Comstock (Eds.), *Sanctions for evil* (pp. 93–101). San Francisco: Jossey-Bass.

Reich, W. (1930/1980). *Character analysis.* New York: Farrar, Straus, and Giroux, Inc.

Reich, W. (1933/1980). *The Mass Psychology of Fascism.* New York: Farrar, Straus, & Giroux.

Reisman, W. M. (1999). *Law in brief encounters.* New Haven, CT: Yale University Press.

Roashan, G. R. (2001). *Loya Jirga: One of the last political tools for bringing peace to Afghanistan.* Institute for Afghan Studies. Retrieved January 3, 2003, from http://institute-for-afghan-studies.org/dev_xyz/jiirga/roashan_loya_jirga_July_2001.htm

Robertson, J. A. L. (2000/2003). *Decide the nuclear issues for yourself: Nuclear need not be unclear.* Retrieved December 31, 2003, from www.magma.ca/~jalrober/Decide.htm

Robinson, D. N. (1993). Is there a Jamesian tradition? *American Psychologist, 48*(6), 638–643.

Rogow, A. (Ed.). (1969a). *Politics, personality and social science in the twentieth century: Essays in honor of Harold D. Lasswell.* Chicago: University of Chicago Press.

Rogow, A. (1969b). A psychiatry of politics. In A. Rogow (Ed.), *Politics, personality and social science in the twentieth century: Essays in honor of Harold D. Lasswell* (pp. 123–145). Chicago: University of Chicago Press.

Rorty, R. (1982). *Consequences of pragmatism.* Minneapolis: University of Minnesota Press.

Rosa, E. (2001). More power to us: Still wary about nuclear energy. *The Public Perspective, 12*(6), 6–8.

Rosenberg, S. W. (1985). Sociology, psychology, and the study of political behavior: The case of the research on political socialization. *Journal of Politics, 47*(2), 715–731.

Ross, M. (2002). The political psychology of competing narratives: September 11 and beyond. In C. Calhoun, P. Price, & A. Timmer (Eds.), *Understanding September 11* (pp. 303–320). New York: New Press.

Rotberg, R. I., & Thompson, D. (Eds.). (2000). *Truth v. justice: The morality of truth commissions.* Princeton, NJ: Princeton University Press.

Russett, B., Alker, H. R., Jr., Deutsch, K. W., & Lasswell, H. D. (1964). *World handbook of political and social indicators.* New Haven, CT: Yale University Press.

Sanford, N., Adorno, T., Frenkel-Brunswik, E., & Levinson, D. (1950). The measuremeent of implicit antidemocratic trends. In T. W. Adorno, D. J. Levinson, R. N. Sanford, & E. Frenkel-Brunswik (Eds.), *The authoritarian personality* (pp. 151–208). New York: Harper.

Sapir, E. (1934). Symbolism. In *The encyclopaedia of the social sciences* (pp. 493–494). New York: MacMillan.

Schiffer, I. (1973). *Charisma: A psychoanalytic look at mass society.* Toronto: University of Toronto Press.

Sears, D. O., Sidanius, J., & Bobo, L. (1999). *Radicalized politics: The debate about racism in America.* Chicago: University of Chicago Press.

Segal, H. (1973). *Introduction to the work of Melanie Klein.* London: Hogarth.

Shamir, B., House, R. J., & Arthur, M. B. (1993). The motivational effects of charismatic leadership—a self-concept based theory. *Organization Science, 4*(4), 577–594.

Shils, E. (1954). Authoritarianism: "Right" and "Left." In R. Christie & M. Jahoda (Eds.), *Studies in the scope and method of the authoritarian personality* (pp. 24–49). Glencoe, IL: Free Press.

Shore, M. F. (2001). How psychiatrists and political scientists have grown up since 1938. *Psychiatry, 64*(3), 192–196.

Sidanius, J., Feshbach, S., Levin, S., & Pratto, F. (1997). The interface between ethnic and national attachment—ethnic pluralism or ethnic dominance? *Public Opinion Quarterly, 61*(1), 102–133.

Silverman, L., & Weinberger, J. (1985). Mommy and I are one: Implications for psychotherapy. *American Psychologist, 40*, 1296–1308.

Slovic, P. (2000). *The perception of risk.* London: Earthscan.

Slovic, P., Fischoff, B., & Lichtenstein, C. (1980). Facts and fears: Understanding perceived risk. In R. C. Schwing & W. A. Albers, Jr. (Eds.), *Societal risk assessment: How safe is safe enough?* (pp. 181–216). New York: Plenum.

Smith, B. L. (1969). The mystifying intellectual history of Harold D. Lasswell. In A. A. Rogow (Ed.), *Politics, personality and social science in the twentieth century: Essays in honor of Harold D. Lasswell* (pp. 41–105). Chicago: University of Chicago Press.

Smith, B. L., Lasswell, H. D., & Casey, R. D. (1946). *Propaganda, communication, and public opinion: A comprehensive reference guide.* Princeton, NJ: Princeton University Press.

Smith, M. B., Bruner, J., & White, R. (1956). *Opinions and personality.* New York: Wiley.

Soldz, S., & Vaillant, G. E. (1999). The big five personality traits and the life course: A 45-year longitudinal study. *Journal of Research in Personality, 33*, 208–232.

Stone, W., Lederer, G., & Christie, R. (1993). *Strength and weakness: The authoritarian personality today.* New York: Springer.

Strachey, J. (1965). Editor's introduction. In S. Freud, *The interpretation of dreams* (pp. xi–xxii). New York: Norton.

Strauss, G. (2000). What's happening inside U.S. Unions: Democracy and union politics. *Journal of Labor Research, 21*(2), 211–225.

Strawson, P. (1975). *Freedom and resentment, and other essays.* London: Methuen.

Sullivan, H. S. (1948). The meaning of anxiety in psychiatry and in life. *Psychiatry, 11,* 1–13.

Swanson, D. R. (1977). A critique of psychic energy as an explanatory concept. *Journal of the American Psychoanalytic Association, 25*(3), 603–633.

Thayer, H. S. (1968). Pramatism. In *Encyclopedia of philosophy* (pp. 430–436). New York: Macmillan/Free Press.

Torgerson, D. (1985). Contextual orientation in policy analysis: The contribution of Harold D. Lasswell. *Policy Sciences, 18,* 241–261.

Torney-Purta, J. (1989). Political cognition and its restructuring in young people. *Human Development, 32*(1), 14–23.

Torney-Purta, J. (2000). Comparative perspectives on political socialization and civic education. *Comparative Education Review, 44*(1), 88–95.

Touraine, A. (1983). *Antinuclear protest: The opposition to nuclear energy in France.* London: Cambridge University Press.

Turque, B. (2000). *Inventing Al Gore: A biography.* Boston: Houghton Mifflin.

Tversky, A., & Kahneman, D. (1974). Judgment under uncertainty: Heuristics and biases. *Science, 185,* 1124–1131.

U.S. Office of Technology Assessment. (1984). *Nuclear power in an age of uncertainty.* Washington, DC: U.S. Government Printing Office.

Valenzuela, A., & Constable, P. (1991). Democracy in Chile. *Current History, 90*(553), 53.

Volkan, V. (1988). *The need to have enemies and allies: From clinical practice to international relationships.* Northvale, NJ: Jason Aronson.

Volkan, V. (1997). *Bloodlines: From ethnic pride to ethnic terrorism.* New York: Farrar, Straus & Giroux.

Volkan, V. (2002, May). *Large-group identity: Border psychology and related societal processes.* Paper presented at the German Psychoanalytic Association annual meeting, Leipzig. Retrieved December 10, 2003, from www.healthsystem.virginia.edu/internet/csmhi/Vol13Volkan.cfm

Waelder, R. (1936). The principle of multiple function. *Psychoanalytic Quarterly, 32,* 15–42.

Waelder, R. (1963). Psychic determinism and the possibility of predictions. *Psychoanalytic Quarterly, 32*(1), 15–42.

Waisbord, S. (1991). Politics and identity in the Argentine army: Cleavages and the generational factor. *Latin American Research Review, 26*(2), 157–170.

Wallerstein, R. S. (1977). Psychic energy reconsidered: Introduction. *Journal of the American Psychoanalytic Association, 25*(3), 529–535.

Walzer, M. (1977/2000). *Just and unjust wars: A moral argument with historical examples.* New York: Basic Books.

Weart, S. R. (1988). *Nuclear fear: A history of images.* Cambridge, MA: Harvard University Press.

Weber, M. (1925/1968). *Economy and society: An outline of interpretive sociology.* New York: Bedminster.

Winnicott, D. W. (1987). *The child, the family, and the outside world.* Reading, MA: Addison-Wesley.

Wyer, R. S., Jr., & Ottati, V. C. (1993). Political information processing. In S. Iyengar & W. McGuire (Eds.), *Explorations in political psychology* (pp. 264–322). Durham, NC: Duke University Press.

Zaleznik, A. (1977/1992). Managers and leaders: Are they different? *Harvard Business Review, 55*(3), 67–76.

Author Index

Subject Index

A

Adenauer, Konrad, 80
Adler, Alfred, 14
Administrator style of leadership, 107, 108, 112, 114
Afghanistan, 80, 133
Aggression
  downward and outward, 44, 45
  moralistic, 141
Agitator style of leadership, 106, 108–110, 112
Alexander, Franz, 14
American Political Science Association, ix, 10
The Analysis of Political Behaviour: An Empirical Approach (Lasswell), 12, 174
Anti-apartheid movement, 81
Anti-Semitism, 25–26, 31, 169
Antidemocratic predispositions
  control of, 74, 78
  traits associated with, 72, 73
Anxiety
  democratic character and, 74, 77, 79, 80, 82, 83
  ego and superego demands and, 56
  management of, 49–50
  meaning of, 87–89, 173
  role of, 68
  social, 76, 88, 173
Anxiety-plagued undemocratic individuals, 82–83
Argentina, 81, 117, 150–152, 154
Aristotle, 41, 77
Armenian Assembly, 140, 141
Armenians, 32–33, 140–142
Ascriptive identifications, 52
Associations, 40–43, 154–158
Atomic Energy Commission, 157, 158
Atoms for Peace program, 157
Attitudes, *See* Political attitudes
Augustine, St., 82
Authoritarian leadership style, 100

Authoritarian personality
  research on, 8–9
  traits and attitudes of, 72, 77, 171, 172

B

Barzani, Massoud, 145
Base values, 104
Battle of Kosovo, 143
Behavioral/attitudinal identifications, 52–53
Benighted undemocratic individuals, 80
Berlin Wall, 61, 117, 118
Beyond the Pleasure Principle (Freud), 37
Bin Laden, Osama, 133, 134
Bosnian Muslims, 117, 143
Brazil, 154
Bryce, James, 172
Bush, George W., 169

C

Carter, Jimmy, 165
Character, *See also* Democratic character
  explanation of, 68–70, 137–138
  political behavior and, 116
Character and Personality, 171
Character-deformed undemocratic individuals, 80–82
Charisma, 175
Charismatic leadership
  collective bargaining and, 159–160
  explanation of, 9, 101–103
  personalized, 175
  problem behavior and, 113–114
  risks of, 110–113
  transformational leadership and, 102, 174
Cioffi, Frank, 167
Civil rights movement, 81
Civilization and Its Discontents (Freud), 12, 168

191

Fenichel, Otto, 172
Ferenczi, Sandor, 14
France, 158
Freudian theory
    anxiety and, 87–89
    condensation symbols and, 42–43
    ego and id and, 47–48
    group process and, 11–12, 116
    identification and, 51, 54
    Lasswell and, 15, 18, 19, 34
    overview of, 35–36
    psychic energy and, 90, 173
    unconscious and, 5, 22–24, 30–35, 38
Functionalist perspective, 13–14

G

Gandhi, Mahatma, 55, 80, 108
"The Garrison State Hypothesis" (Lasswell),
    15, 84
Generalization, erroneous, 32
Germany, 117, 128, 137
Gore, Albert, 169
Great Society, 58
Group Psychology and the Analysis of the Ego
    (Freud), 54, 116
Gypsies, 31

H

Hart, Gary, 113
Heuristics, 1, 128
Hitler, Adolf, 4, 64
Horney, Karen, 14, 170–171
Human relations-oriented leadership, 101
Hussein, Saddam, 144

I

Ichheiser, Gustav, 84
Identifications
    ascriptive, 52
    behavioral/attitudinal, 52–53
    democratic character and, 74
    democratic symbols and, 46
    explanation of, 50, 53
    formation of, 53–56
    mood/mood swings and, 121–122, 126
    negative, 170
    psychoanalytic theory and, 47–48
    salience of, 144–146
    symbols of, 51, 53
    totalitarian regimes and, 44
Impostorship, 109–112

Impulses
    democratic character and, 75–78
    from id, ego, or superego, 45, 51
    mapping of, 50
    mood/mood swings and, 123, 136–137
    psychology of, 56
Indignation crisis, 124
Information bias, 32–33
Insecurity crisis, 124
Intensity
    explanation of, 69
    manipulation of, 133–134
Intergroup conflict
    attitudes and, 140–143
    Iraq and, 144–146
    Northern Ireland and, 140–142
    symbol manipulation and, 142–143
International Society for Political Psychol-
    ogy, ix, 6, 10
Interpretation of Dreams (Freud), 42
Inventing Al Gore (Turque), 169
Iran, 55, 117
Iraq, 144–146
Ireland, 140, 141
Irish Republican Army, 140, 142
Islamic fundamentalism, 51–53, 122, 134
Israel, 41

J

James, William, 7, 13
Japan, 80, 128
Johnson, Walter, 82
Journal of Personality, 171
Jurisprudence for a Free Society (Lasswell &
    McDougal), ix

K

Kaplan, Abraham, 12
Kelsen, Hans, 172
Kluckhorn, Clyde, 13
Kosovar Muslims, 143
Kurdish Workers Party (PKK), 145
Kurds, 145

L

Labor Attitudes and Problems (Atkins &
    Lasswell), 14
Labor unions, 159–161
*Language of Politics: Studies in Quantitative
    Semantics* (Lasswell, Leites, & Associ-
    ates), 15, 19